# Airline Odyssey

# JAMES OTT
# RAYMOND E. NEIDL

# Airline Odyssey

## The Airline Industry's Turbulent Flight into the Future

**McGraw-Hill, Inc.**

New York   San Francisco   Washington, D.C.   Auckland   Bogotá
Caracas   Lisbon   London   Madrid   Mexico City   Milan
Montreal   New Delhi   San Juan   Singapore
Sydney   Tokyo   Toronto

Library of Congress Cataloging-in-Publication Data

Ott, James.
    Airline odyssey : the airline industry's turbulent flight into the
future / James Ott and Raymond E. Neidl.
            p.      cm.
    Includes index.
    ISBN 0-07-048030-3
    1. Airlines.   2. Aeronautics, Commercial.   I. Neidl, Raymond E.
II. Title.
HE9780.088   1995
387.7—dc20                                                      95-6656
                                                                   CIP

1 2 3 4 5 6 7 8 9 0   DOC/DOC   9 0 0 9 8 7 6 5

ISBN 0-07-048030-3

*The sponsoring editor for this book was David Conti, the editing supervisor was
Virginia Carroll, and the production supervisor was Pamela Pelton. It was set in
Bembo by North Market Street Graphics.*

*Printed and bound by R. R. Donnelley & Sons Company.*

*To the railroaders in each of our families who instilled in us
early an interest in the movement of people and goods.*

*To our colleagues among the airline analysts and journalists who
cover this great airline industry.*

*To the people who fly.*

# Contents

# Preface

Over the last five years, the world airline industry has endured more upheaval than in any other comparable period of the post–world war era. New airlines offering low fares are springing up around the globe. The jet aircraft of the pioneers, Pan American World Airways and Eastern Airlines, no longer ply the skyways. Following the deregulation trend that began in 1978 in the United States, nations in Europe and other key areas have turned away from economic regulation of the industry. Instead, they are relying on market forces to mold the industry. In unregulated markets, the new, high level of competition among airlines is winnowing out the inefficient. While trade barriers are slowly coming down, the aviation world at mid-decade is, however, far from the free trade goal of Open Skies favored by leading industrial nations.

Where governments have pulled away from strict economic oversight, the airline industry is transforming. The efficient, low-cost carriers, structured to offer low fares, are catalysts for change. The veteran airlines, hampered by high costs and other ills, have been jolted into looking for new ways to compete. Many large carriers, household names around the world, have launched programs to expand their international presence and are forging alliances with other carriers from other regions.

At all times in its history, the airline industry has been acutely sensitive to the state of the economy. Booms have produced a spate of passengers; recessions inevitably have deflated traffic and cargo movements. And, in the strange economy of the 1990s, with its deep, lingering recession and slow recovery, the airlines have been sent reeling from unprecedented earnings losses, layoffs, and delays in delivery of aircraft.

This book offers an analysis of the industry to aid in the understanding of the major forces reshaping it. The book has been written
for the general public, but we have remained aware of an audience of
investors interested in long-term trends. We have focused on certain
airlines because their experiences offer clues to these trends. We have
discussed the impact of change on today's airlines and projected a
vision of the industry as it moves toward the twenty-first century.

James Ott and Raymond E. Neidl
February 1, 1995

# Acknowledgments

The authors wish to thank hundreds of individuals who have helped guide us in innumerable ways to present this story. They have contributed greatly to this book and to our understanding of the airline industry.

We are especially grateful to Washington consultant George Aste, former vice president, government affairs, for United Airlines; Joe Hopkins, media relations manager, United Airlines; John (Jack) Pope, former president and chief operating officer of United; John Adams, former Continental Airlines personnel chief and consultant; John Walsh, aerospace forecaster, former head of forecasting at Rohr, Inc.; Vern Thomas, chief forecaster at General Electric Aircraft Engines; Dwight Weber, formerly of GE, and Rick Kennedy, of GE public relations; Henry (Hank) Duffy, former president, Air Line Pilots Association; Al Becker, managing director, public affairs, American Airlines; Michael E. Levine, executive vice president, marketing, Northwest Airlines; Jos Kamp, the coordinator in charge of negotiations with Northwest Airlines for KLM Royal Dutch Airlines; Jim Faulkner of Northwest's public relations, and Odette Fodor, of KLM's public relations in New York; Charles Curran, senior vice president, marketing, Comair, the Delta Connection; Gordon Bethune, president and chief operating officer, Continental Airlines; Ginger Hardage, director of public relations, Southwest Airlines; Herbert J. Kelleher, chairman and president, Southwest Airlines; aviation consultant John Eichner of Simat Helleisen & Eichner, New York City; Tom Parsons, publisher, *Best Fares* magazine; airline consultant Edmund S. Greenslet, ESG Aviation Services, Ponte Vedra Beach, Florida, and Gary Church, president, Aviation Management Associates, Springfield, Virginia.

Special thanks go to Paul Proctor, U.S. Northwest bureau chief, *Aviation Week & Space Technology,* Jeffrey Lenorovitz, former senior international editor at *Aviation Week,* and Donald Lang, president, Pratt & Whitney, China, each of whom provided insightful information on Russia and China. We are obliged to Ed Cowles of Pratt & Whitney; to Donald E. Fink, editor-in-chief of *Aviation Week* for his expert guidance, and Kenneth E. Gazzola, *Aviation Week* publisher for his support; to consultant Jon Ash, managing director, Global Aviation Associates, Inc., Washington, D.C., for expert help over the years; to Mary Downs, vice president and general counsel, the Air Transport Association of America; to Marion Mistrik, librarian, and David A. Swierenga, chief economist, each with the ATA; to Dr. Assad Kotaite, president of the Council, International Civil Aviation Organization (ICAO); to Dr. Philippe Rochat, secretary general, Hutton Archer, public information director, and Chris Lyle, chief, economics branch, all with ICAO.

We are indebted to Willis Player, the aviation consultant and retired Pan American World Airways executive who learned the business as an aide to C. R. Smith, the aviation pioneer of American Airlines. We owe a debt of gratitude to Furman Selz Incorporated and to *Aviation Week & Space Technology* for their support of this project. For professional guidance on the organization of this book and for helpful editorial suggestions, we thank David J. Conti, editorial director, Business McGraw-Hill.

# Airline Odyssey

# Prologue

Nationalization of the nation's airline industry cannot be discounted as a possible eventuality. Once the public is faced with the chaos, disruption of service, economic demoralization of carriers, and concentration of service in the hands of the remaining few air carriers . . . a demand would arise that the government take restorative action.

—W. T. BEEBE,
   Former Chairman and Chief Executive Officer,
   Delta Air Lines

THESE WORDS, written over 18 years ago, reflect the worst fears of any chief executive. Most top managers of the elite major airlines during the latter part of the 1970s shared many of W. T. Beebe's concerns. Federal regulators had ruled over the U.S. airlines for 40 years. They set the levels of air fares and acted as final arbiters on critical business issues such as what cities the airlines served and with how many flights. Competition existed among the air carriers, but it was limited to heavily traveled routes and was carefully controlled by the regulators at the Civil Aeronautics Board. When Beebe penned his concern, Congress was debating whether it should withdraw the protective hand of government from the airline business. Epochal change was blowing in the wind, and airline officials foretold of chaos. For all in industry and government, the late 1970s were a time of uncertainty.

The Delta executive adopted a harder line against deregulation than most opponents. He claimed the airlines would become the victim of academic idealogues and political theorists, and he doubted their integrity. He wrote that they had "cleverly conceived and disguised" deregulation as a matter of free enterprise and regulatory reform. He predicted that, in time, it would foster a reverse effect, and that new regulations would multiply. He couldn't fathom how increased competition and new start-up airlines would benefit the industry's profit margins. The system wasn't broken, he argued; it needed no fixing.

Beebe worried that airlines were heading for insolvency and the disruption of their ability to serve passengers, pay bills, fly safely, and continue the costly process of fleet modernization. "America's airline industry is an extremely complicated, interrelated, and technological business," he wrote. "It is a quasi-public utility. It is a business wherein if any one 'cog' in any of its 'wheels' is broken, the entire apparatus is jeopardized." His concerns were so great that he resorted to portraying deregulation as a step on a hazardous road to a government takeover of the industry.

Today Beebe's manifesto seems antiquated after 16 years of deregulation, though he was correct in his prediction of turmoil and of the broad effects it would engender. He died of a heart attack in June 1984, just as the U.S. industry recovered from the first economic slump of the deregulation era and stood at the threshold of great expansion into international markets. The nationalization he feared was never threatened. To make an Amtrak out of the airlines seems as remote a possibility, then and now, as the investiture of a monarchy in the U.S. It simply isn't going to happen.

Few in industry, academe, or government, however, foresaw the ceaseless ferment that deregulation would create. From the first easing of the government's regulatory hold in 1978 to today, the chain of shocks has rattled even the most secure and best-managed airlines. No longer considered public utilities, the U.S. airlines have become very much like any other American business operating largely free of government economic controls, on their own in the competitive environment of the day. Rivalries have intensified. Airlines have competed with each other for passengers and cargo, and for support from financial markets. Absent any government controls, the weight of responsibility and accountability for airline performance fell more heavily on the executive suite.

Under the pressures of this sea-change, a few among the great pioneer carriers have departed like extinct bird species, unable to adjust to the new and more demanding environment. The major airlines have consolidated to fewer than 10, and ultimately the number of survivors will be even smaller. New strategies have emerged. America's big airlines are seeking out international markets as the tide of competition—and protectionism—is rising all around the world. Airlines have found niches in the marketplace. A goodly number of commuter-regional carriers and recent new-start airlines have thrived in the short-haul market, the flights of 1000 miles or less. Over the years, however, most of the hundreds of new-entrant carriers have become victims of failure, merger, or liquidation.

In this recent period, the U.S. airline industry has endured layoffs and strikes, fuel crises and international terrorism, labor problems, rising costs and soaring taxes, restrictions on market access, foreign protectionism, and the fiercest competition on domestic soil that free enterprise could muster. In the latter part of the 1980s, the Big Three carriers—American, Delta, and United Airlines—appeared impregnable. A major advantage for airlines during the middle and latter part of the 1980s was the comparatively low price of fuel. Prices in 1988 were as low as they were in 1979. In a prosperous period, the airlines were making hay while the sun shone. The orders for new aircraft kept the production lines humming at airframe and engine manufacturers.

Yet as the 1980s closed down, the airlines found themselves caught up in an ugly spiral of rising costs and declining revenues. Labor costs climbed significantly. Over five years, average wages and benefits increased an average of nearly $10,000 per employee. Suddenly, with the Iraqi invasion of Kuwait in 1990, the price advantage for fuel disappeared. The economic recession began to cut into travel budgets, depriving airlines of passengers, and the threat of terrorism scared more people away. In 1991, airline traffic declined from the previous year for the first time in aviation history. By 1992, earnings losses were so great that they exceeded all the profits earned by the industry in its then 67-year history. While the greatest share of the airline deficit may be attributed to steady losses by a handful of defunct carriers, most airlines suffered, and all took on heavy debt loads. Only in 1994 were there signs of a slow recovery.

In this book, we have attempted to establish the major trends in the industry and chronicle their impact, as of this writing (February

1995) on the U.S. and world airlines. It is our position that the upheavals of the last five years are just a taste of what lies in store for the international airline industry: "The past is prologue." The shocks will continue, and even many of the famous names will be no more. In the current period of soft economic rebound, the jolting changes have picked up speed and have caused the industry to invert: Ironically, earnings hold more promise at the lower end of the industry than at the top. On domestic runways, traffic is still in a slow-growth pattern. The once-vaunted market power of the Big Three carriers has dissipated in the wind of consumer demand for low prices. For a time in 1993–1994, the elite carriers seemed ready to topple of their own weight. Still carrying the burden of high labor cost structures, they couldn't compete on a sustaining basis with low-cost competitors on routes of short to medium length. Now the Big Three all are living out their own solutions to their problems.

All across the globe, Airlines both large and small are engaged in a great competition to become profitable and survive. What falls out in the next few years will define the industry for many more years to come. In this book, we provide a picture of the future world airline industry. To buttress our own knowledge of the business, we have conducted hundreds of interviews with airline, aerospace, and government officials.

In the early chapters, we explore the dilemmas of key U.S. airlines, detail some success stories, and provide some insights into future plans. No contemporary account of the U.S. airline business would be complete without an examination of the phenomenon of Southwest Airlines of Dallas, Texas, the avatar of the new domestic carrier. We critically review airline pricing strategies, and offer our observations on the unusual relationship between the United States' airlines and its government.

Later chapters are devoted to the spread of the spirit of deregulation around the world. We focus on Europe, which has adopted its own brand of deregulation, and on the Netherlands, whose government has set the pace toward free trade in the air. The development of the high-speed commercial transport is traced, and we explore several proposals for future aircraft. Anecdotal stories of aviation in

China and in the newly independent states of the former Soviet Union are presented to provide portraits of these emerging markets.

Deregulation of the airline industry has provided the American public with the rare sight of government in retreat. In 1983, the Civil Aeronautics Board, the chief regulatory body, lost authority over domestic routes and fares. It closed its doors on December 31, 1984, ending 46 years as a regulatory body. The Department of Transportation inherited some CAB roles, and the Federal Aviation Administration continues to be the watchdog of air safety.

While deregulation has loosened government's grip, the hand of the U.S. government on the airlines remains strong. Those who regard the airlines as a public utility, such as the companies that provide gas and electricity, cry out for reregulation every time the industry gets into trouble. Thus far, Chairman Beebe's dire forecast that the airlines will be nationalized has proved untrue. But then, flying the airlines really hasn't been as bad as some like Beebe predicted it would be. Even in the worst of times, the airlines still provide a safe means to get from here to there, faster and better than any other mode of transportation.

# ONE

# Flying in
# the Future

Whether the industry as a whole will be in a better financial position ten years from now than it is today remains an open question.

— *A report of the* Organization for Economic Cooperation and Development (OECD), Paris, 1992

## A GLIMPSE OF THE BRIGHT SIDE
### *New York City:* Fall 2005

JOHN CARLTON STARTS WORK EARLY at MegaLux Corporation on Third Avenue. It is 7:35 A.M., and he has just ended an important telephone conversation with a business associate in Atlanta. The office administrator, Ms. Sheila Casey, walks into Carlton's office to follow up on that telephone call. She knows that she will be representing MegaLux at a noon luncheon meeting in Atlanta. The trip was worked out at the last minute on the telephone. Sheila doesn't mind. She'll be back in New York well before 5 P.M., with documents that her boss will need to sign before he catches a 7 P.M. flight to Tokyo on the new supersonic transport.

Sheila heads for the automated "travel agent" machine in the lobby of the MegaLux Building and reserves a Business Class seat on a 9 A.M. flight to Atlanta. She inserts a company debit card to reserve the seat. A printer in the automated machine rolls out a confirmation number, departure times, and the gates at LaGuardia Airport and at

Atlanta's Hartsfield International Airport. Within minutes, she is on her way to the airport.

John Carlton leans back in his chair. He has a full day's work ahead of him, preparing for his Tokyo meeting. He will meet Sheila at the TransGlobal Airlines lounge at John F. Kennedy International Airport any time after 5 P.M., to put his signature on the Atlanta documents. Sheila took the Atlanta assignment so John could manage with his appointment-filled day and prepare for Tokyo. He has been talking with his Japanese contact for several weeks, by teleconference with the London office. He wants to discuss a project in detail and watch his contact's reactions to several complicated proposals.

The day passes quickly. Sheila's flight connections to and from Atlanta are without incident. The privatization of the air-traffic-control system has improved its efficiency remarkably. She walks into the TransGlobal lounge at 5:30 P.M. Carlton signs the papers, and together the two of them check over his itinerary: TransGlobal to Tokyo for two days; a return trip on European International Airways to Bahrain for a quick visit; then to London on EIA for two days. By the way, Sheila mentions to Carlton, TransGlobal and EIA have a code-sharing relationship. In fact, the SST he will be flying in are some of the new ones the two airlines are co-leasing.

A few hours later, Carlton boards the aircraft and takes a spacious seat in the first-class cabin. The ticket was expensive, but the cost is worth it. MegaLux is several million dollars richer because of the Atlanta deal alone. Carlton's Bahrain and London stops are important, and time is of the essence. Flight times are cut in half on the SST. Jet lag is minimized. The personal visits in the Far and Middle East will put sealing touches on business relationships that developed slowly through teleconferences. Face-to-face handshakes definitely were needed. Still, MegaLux will get full use of Carlton. He will be working during most of his flight time, in contact with Sheila by telephone and fax. He wants to write a speech anyway, and the hours in the air will give him time to gather his thoughts.

John Carlton and his wife, Kim, are looking forward to a vacation after these deals have been completed. In spite of all of his flying hours, Carlton can't earn frequent-flier miles toward free flights.

TransGlobal and EIA gave up their frequent-flier programs several years ago, when the demand for free flights became too much of a burden. Carlton has decided instead to buy an advance-purchase discount ticket, on a point-to-point domestic carrier that will leave him and his wife an hour or so away from a favorite mountain resort. The domestic fares are so cheap, they could have taken the kids. Next year, maybe.

Transporation worth many thousands of dollars was bought in these few exchanges, but neither John Carlton, his wife Kim, nor the office administrator Sheila has realized that most of the interaction and transactions happen with independent companies under contract with the airlines. The aircraft operated by the airlines are leased. Sheila made reservations on a computer reservations system (CRS) that the airlines partly owned in a consortium. The aircraft are maintained by private companies established to serve. the airlines leasing the SSTs. The people at the airport gates and the airplane crews are associated with the airlines but operate on a contract basis, and are interchangeable between the two carriers.

Such scenarios will be played out routinely in the next century. World commerce will be tied together efficiently to nearly everyone's benefit. Telecommunications will diminish the need for business travel, but the ability to communicate electronically will not eliminate the need altogether. Face-to-face meetings, especially between people with cultural differences, will be a necessity justifying cost and time. Tourism will continue to grow, in any case. Leisure travel will accelerate, even as business flying declines in rates of growth.

## A GLIMPSE OF THE DARK SIDE
### *New York City:* Fall 2005

It's 7:35 A.M., and John Carlton is at his desk in the MegaLux Building. The deal with the Atlanta group is about to close, and Ms. Sheila Casey, the office administrator, must go to a luncheon meeting that day in Atlanta to collect documents for Carlton's signature. Sheila calls the MegaLux travel agent, who checks on the flights to Atlanta and the prices. Sheila needs to know the actual fare, because she must know how much of a bite it will take out of the office budget. The price will be high, since there is no competition in the market. A seat is available on the 11 A.M. flight—too late for Sheila to arrive at the downtown Atlanta office building by noon, but the seat is reserved anyway. She'll be late for the luncheon, but she'll collect the documents that need Carlton's signature and head back to the airport, where she'll wait as a standby for a return flight to New York that afternoon.

Meanwhile, Carlton is trying to work out a way to meet Sheila and sign the documents before departing on a 7 P.M. flight to Tokyo. He isn't looking forward to a long and tiresome trip. He wants to stop at Bahrain and at London. The contacts in each of the foreign cities could prove useful, but he wonders whether the extra hassle is worth it. He decides to make the stops, and arranges the itinerary over a 10-day period that will take him around the world. He only hopes that Sheila will manage to find a seat on the return flight, so that the Atlanta deal can be completed and gotten under way.

Carlton is really looking forward to a vacation after completing this grueling schedule. He is out of luck for a nice flying trip to an exotic place, however. Ever since reregulation of the airlines, prices have skyrocketed due to all the inefficiencies that have crept back into airline operations. Vacations are now limited to the shore or the in-laws' lakeside cottage, all within driving distance.

When the airlines reregulated, their schedules and pricing were fixed by a new government agency. Airlines now have no incentive to offer real discounts, and few are available. The government agency bases airline fares on costs, which have grown enormously. Airline executives feel no compunction about seeking government approval of every cost increase, from fuel to labor. They file their cost records in the new Docket Room at the new federal agency, and the new board rarely makes any comment.

Labor officials love the new regime. Ever-rising cycles of wage increases and featherbedding work rules are built into the airline calendar. Pilots of the large transports are making a half-million dollars a year. A whole new industry has developed in Washington, D.C., as representatives of the airlines battle with each other to get a favorable edge in decisions from the new airline board.

A historian says that the whole scene is reminiscent of the early days of the regulated industry during the FDR era. The flying public now comprises business fliers and the wealthy who can afford the ticket prices. Accordingly, passenger traffic has fallen off drastically. No longer a growth industry, the airlines have slipped into permanent financial trouble due to lost business and bureaucratic inefficiencies. The talk has started up in Washington about the need for a public air-transport company. AMAIR, someone suggested, would be a good name, a parallel to AMTRAK.

*    *    *

The air-transport systems just described are extreme examples of what travelers may experience in the next decade. In the United States and across the world, the industry has reached a crossroads, one of many since its founding seven decades ago in the post–World War I era. Since those pioneering days, the commercial industry has steered a jagged course of boom and bust, through one Great Depression, global wars, a Cold War, and many recessions. The most recent economic downturn, which started in late 1989 and lingered through the 1990s, has damaged the industry and given it a severe shaking. Global airline losses have topped $15 billion since 1990. In the United States alone, the $10 billion deficit from 1990–1992 exceeded the total amount of profits earned by the American carriers since the 1920s.

Airline earnings reflect the many periods of financial chaos over the years. Why can't the airlines make a dollar? The question is haunting to those in the business. Turmoil and heavy losses have marked the first years of the last two decades. In recent history, the U.S. airlines last performed well in the mid-to-later 1980s. But even in the better years, airline profit margins have been among the lowest of any industry, and the prospects for improvement are not good.

Today, at mid-decade, earnings are trending up but are still uneven. Forecasts by manufacturers, which have much to gain or lose from the financial condition of airlines, indicate continued struggles for them.

Much of the answer to today's airlines' financial dilemma should be plain. Many carriers have grown too large, spreading well beyond the borders of their home markets. They have overbought new aircraft and let their costs rise out of control. Unions are partly to blame for high costs, but managements, inadequate to their tasks, must share that blame. The loss of once-great carriers in civil aviation, Pan American World Airways and Eastern Airlines, testify to dismal failures of labor and management to solve their problems.

The industry upheaval can be witnessed in every part of the globe. Privatized airlines are competing in a one-sided battle with government-owned carriers. Protectionist policies are commonplace. The concept of free trade in the air has made few advances. Airlines are caught in a web of inherently restrictive bilateral air service agreements between nations. Some 3000 or more such agreements crisscross the globe.

In response to the '90s shakeup, airlines around the world are pulling back, cutting down, restructuring, and in most cases, preparing for a future of constant low fares and increasing competition. These changes have come about as the industry, in 1993, carried 1.170 billion passengers and generated revenues of $230 billion. What has caused the airlines to take these measures? Why are executives trying to reinvent their airlines?

Some of the answer can be traced to airline deregulation, the epoch-making trend that began in earnest in academic circles 30 years ago in the United States, and took hold in Congress during the 1970s. Deregulation of the airline industry, which occurred on October 24, 1978, became the modern-day equivalent of the American "shot heard around the world." When the government withdrew from economic regulation of the U.S. industry, the airlines became free to take action in two areas that 40 years of regulation had denied them: they were able to set fares at the prices the market would bear and to choose their own destinations. Deregulation found a home in the United States, but neither the airlines nor the government were prepared for the massive fallout from the exercise of these new freedoms.

## FEW WERE PREPARED FOR THE DRASTIC CHANGE
### *Washington, D.C.:* October 1978

The offices of the Civil Aeronautics Board occupy a building on the sloping and broad Connecticut Avenue. The CAB is the federal agency that had regulated the airlines for 40 years. On October 24, 1978, some 28 or more airline representatives stood in line outside of the CAB's front doors as they had for five days through cool, sometimes damp, fall nights. They lined up in front of a makeshift sign, DORMANT AUTHORITY LINE STARTS HERE, which had been written in grease pencil and pasted on one of the doors. On that day, at 1600 Pennsylvania Avenue, President Jimmy Carter had penned his signature to the Airline Deregulation Act of 1978, which was to forever change the relationship between the U.S. government and the nation's airlines, eventually ending the CAB's regulatory powers.

The representatives had begun to queue up outside the CAB on the previous Friday, October 20, in anticipation of the Board implementing one of the deregulation act's provisions. The new law had authorized the Board, for the first time in its 40 years, to issue route authority to the airlines in an unusual way: not by an evaluation of airline service proposals in long, laborious procedures, but on a first-come, first-served basis. The routes involved were by no means premium ones. Rather, the board was clearing its books of routes that the airlines had the authority to operate but weren't flying. In the language of the bureaucrats and lawmakers, these routes were "dormant authority" routes.

Virtually every airline had dormant routes. They weren't being flown simply because they weren't very promising. Insufficient traffic demand had made them unworkable and inactive. Under the new law, any airline could apply for the dormant routes or protect the ones it had.

The queue of airline representatives consisted of Washington lobbyists and other agents who had been deputized by the carriers, even a squadron of Washington bicycle messengers. Those in the queue had been given one general order from their superiors: do not relinquish your place in the line, no matter what the hardships. The airline bosses had feared that by losing a place, an agent for another airline would move up in line and have first crack at the routes coming available under the law.

Why did the airlines dispatch representatives to line up for routes that had little value? Many of the airlines' Washington representatives knew that the routes offered their companies little or nothing.

Some weren't so sure, however. In executive suites far from Washington, airline officials had no idea what to expect from deregulation. They were worried that somehow they might strike out in this first inning of the new deregulation ballgame.

Officials at United Airlines had a better sense of the future than most. George Aste, the airline's federal liaison officer, had guessed that the CAB would allow a queue to form and, at some point, issue the route authority as the law required. He took the first place. The line formed behind him and lengthened as the hours passed. It remained intact for approximately 120 hours, over the weekend through to the morning after Carter signed the act.

Queue-keepers came up with a fun competition to ease the boredom. They competed with one another as to the size of the cardboard boxes in which they carried route applications. They wanted to make it look as if they were going to apply for a large number of routes; some, indeed, were going to grab as many routes as possible. Old Allegheny Airlines sought approval for 125 routes, and Braniff for more than 300. United played along with this farcical competition. Aste and other agents who relieved him on the line carried a large box, but it contained only a one-sheet document comprising United's lone route application, for nonstop rights between Buffalo and Miami.

On that first morning of deregulation, CAB officials at last permitted the line to move inside the building. Aste led the airline representatives to the Docket Room on the upper floors of the CAB building. As required by law, the CAB rubber-stamped the route authorizations on a first-come, first-served basis. United was authorized the Buffalo–Miami route. It started nonstop service, but it never proved workable and eventually the carrier withdrew.

Characterizing the banzai approach to deregulation's new freedoms, Braniff International topped the 28 carriers in applications. It received CAB approval to operate 17 routes. In May 1982, when Braniff filed bankruptcy papers, many in aerospace circles recalled Braniff's ambitious grab for routes of such dubious quality. It became an emblem of the general ineptitude with which that carrier's executives had greeted deregulation.

The CAB's bureaucratic response to deregulation, forcing the representatives to queue up for so many days, had revealed the government agency for what it was: a part of the entrenched bureaucracy unprepared for the great changes deregulation would bring to airports, airways, and the airlines. The airlines' own deficit of direction matched the government's lack of readiness. While the airline people maintained their sidewalk queue, route analysts at the air carriers spent the days trying to figure out which of the unused routes might be served with some semblance of profitability. It was a tough job, since few of the routes were worth preserving or, for that matter, applying for.

## AN INDUSTRY TURNED UPSIDE DOWN
### *Chicago:* November 1, 1994

Robert Rosati, the chief executive officer of International Aero Engines AG, of Glastonbury, Connecticut, takes frequent barometer readings of the state of the airline industry. He has spent many hours in his 40-year aerospace career in executive suites, trying to sell aircraft engines. His company, an international consortium, builds power plants for the small- to middle-size Airbus Industrie jets. Rosati, a panel member at a conference sponsored by the industry journal, *Aviation Week & Space Technology,* speaks of the great change that has occurred in the industry he has served. He recalls a conversation with a veteran executive, a keen, salty operations chief whose name is lost among thousands of industry contacts:

When we first started flying, we launched an airplane to a destination in the hope that it would get there. A few years later, we launched an airplane in the hope it would get there *on time.* Today, we launch an airplane and hope it will make a dollar.

For Rosati, that executive summarized the essence of the airline industry. He spoke of its audacious beginning six decades ago, of the persistence of people in building a workable system, and of the great challenge of today—the struggle for profitability. The last one may be the airlines' greatest challenge. Producing a profit in commercial aviation, a hard task since the pioneers flew, seems even tougher today.

"From the business school perspective, everything is wrong with the airline business," says Jack Pope, the former president of United Airlines. "It is capital-intensive, labor-intensive, and fuel-intensive. It is intensive in everything."

Passenger traffic is growing fastest in the low-yield leisure end of the business—fine for consumers but not so for the airlines. The passengers referred to in airline lingo as VFRs—Visiting Friends and Relatives—are outpacing the market for those business fliers on whom most airlines traditionally have depended to pay a premium price. Julius Maldutis, an airline analyst with Salomon Brothers, New York City, noting the absence of necktie-wearing businessmen on recent U.S. flights, puts it succinctly: "The high-paying suckers aren't there anymore."

In the United States, where many world trends have begun, the airline business is undergoing a thorough transformation. The market for short-haul flying, from point to point, once deserted by the major airlines, has been rediscovered. United and Continental are competing in the short-flight market, offering low-fare, no-frills alternatives. Southwest Airlines of Dallas, the discoverer of the short-haul niche, and, with a uniquely simple and productive operation, is leapfrogging across the U.S. New-entrant airlines and some of the regional/commuters now in jet aircraft are boosting competition and avoiding the big and busy airport hubs.

Some positives are emerging. Even within the competitive pressure cooker of today's businessworld, labor-management relations are showing signs of improvement. There is widespread recognition that the confrontations that destroyed Eastern and Pan Am served no one's interests. In recent times, employees at United Airlines and Northwest Airlines have become part of the solution to financial dilemmas. In some cases, airline employees have taken the risk of hinging their salaries and pensions on the success of their carriers.

In their search for new paths to profitability, airline executives are contemplating some radical steps, and they're restructuring their carriers along the way. In America, the airlines are more competitive and dynamic than in any of the 17 years since the U.S. Congress set the airlines on a new course with deregulation. Reflecting the dynamism, airline revenues have doubled over the last 10 years to nearly $80 billion a year.

Then, too, while many of the big airlines have sustained heavy losses, year after year, some carriers have performed well. Southwest Airlines found the short-haul niche and exploited it so expertly. When it found the secret to profitability, Southwest grew from its regional base in Texas to major-carrier status.

A few others have paralleled Southwest's records, but on a smaller scale. Comair, a regional carrier based in the Midwest and affiliated with the major Delta Air Lines, and ValuJet, of Atlanta, have practiced the fine art of making money. Comair and ValuJet demonstrate that U.S. airlines can be profitable even in the worst of times. (For more on these carriers, see Chapter 4.) Their advantages lay in their size and, perhaps, in the management ability to communicate ideas and oversee their execution. Moreover, Comair was undisturbed by the calamity that affected most other airlines in the early 1990s—a situation called overcapacity. ValuJet actually benefitted from the situation, acquiring used aircraft at reasonable prices. Too many airlines offered too many seats in major city markets, and the surplus contributed to prolonged and damaging fare wars.

The chronic state of overcapacity was a product of a widespread industry miscalculation. Traffic forecasts had predicted a travel boom in the 1990s that did not materialize. Forecasters at aircraft manufacturers were as wrong as those at the airlines.

Boeing's forecasts were the most upbeat of all. Between 1987 and 1989, the Seattle manufacturer looked out over a 15-year span and saw a boom in aircraft production. Boeing was virtually alone in predicting increases of between 15 and 25 percent.

Traffic flattened, though, as the world economy slowed in late 1989. When the 1991 Persian Gulf War broke out and the threat of terrorism was heightened, international travel from the United States dropped more than 20 percent. When the war was over and the troops came home, the predicted traffic turnaround did not materialize.

Even after two years of a clear down cycle, the airlines continued to take delivery of new aircraft and failed to adjust to the unexpected, even when it had become apparent that times had changed for them.

# Boeing Forecasting Philosophy Reflects Fundamental Long Term Trends

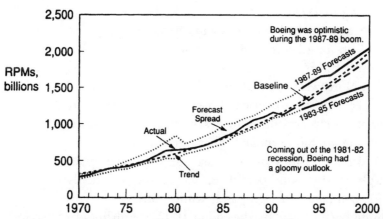

**A Boeing Miscalculation.**    The chart from the aircraft manufacturer, the Boeing Co. of Seattle, illustrates the shift toward optimism in 1987–1989 company forecasts of world airline traffic trends. In actuality, traffic declined in 1991. While traffic demand remained fairly static in 1990 and in 1991, world airlines took delivery of 1450 new passenger aircraft, aggravating an already severe state of overcapacity of airline seats. Overcapacity is a primary cause of fare wars.

As airlines struggled in the poor 1990s' economy, they were caught in a squeeze play. Passengers had turned away from flying even as the airlines prepared the mythical traffic boom. They began to flood the surplus aircraft market with transport aircraft. The number of transports available for sale or lease peaked at 854 in mid-1991 and remained at approximately 700 through 1993. Available at low prices, the used aircraft were to return to haunt the big carriers that shed them.

Vern Thomas, the forecaster for General Electric's GE Aircraft Engines in the Cincinnati suburb of Evendale, Ohio, estimates that the forecasters' miscalculation points to a mistake of at least $65 billion, the value of the 1024 aircraft in limbo.

Manufacturers still suffer from this miscalculation. The world airlines continued to build the fleet through 1992. The 669 aircraft delivered that year broke all records. Then deliveries dropped to less than 200 aircraft in each of the next two years. The prime manufacturers—Boeing, McDonnell Douglas, Fokker, and Airbus Industrie—found themselves in a widening competition in a declining market.

The airlines had gotten themselves into this mess. They had geared up for a boom, ordering new aircraft in record numbers. To accomplish this, even the most financially sound among American, Delta, Northwest, United, and USAir had more than doubled their long-term debt and capital leases between 1987 and 1991, from approximately $6 billion to nearly $15 billion, and committed to acquiring aircraft at much higher figures.

Adding pressures on the carriers, wage and salary levels rose sharply in this same period. Passenger traffic actually declined in 1991, compared to 1990; and, while traffic was recovering, it was coming back slowly. By the end of 1992, the airlines had had losing years for three years in a row, totaling nearly $10 billion in net losses. Competition was growing more intense, especially from the low-fare carriers entering the market.

Thus, a combination of forces closed in on airline management, prompting reevaluation of the cost of every operation and the display of very sharp paring knives. Airline executives began to realize that their carriers had grown too large, had spread out of their natural business areas, had overbought in aircraft, and had let costs grow out of control. One of the first steps taken by the major carriers was a rollback of scheduled new aircraft deliveries to dates later in the decade, accompanied by wholesale cancellations of aircraft orders.

Restructuring was next on the agenda. By the spring of 1994, most airlines had developed a survival kit for the rest of the decade. Common to each kit was an understanding that America needed more airlines like one of its own, Southwest Airlines, a short-haul carrier that became a major airline. It was the model domestic carrier of the future: a low-cost airline designed to transport people safely and reliably at low prices. Each of the full-service major carriers approached this new need in a unique way, which is the subject of Chapter 2.

# TWO

# The Big Three Face the Crisis

It is quite possible that United would become the General Motors of the airline industry. American Airlines would become the Ford. Delta might equate with Chrysler.

—HARDING L. LAWRENCE,
  president and chairman of the board, Braniff International,
  Dallas, to the Congressional Committee on Commerce,
  Science and Transportation, Subcommittee on Aviation;
  March 31, 1977

We can expect more change in the next two or three years than we have experienced in the last fifteen.

—STEPHEN M. WOLF,
  former Chairman and CEO, UAL Corp. and United Airlines,
  speaking on his expectations for the world's airlines

## UNITED'S DILEMMA: REDUCE FARES, OR DIE
### *Chicago:* April 29, 1993

THE FEW HUNDRED PEOPLE assembled for UAL Corporation's Annual Shareholders Meeting were performers in an American ritual. Dark-suited executives hurried across the richly appointed eighth-floor anteroom of the Grand Ballroom at the Chicago Four

Seasons on Delaware Place—men on a mission. The dark suits contrasted with the casual colored clothing worn by a bevy of retired folks, who sat in chairs along a mirrored wall. An older man in a billed leather cap munched on a sweet roll, taken from a long table loaded with handy-to-eat breakfast food. The shareholders of United picked at the food and moved off with their coffee cups to form talkative groups. A line of union pilots in mufti appeared eager to get the show on the road. The air in the anteroom that morning of April 29, 1993, was filled with anticipation.

Stephen M. Wolf, chairman and chief executive officer of UAL Corp. and United Airlines, called the meeting to order. He dominated the dais in the Grand Ballroom. His 6'6" frame towered well above the lighted reading desk of the hotel lectern. After a few preliminaries, he began solemnly, "The situation at United—and indeed throughout the industry—has both worsened and grown more complex." The audience listened intently as he intoned the contents of his report. The bad news outweighed the good. But Wolf, making eye contact with his audience over half-glasses, presented the bad news in the form of a challenge.

United stood at a crossroads. It was not alone. All traditional, full-service U.S. airlines stood there. A substantial change had occurred in the marketplace since his shareholders' report of 1992. The airline was encountering its stiffest competition in the domestic market, from other airlines offering low fares.

The new opposition was an odd assortment. Some were new carriers that had taken advantage of low-priced used aircraft and the availability of experienced personnel, refugees from continued upheavals in the industry. A few others, notably the low-cost Southwest Airlines, had been around for years and were expanding domestically. A few more had been around for even longer. Actually they were pioneer carriers, Continental Airlines and Trans World Airlines. Against all odds, they were emerging from lengthy reorganizations in bankruptcy. The last survivor of the new entrants of the 1980s, America West of Phoenix, was making a comeback. Another pioneer carrier, Northwest Airlines, had narrowly escaped bankruptcy. It was becoming a low-cost carrier, as its employees volunteered pay cuts and work-rule revisions to reduce costs.

Whatever their status or previous condition, these airlines could afford to charge low fares. Their unit costs, one of the primary measures being the cost to produce available seat miles (ASMs), were as much as 25 percent below United's. United could match the low fares, but only at a heavy loss. Wolf had gone to the unions for help. Some labor leaders said no; others were studying the issue. Wolf calculated that United was battling the new competition over 63 percent of its route system. The situation was untenable. United could not hold up under such an assault on its domestic feeder system.

Wolf faced a choice of directions. By taking one path, United could restructure itself, sell off assets, and hope to obtain significant reductions in labor contracts. Wage concessions would be required, and costly work rules would have to be eliminated. The paid lunch for mechanics of the International Association of Machinists and Aerospace Workers (IAM) would have to be abolished, work rules that hindered employee productivity eliminated. Such a change would require union and rank-and-file support. That kind of support wasn't forthcoming, at least not back then.

Wolf's other possible direction was less defined, and portended a greater challenge and change. United would sell its major assets, possibly even its maintenance and training bases. It would trim down to the essentials, and acquire needed services through third-party contracts for everything else.

The alternative to taking some kind of action was to stand by as United withered away, stranded in the crosswinds of change, a high-cost producer in an increasingly competitive marketplace.

Some in that shareholder audience may have understood United's plight, and wanted to hear Wolf articulate it. Wolf didn't relish delivering his challenge, but he didn't flinch even as labor shareholders leveled their criticisms from the floor.

One shareholder adopted an old-line union position, and hit on executive compensation as "a problem for employees." The critical shareholder probed a conspicuous weak spot in United's armor. It lay in a report on directors' compensation in the Proxy Statement that listed the cash payments United had made to 13 directors. Each director was recompensed for 1992 income-tax liabilities arising from the free transportation taken by them and their families, one of the perquisites of being a United director. Two board members, Andrew F. Brimmer, a Washington, D.C., financial analyst, and Paul E. Tierney, Jr., an investment banker, had received cash payments from United of $41,686.41 and $39,329.10, respectively, to cover 1992 income tax liabilities arising from the free transportation. Other directors were paid lesser amounts, such as Wolf's $6,173.50. To union shareholders in the audience, the payments were a symbol of executive extravagance.

Wolf handled the touchy issue with aplomb. Directors had been selected for their record of accomplishments and for their ability to serve United. They were respected, qualified individuals who provided oversight and direction to the company. The free transportation served as a perquisite. It enabled the directors to get to know the company, and it served to compensate for the shortcomings of United's rather average compensation for directors. Still, the union leader thought that payment of such costs was "sending the wrong message" to employees who, once again under deregulation, were being asked to bail out the company.

Wolf treated the labor shareholders employees with businesslike dignity. "No one is blaming anybody. The unions are not at fault. There has been a gradual change in the marketplace. Pan American, the widest-known corporation in the world, is now gone. The consumer is telling us, 'We want to pay less for fares.' "

The employee shareholders pressed for other alternatives to United's dilemma. One suggested that the company should dismantle the hub-and-spoke network and reorganize United in the pattern of Southwest Airlines, flying a simple point-to-point network. That might sound easy, Wolf said, but a change of that sort wasn't possible at United given its labor contracts. The contracts reduced productivity and allowed little flexibility.

After nearly an hour, Wolf in desperation called for labor leaders and United's managers to meet and sort out how productivity gains could be achieved. He repeated his call at a press conference. It was like howling into a desert wind. A retired United employee classified the 1993 shareholders' meeting as the most confrontational he had known in over two decades. A reporter at the press conference asked about employee discontent. "There *should* be a lot of discontent," Wolf remarked. "This is a strange time."

Eight months later, United had a new direction, a union-led employee buyout.

## THE TIMES, INDEED, WERE STRANGE

The U.S. airlines battled against a series of reversals starting with the economic recession in late 1989. In the summer of 1990, Iraqi troops invaded Kuwait, and the airline fuel bill soared $4 billion in two quarters. During the Persian Gulf War, international airline traffic declined by 25 percent. The number of airline passengers in the United States, fell in 1991 on an annual basis for the first time in aviation's history. Three airlines—Continental, Trans World, and America West—were reorganizing under protection of the bankruptcy law. Before 1991 ended, three carriers had ceased operations; namely, the pioneers Pan American World Airways and Eastern Airlines, and Chicago's Midway Airlines.

Debt for the U.S. carriers accumulated to a record total of $35 billion. Airlines had embarked on a buying binge for new aircraft in anticipation of continued growth in the 1990s. Capital markets grew uneasy. When new, low-cost, low-fare airlines entered the marketplace in the 1990s, stealing the domestic traffic base out from under the traditional carriers, Standard & Poors and Moody's lowered credit ratings. Under fiscal and credit pressures, and more combative than ever, the airlines drew battle lines over fares. That summer of 1992, they tangled in the most destructive fare war in history, and the carriers lost $4 billion on the year. The time had come for drastic action.

Three airlines emerged as industry leaders in the late 1980s, to become known as The Big Three: American, Delta, and United. Each had a market share of close to 20 percent, and each was expanding in the international market. But the low-cost carriers were forcing them to make changes. Although each is U.S.-bred, they are nearly as different as Lufthansa is from Air France. Their responses to the dilemma they faced in terms of an eroding domestic market reflect their different cultures.

American is the tough competitor—a carrier whose employees, to use the vernacular, play hardball. The chief executive, Robert L. Crandall, has fostered the competitive spirit that pushed American to first place among U.S. airlines in the 1980s.

Delta Air Lines betrays its Southern, conservative origins in nearly every act. It still splits in two the word *air lines,* following the style of the 1930s. Topside appointments usually come from within the company, and employees have been among the most loyal of any carrier. Among the large employee groups, only the pilots are organized in a labor union. Delta sometimes is slow to respond to changing trends, but usually its sights are on the long term.

United Airlines, with its Chicago base, represents Middle America. Nonetheless its strategy since the mid-1980s has been global, and it has been the most successful carrier beyond U.S. borders. United has gained footholds in the major cities of the Orient, North and South America, and Europe. Its labor battles are legendary. Two of the longer of the 18 strikes since deregulation happened at United: the machinists for 58 days in 1979, and the pilots for 29 days in 1985.

Each of The Big Three responded individually to the fiscal and credit crises of 1990–1994, but American was stymied by its unions, Delta was preoccupied with a long and slow course of restructuring, while United adopted the most radical approach, one sanctioned by the Clinton Administration.

## UNITED'S **ESOP,** BORN OF A BITTER STRIKE
### *Chicago:* Spring 1987

The Employee Stock Ownership Plan (ESOP), the key to the 1994 employee takeover of United Airlines, had its beginnings in the 1985 pilots' strike. The 29-day walkout was a bitter confrontation between the Air Line Pilots Association and management over the direction of United and its parent corporation, UAL, Inc. Former hotelman Richard Ferris, then at UAL Inc.'s helm, had diversified its holdings into the hotel and car-rental businesses.

In Ferris's view, such a diversification strategy protected and strengthened the airline. But the union pilots regarded UAL's spread into other businesses as foolhardy and detrimental, above all to the airline. An aggressive, eager executive, Ferris early in his tenure developed a rapport with the pilot group. He took up flying and earned a pilot's license. In the heyday of the relationship, when he turned over United's financial books for the pilots to review, Ferris was granted the rare courtesy of being given an honorary pilot's seniority number.

The rift between Ferris and the pilots couldn't be bridged unless either Ferris reversed the strategy or the pilots caved in. Neither had much chance of happening. Ferris was under strong pressure when United's chief rival, American Airlines, challenged the carrier by establishing a hub at Chicago's O'Hare International Airport near the United headquarters. The challenge came not only from new American flights but from the sheer fact that American had a lower cost structure than United. American's President, Bob Crandall, had transformed the competitive landscape in those years by obtaining a two-tier salary scale for American's employees, an "A" scale for veterans and a "B" scale, with lower salaries, for new hires. The Dallas carrier expanded considerably in this period, taking advantage of its low costs. Ferris was obliged to secure a similar cost structure from the very union officials who were in bitter disagreement with him over long-term strategy.

United's union pilots are a tough lot. In the 1970s, they fought a losing and expensive battle with management over the crewing of the Boeing 737. Management regarded the three-crew aircraft an example of union featherbedding. The unions saw the potential of job loss and labor officials waved "the bloody shirt," alleging a derogation of safety margins. United was alone among U.S. carriers in staffing a third crew member to fly in 737s until 1981. The crew complement battle was renewed just before United received its first Boeing 767 in 1983, but today two-crew aircraft are the rule.

The same feisty spirit was seen in the pilots when they struck United for nearly a month in 1985. United tried to get by, using management pilots and hiring replacements, but the walkout was effective; even most of the 500 pilots in training joined the strikers. Bitterness over the hiring of replacement workers—*scabs,* to use union lingo—lingered for years. Some union pilots carried hand devices on their person that made a clicking sound. They clicked them whenever they were in the presence of one of the replacements, even several years after the strike. Many employees deplored this grudging behavior, but it revealed that depth of feeling in the union ranks which gave birth to the idea of an ESOP.

Two years later, on April 5, 1987, the pilots' union, still dissatis-
fied with United management, proposed an employee stockowner-
ship plan (ESOP) as the long-term solution for United. The first
pilots' buyout attempt, valued at $4.5 billion, fizzled upon their
failure to obtain adequate private financing. Ferris battled the ESOP
from the start. He called it "unclear on its face."

That wasn't all that fizzled for United during that period. Ferris
changed the name of UAL Inc., the parent company, to Allegis.
Donald Trump remarked that the name sounded like a disease from
the Third World. Upon hearing the name, pilots either sighed or
laughed. Since the term "Allegis" had no clear connection with any
of the famous companies within the corporation—Hertz, Hilton,
Westin, Covia, or United—it seemed meaningless, and seemed to
bear out the pilots' notion that the corporation was mismanaged and
heading for disaster.

Actually, Ferris had a real purpose in mind, at least initially. The
new name was directed at a specific audience, the financial community. Ferris had been disappointed at the lack of support for his diversification plan. In Allegis, he saw a way to better identify the
diversification of the corporation on the stock market. The corporate
name UAL would always be associated with the airline, limiting an
apprehension of the corporation's broad base. In Ferris's mind, the
old name simply didn't reflect the company's real value.

Ferris introduced the Allegis concept in the grand ballroom of the
Plaza Hotel to 100 Wall Street analysts, the main audience for the
impending change. Ferris made his points in a verbal presentation
from the podium. Allegis represented more than just an airline: It
was a total transportation company, a company for a globalized
future. He relied on a professionally crafted media display to drive
his points home. At the end of the nearly hour-long program, in his
summing up of all of what Allegis stood for, a foreboding quiet fell
across the ballroom. The analysts looked to one another in amazement. They were appalled, and many asked, "What on earth is he
trying to do?"

The name Allegis had emerged from a New York firm that spe-
cializes in identity and image management, Lippincott & Margulies.
It was understood at Lippincott & Margulies that the new name was

in no way intended to replace the irreplaceable brand names of Hertz, Hilton, Westin, Covia, or United. "It was a classic case of the operation being a success and the patient dying." Thus Clive Chajet, a principal with Lippincott & Margulies, later described the fiasco that ensued over Allegis. Chajet believes that Allegis could have been successful if well enough had been left alone. "In fact, if the company had remained faithful to the idea of changing the name for the financial community only, there would have been no problem," he said. "What was a problem was that somebody persuaded somebody that there was another master to be served, and that is the consumer."

Allegis suddenly became promoted as a total transportation and travel company. Soon, Chajet added, "a plan was in place that if you checked a bag at the Hertz station in New York and you were traveling to San Francisco, it would magically appear at the Mark Hopkins." Allegis lived for only a few short months, and was written off as a mistake. Ferris left United later that year (1987), to be replaced by Stephen Wolf.

The employee ownership plan never really died. Other investment interests negotiated to acquire United in the next few years. The Conniston Partners and the entrepreneur Marvin Davis sought ownership, but the union pilots remained an obstacle, outbidding Davis in a 1989 takeover attempt. This buyout effort looked stronger than the first, since it had gained the approval of United's management and the support of British Airways. United and the British carrier were then working in close cooperation under a marketing agreement for exchanging passengers at Chicago. The ownership formula would have been 75 percent employees and 15 percent British Airways, with management owning another 10 percent. The union-management consortium that developed appeared invincible, and it offered a substantial $300 a share for United stock, enough money for everybody. But the offer was ill-timed. The 1980s were coming to an end, leveraged buyouts had had their day, and concerns were on the rise in Washington and New York for the financial health of U.S. airlines. Jointly, these factors deprived unions of their prize. The failure of the United buyout coincided with a mini-crash of the stock market on October 13, 1989, that brought an end to the leveraged buyout (LBO) activity.

United returned to a normal pace as the new decade began. The managers concentrated on building the routes to the Far East it had acquired under Ferris from Pan American in 1985. New transatlantic routes it acquired in 1991 under Wolf, again from Pan Am, also needed attention. In this period, United completed a phase of international growth and secured a strong geographical network based in three of the world's greatest metropolitan areas: London, Chicago, and Tokyo.

"If you want to know about United's strategy," a top official observed a few years ago, "just look at the large population centers and that's where United will be."

Given the unusual circumstances of the market, United in 1993 chose to bide its time. It adopted a slow-growth plan through 1996, reducing its domestic flights wherever low-cost competitors had been making inroads. At the same time, United management was looking for ways to reduce costs, at least by 10 percent, to better equip itself for tougher competition. A restructured, lower-cost United was the goal of United's executives. Already feeling the vise closing on them, the executives developed a list of 125 target items. The sale of United's maintenance base and the Denver training center was among the options considered. The unionized kitchens were the first to be sold.

"This was a means to an end," says Jack Pope, the former president and chief operating officer. "There was recognition that with every service we performed, United's costs were higher by a significant margin than the lowest-cost producer in the business." The 125 items were divided on a two-dimensional scale: those that carried the smallest impact and the greatest, those that were the easiest to accomplish and the hardest to carry out. Many items involved labor unions, which made changes hard to come by.

To their amazement at United, a contract for Sky Caps at Boston's Logan Airport was dropped from the United rate of $13 an hour to $4 an hour. The Sky Caps contractor originally bid $2 an hour, well below the minimum wage requirement, which surprised the United executives. It developed that the contractor hired people in Boston who paid him for the opportunity to work the curbside check-in area at United for the tips alone. Jack Pope said it was rumored that Sky Caps made as much as $80,000 a year there, mostly from tips.

United began to contract out for services that had been performed in-house. Under an outside contract, the 63 janitors at United's headquarters were replaced by 39 employees, who accepted $10 as opposed to $17 an hour. The winning contractor also submitted a cache of supplies to cinch the contract.

The biggest change came with the sale of the United kitchens. The International Association of Machinists and Aerospace Workers (IAM) lost more than 5000 dues-paying members with the sale of the kitchens. The former United executives who directed the sale remain puzzled as to why the IAM did not, in union parlance, "go to the mat" over the loss of personnel. United offered to sell the kitchens to the union and its members, on the condition that there be wage and productivity concessions. The union leaders refused. United executives regarded their refusal as a sign that they feared the spread of a buyout mentality that could endanger the union itself. If the kitchens were sold to employees and the union, what of the sale of other United operations to unionized ramp workers and others covered by the IAM? One possible answer is that union leaders elected the status quo for the sake of stability in the rest of the ranks. One IAM official said that the sale of the kitchens was regrettable, but he insisted that the union was restricted from taking forceful action in this case. The IAM contract with United had elements in it dating back to the days of United president (1934–1963) Pat Patterson, which provided them with no legal leg on which to stand and fight.

In this steamy atmosphere of deal-cutting and cost reductions, the union pilots, in the company of the machinists and flight attendants represented by the Association of Flight Attendants (AFA), came to the table with the ESOP plan. Negotiations lasted from May 1993 to a tentative agreement in December of that year. But as the specifics were being ironed out, negotiations continued on until July 1994, prior to the stockholders' meeting.

One of the most contentious issues was the cost of the transaction, which finally was approved at a cost of $79 million, largely to take care of legal, financial, and accounting fees. Each party was served by advisors, both legal and financial. Jack Pope said that negotiations never did reveal the details of the fees the Air Line Pilots Association had agreed to pay. The high cost of the transaction nearly scuttled the deal several times. Perturbations in the stock market posed problems for the financial transaction, prompting a bid by the unions for a renegotiation. The flight attendants withdrew, but the loss didn't deter the remaining unions from offering to acquire United. The offer was accepted by the board of directors in the days just before Christmas of 1993. The takeover plan envisioned a new low-cost United, born of wage and benefit cuts and a revision of work rules. One of the jewels of the transaction was union support for the start-up of a satellite short-haul airline, now known as The United Shuttle, as a way of directly competing on the home front.

## UNITED'S UNIONS AND EMPLOYEES TAKE A RISKY, EXPENSIVE RIDE
### *Chicago:* July 12, 1994

United Airlines was launched into a new era of majority employee ownership on this day, and it was clear that the employees were deeply split over it. Shareholders voted 70 percent in favor of the Employee Stock Ownership Plan (ESOP), hinged to the employee investment of pay and benefit cuts averaging 14 percent over a period of five to six years. The owners of the UAL Inc. stock, which numbered 24 million shares on the day of the transfer, received $84.81 in cash for each share owned, plus a half of a share of new UAL common. The sale of a company for that price was a good deal for the employee buyers, when one considers that the assets alone could have raised at least $200 a share. In exchange for the value of pay cuts and benefits, estimated to total $4.9 billion, the participating employees gained 55 percent of United's common stock and three seats on the board of directors.

The ballroom at Chicago's Fairmont Hotel was jammed with airline executives, union officials, and members of the press eager to cover United's transformation into the largest employee-owned company in the world. Typical shareholders, who had dominated the 1993 meeting, seemed to be in the minority. Even as the crowd gathered in an anteroom before the meeting started, word spread from United officials that the deal was done. The meeting was under way at the scheduled 8:30 A.M. start, and Chairman Wolf made it official with his first words.

After the signing of the transaction papers that day, Wolf and his colleague, Jack Pope, the president and chief operating officer, found millions of dollars in their personal coffers. Wolf's "golden parachute" clause in his personal contract brought him $20 million. Pope got $16 million. These outlays were in addition to the $79 million in expenses associated with the buyout, which included legal, accounting, and financial fees.

The shareholders' meeting lasted two hours. The only spark came from salaried, nonunion employees who were soured over their disenfranchisement by management. The salaried employees, numbering 27,000 people, weren't given a chance to vote on the transaction. One after another, they stood up at the shareholders' meeting and questioned the validity of what had happened. The board of directors was being reconstituted, in part staffed by a strong union contingent—still a novel way to do business. Wolf had several heated exchanges with shareholders and employees over transaction costs, but given the dimensions of the cash involved (United added $758 million in debt, increasing long-term debt to $3.4 billion; shareholders' equity slipped from over $1 billion to a negative value of $448 million), the meeting went on smoothly.

Within two weeks, the new United start-up had been rocked by a revelation involving the member of the board of directors appointed by the union pilots. Roger Hall, chairman of the union's ruling body known as the Master Executive Council (MEC), was the chief architect of the buyout plan. He had been associated with buyouts since 1985. Dissident pilots looking into the legal fees discovered that one of ALPA's legal advisors, Charles Goldstein, had been authorized a $2 million fee if the transaction was approved. Hall had authorized the fee; the Master Executive Council had not. After a stormy MEC meeting over July 23–24 in Chicago, Hall resigned his MEC post and returned to flying Boeing 747s based in Hawaii. He also resigned as a member of the board of directors. The legality of the fee soon came under close scrutiny by the pilots' MEC.

Several union members brought charges that Hall had violated union rules of procedure in authorizing the fee to Goldstein without MEC concurrence. The rules prohibit any union staff member from receiving special remuneration for union-related work. Internal hearings on the matter turned up new information. Hall had been following a precedent. In 1991, the previous MEC chairman, Rick Dubinsky, had authorized a $375,000 fee to Goldstein for extensive work associated with the failed 1991 buyout.

According to a spokesman for the Master Executive Council, Hall has been exonerated of the charges. He is a line pilot for United.

In January 1995, the MEC dismissed Goldstein as a staff lawyer, but the termination was under appeal. The disposition of the $2 million fee had not been determined at that time. The funds were being held in escrow. The spokesman said the fee was proportionately similar to fees paid to other lawyers, accountants, and advisors who had worked on the buyout. The problem, he said, was that the MEC did not know about it.

Sadly, it appears that the ESOP represented the only course left for United. In 1993, the prospect of continuing labor strife swung like a Damoclean sword over union-management negotiations. If United had sold assets and trimmed down, as Wolf had hinted it might, management would have had to confront the obstinate unions to win concessions, and who knows what would have happened. The Clinton Administration's blessing of the ESOP buyout cast a rosy glow over the transaction. For the ordinary employee, whose pay and benefits were cut through the turn of the century, the risk of a new venture seemed high.

## HAIRCUT FOR AMERICAN'S SAMSON
### *Dallas:* **May 18, 1994**

Spring days start early in Dallas. Light is barely creeping over the eastern horizon when sleepers in the hotels on the grounds of the Dallas/Fort Worth International Airport are jolted awake by alarms, telephone calls, or the muffled roar of aircraft. Hotel windows facing east look down on the active runways. One by one in the dusky half-light, silver-toned American Airlines transports lift off. Engines bellow and bring the heads of the barely awake up from their pillows.

American launches 2500 jet-aircraft flights every day (see photo). Dallas is its home hub. Of all the full-service majors, American takes home one gold medal as the most efficient carrier, and another as the most operationally adroit. The shrewdest team in the business over-

**An American Bank.** Jets of American Airlines, distinctive for their buffed aluminum exteriors with red, white, and blue trim, nose into gates at Dallas/Fort Worth International Airport, the carrier's main hub. The aircraft are part of a bank of flights that have converged at Dallas in American's hub-and-spoke operation. American operates 2500 flights each day. (*Photo provided by American Airlines*)

sees the airline and the affiliated non-airline companies, the SABRE computer and information affiliate included. It has served as a virtual graduate school for U.S. airline managers who left American in search of high-level positions, independence, Wall Street, or their own shop in other corporate malls.

During the 1980s, American achieved top rank in all phases of airline operations: planning, finance, scheduling, pricing, marketing, maintenance, fleet development, communications, and facilities. American supports an academy of researchers who provide complete background for management decisions. In the past, American's engineers defined the airplanes the carrier needed, launching such staples as the McDonnell Douglas DC-10. Today, the tradition of thorough research continues in the arcane areas of pricing and revenue management. But it is their thorough working through of an issue, and their clear sense of direction, that has enabled American's managers to forge ahead. It is no accident that American occupies a premier place on almost all lists of world-class carriers, and with total liquidity of well over $1 billion, it needs no one's sympathy.

Owners of AMR (the parent of American Airlines) stock owe much of the credit for the company's success to Bob Crandall, who developed the team that lifted American to first place. He made ripples after he became president in 1980, by separating the airline from non-airline businesses such as training, computer reservations, and information services. He made *waves,* by adopting in 1984 a grow-from-within strategy that stood American apart from its merger-minded airline partners. That same year Crandall found a way to ease the path toward growth. He wrangled a two-tier pay scale from the company's unions, the Allied Pilots Association (APA), the Association of Professional Flight Attendants (APFA), and the Transport Workers Union (TWU). As a result of contract changes, the newly hired at American were employed at low, entry-level rates, known as the "B" scale. American's practice in this area swept the rest of the industry through the decade. In this period, American also developed its regional/commuter operation and acquired the workhorse of its domestic fleet, the McDonnell Douglas MD-80. (As of March 1994, American's fleet of 663 jet aircraft comprised 260 MD-80s.) In the 1980s, American was the fastest-growing U.S. airline and also the richest, with total profits in that decade of well over $2 billion.

The four-and-a-half-year span between 1989 and the shareholders' meeting on May 18, 1994, saw a series of developments that put a halt to American's growth plan and changed the industry forever. The airlines were peaking in the latter 1980s, as the U.S. economy staggered; then the Persian Gulf War and terrorism took a heavy toll. An oil-price increase raised fuel prices. Labor costs got out of hand as the B-scale employees shifted to A-scale status. The economic recession spread around the world. Traffic dropped. Low-cost, low-fare airlines took root all over the country. Therefore, May 18 in Dallas was not a time or a place for rejoicing at American Airlines.

At the podium, Crandall looks, acts, and sounds like someone born to be the head of a U.S. company. Here is a man with a plan, a formidable advocate, a Samson among the heads of the major carriers. But he can irritate as well, and easily overwhelm an audience. He has his harsh critics but also his strong admirers, particularly since, until recent years, he has been wildly successful. His comments in the cool, low light of the Park West Ballroom, in the Double Tree Hotel on LBJ Freeway, were typically straightforward, nearly blunt, but never defensive. He always has a well-stated position on all things related to the airline's dilemmas, and in his comments he fires not from the hip but with calculated aim. His firepower stems from facts, comparisons, outlooks.

Crandall calls the shareholders' meeting promptly to order at 10 A.M. "As you all know, we are still struggling with the problem of how to wring profits out of the airline business. 1993 was not a good year. . . . Our problems are a consequence of the fact that our fares are being set by carriers whose costs are far below ours. Thus, despite achieving a substantial unit revenue premium over most of our competitors, we have been unable to match revenues and costs well enough to become profitable."

He mentions the flight attendants' strike that partially paralyzed American in the days leading up to Thanksgiving of 1993, before President Clinton intervened in the strike, ending it under the requirement that management and the flight attendants accept binding arbitration. Crandall doesn't mention Denise Hedges, the president of the flight attendants union, or even the flight attendants whose resolve he and others had underestimated. His comments are kernels of truths encased in age-old business rhetoric. He doesn't ignore the facts; rather, he places them in the context of a response to what has happened. "1993's performance, of course, was marred by a fall strike that was truly tragic for everyone except our competitors, and made clear that we must find ways to persuade all the company's people that we have a shared responsibility for the company's success."

In May of 1994, American's senior managers were on the road, touring company facilities so as to lay a groundwork for labor contract negotiations. The tenor of those contracts will affect American's productivity and profit margins for the remainder of the decade, and influence negotiations at other major carriers. While the President's intervention prevented what would have been a disruption for thousands of passengers that Thanksgiving, it was a blundering intrusion into the most challenging labor-management struggle of this decade, for it strengthened labor's hand in the debate over productivity and fair wage scales.

Crandall wanted to hold out against the flight attendants' union, replacing the strikers if necessary. During the walkout, he turned down a proposal for binding arbitration of the labor-management dispute that Ms. Hedges had requested. A day before the President intervened, Crandall also had rejected the appointment of a presidential emergency board, another union proposal. Crandall didn't want any individuals who could be politically susceptible and had no long-term interest in American Airlines making decisions that risked American Airlines' future.

But the tide had turned against Crandall. Regulations require that there be a certain number of flight attendants on every flight. The lack of available attendants forced American to stop selling tickets for 20 percent of its flights, and caused cancellations across another 40 percent of the system. Losses were calculated at $10 million a day for the five-day outing. Crandall had two public reactions to Clinton's intervention.

"In view of his national responsibilities, we think his requests are entitled to great deference," he said at the time. But later, he felt he had been "leaned on." Another view is that the board of directors at American, concerned over miscalculations by management and appalled at the daily hemorrhage of money, prompted Crandall to seek a solution. In any case, Ms. Hedges played the Delilah who gave this Samson a metaphorical haircut, one that thwarted him from restructuring American, at least at that time when it needed it most.

As a consequence, Crandall's Transition Plan, an interim operating plan conceived in 1993, will remain in force until the airline has obtained competitive costs. Thus, a new AMR Corporation is evolving. The airline is prepared to shrink, if need be, for according to the plan other more profitable businesses under the AMR umbrella will prosper. By the fall of 1994, American had furloughed 5000 employees, and more employees will be released unless American can make drastic changes in labor contracts. San Jose and Raleigh-Durham are no longer hubs for American, and other hubs may go. Under the plan, some 94 aircraft (35 DC-10s and 59 Boeing 727s) have been retired through the middle of the decade. Services that aren't profitable or that are marginally so have been and will continue to be eliminated. By the fall of 1994, American had withdrawn from 61 markets, substituted short-haul turboprop aircraft in 28 of them, and discontinued service to 25 cities.

In September of 1994, American took a small but real step toward what could be a new trend, becoming an airline without assets. The carrier adopted a new approach to the operation of its reservations and gate operations at airports. Wages were frozen and new automation introduced, and a new pay plan went into effect. More important, American began to outsource for personnel. Crandall said he was looking at a $130 million annual savings, part of the $750 million in annual labor costs that had to be eliminated.

In 1994, under its Transition Plan, American's managers accomplished the nearly impossible. They reduced the work force and shrank the airline in terms of flights and seat capacity. Yet American was able to report positive earnings in 1994, while at the same time reducing its unit costs. Skillful surgery and cost-cutting, by a band of dedicated achievers, accomplished this distasteful mission.

## GOOD OLD DELTA
### *Cincinnati:* October 5, 1993

Ronald W. Allen, chairman and chief executive officer of Delta Air Lines, clearly understood the competitive problem. He had just cut a ribbon before the new 28-gate concourse at the Cincinnati Northern Kentucky International Airport, situated on the flat highlands of Boone County amid the distant Kentucky hills. He knew then, but couldn't say, that in the next six months Delta would change radically. Good Old Delta was working at its usual slow pace, looking for some way to combat the new domestic competition at its hub at Salt Lake City, Utah. Morris Air had been tough enough, but now Southwest had acquired Morris and spread the competition over a wider field. Southwest's presence at Salt Lake City was a sign of tough new times ahead.

For nearly a year, Delta had been chipping away at the periphery of its problem of rising costs in the face of low-fare competition. It had laid off part-time and seasonal employees, and 600 ALPA pilots. The airline put a strain on credulity by claiming that it had identified cutbacks valued at $6.6 billion, though much of this savings was the consequence of the rollback of new aircraft to delivery dates of 1997 and beyond.

By 1994, it was clear that Delta hadn't done enough. Its own costs were still too high (about 9.26 cents per ASM) to compete with the low-cost carriers. More and deeper cuts would come from layoffs, the first large-scale layoffs for this major, largely nonunion carrier. Through 1997, Delta will reduce payroll by as many as 16,000 positions, 20 percent of its entire work force. The target of this necessary surgery is an ASM cost of 7.5 cents, which will bring Delta's costs close to those of its low-fare competitors.

Delta officials thought about forming within the airline itself a new low-cost, low-fare, short-haul carrier, similar to United's Shuttle and Continental's Continental Lite. It was one option under study by a special committee named by Allen and headed by Hiram Cox, a company officer. Quite simply, the committee recommended against it. A separate low-fare operation would solve only the domestic, short-haul half of Delta's problem. By remaining one airline, operating at the lowest possible cost, Delta believes it is in a stronger strategic position to defend itself against all comers and to become a long-term force in the marketplace. Questions remain as to whether such a drastic cut is achievable without damaging the morale of its employees, who are known as the most loyal in the business.

But the Atlanta carrier is well equipped for its next challenge. Since it is largely nonunion, Delta officials have more flexibility to downsize and trim than most other major airlines. Further, the carrier is making adjustments: eliminating marginal-to-losing long-haul flights, and turning over short-haul routes to the commuter/regional airline partners that are closely allied to Delta. Cutbacks amounting to hundreds of millions of dollars are projected for flight operations, technical support, on-board services, marketing, administration, and personnel. While Delta's management is slow-moving, it is deliberate, and its decisions are based on long-term strategy. The restructuring of its operations stretches over a three-year period through 1997, and will target the $6-billion goal first identified in 1993.

A further advantage for Delta is its financial strength. In late 1994, it had available to it $1.38 billion in cash and about $1.25 billion in bank lines. Such a cash position allows for reform with a protective cushion. The $6-billion cutback is aggressive but achievable, with considerable pain. If it falls short but still has the effect of narrowing the gap between its fares and those of its competitors, Delta will benefit. But all are braced to monitor the effects of radical surgery on the now complex, worldwide organization that Delta, the one-time crop-dusting operation, has become.

Surrounded by reporters at the new Cincinnati concourse, Allen observed that the $375-million airport project, which added 10 new international gates to Delta's Cincinnati holdings, had eluded the Delta paring knife. The outlay has secured the Cincinnati hub as the locus of Delta's midwest operations, and has conveyed the carrier's regard and need for hub-and-spoke operations. The midwestern Cincinnati hub, and its equivalent western hub in Salt Lake City, each have been profitable. But each needs a more robust flight schedule than the 160-plus daily operations of recent years if greater returns are to be achieved. On December 1, 1994, when Allen dedicated the new Cincinnati facilities, he predicted that Delta would be flying 200 flights a day into and out of the Cincinnati airport by the end of 1995.

Delta employees know hubbing, and they know when it works. The carrier developed its hub system more than 30 years ago, when propeller-driven airplanes served small communities in the South and moved passengers to Atlanta. From Atlanta, Delta carried passengers to large cities in jet aircraft that arrived in banks of flights, also known as "waves" or "rushes." Changing airplanes at Atlanta became commonplace, and a favorite target of comedians. Jokes portrayed people in all sorts of dilemmas or under a mandate of one kind or another, but no matter what, they first had to change planes in Atlanta.

Deregulation only enhanced the appeal of the hub-and-spoke concept. Delta's oldest hub at Atlanta's Hartsfield International Airport now operates as a continuous hub, serving more than 500 Delta flights a day.

Allen, who could pass for a football coach at a southern university, is a quiet, soft-spoken individual who has little contact with the world outside of Delta. His public appearances are related largely to official pronouncements on major steps taken by the airline. His contact with the press also is limited, a source of complaint from the major business newspapers. Allen has piloted the spread of Delta through a merger with Western Airlines and the partial acquisition of Pan American World Airways. The acquisition of Western was one of the few sensible mergers of the 1980s. Its success lay in the welcoming attitude of Delta employees to the former Western employees, an attitude that was born in Allen's office.

In recent years, Allen has championed the practice of sharing computer reservation system (CRS) codes to extend Delta's presence, even to London's Heathrow Airport, the busiest port in Europe. This connection was accomplished through a partnership with Britain's Virgin Atlantic Airlines, a shrewd move that could block American and USAir from gaining larger market shares. Delta is strengthening its European connections, placing Airbus A310s at Frankfurt for its Far East operations. Its alliances with other international airlines are among the most extensive of all those in international aviation.

Under joint marketing agreements, Delta and its allies sell tickets for trips on one another's airplanes. (For a thorough discussion of these arrangements, see page 51.)

The executives at slow-to-move, conservative Delta have responded to the nineties' competitive dilemma in a more decisive way than their counterparts at either United or American. Dealings with the ALPA union have been strained, but they improved in 1994 when the pilots rejected the 2 percent pay increase that their contracts had authorized. Delta will emerge at the end of the decade as a global air carrier, one of the U.S. successors to the old Pan American. Its mutual coinvestment in Singapore Airlines and Swissair has paid off for Delta by introducing it to the broader world. These international alliances are a foundation on which Delta can build.

**The other players.**   Other U.S. major airlines in the early '90s did not fare as well as The Big Three. USAir peaked in earnings performance in 1987 and 1988, then slid into a performance decline until 1994. Northwest Airlines was acquired in a 1989 leveraged buyout, and came close to insolvency before its employees and bankers bailed out the carrier with large concessions. Continental went bankrupt twice in less than a decade, emerging for the second time in 1993. Ineptitude played a role in forcing both Trans World and America West into bankruptcy. Their responses to the new world of the 1990s are a separate tale told in the next chapter.

# THREE

# Industry Hot Spot: The Middle Three Airlines

Fortune brings in some boats that are not steered.

—FRANCIS BACON

AIRLINES IN THE BROAD MIDDLE of the U.S. airline industry are indeed the stuff of a separate tale. These carriers took the biggest hit from the heightened competition of deregulation. The middle-size, regional airlines, known as "the Nationals" under the old Civil Aeronautics Board hierarchy, virtually disappeared during the 1980s. For the most part, they merged with larger carriers that had been seeking broad market power. Old names such as Air California, Hughes Air West, North Central, Southern, Ozark, Piedmont, and Pacific Southwest have become entwined in the history of the surviving carriers.

Competition has been harsh in this middle ground between The Big Three airlines and the commuter/regional carriers. The airlines at the top end of the middle—Northwest, Continental, and USAir—operate in much the same fashion as American, Delta, or United. But unlike The Big Three, their networks are tied closely to regions of the United States. Northwest is linked to the Midwest, for example; Continental traditionally to Texas and the West; and USAir to the East Coast.

Under strong competitive pressures from The Big Three in the late 1980s, The Middle Three became vulnerable to takeover, weakened financially, and became prime targets for investment by foreign airlines. Investments and affiliations by foreign carriers in Northwest, Continental, and USAir provided the non-U.S. carriers with improved access to the lucrative U.S. market. Cash infusions from abroad were welcomed by these U.S. carriers, each of which was threatened with extinction in the downturn of the early 1990s. KLM-backed Northwest turned to its employees for help. Continental won support from Air Canada and a stream of cash from new owners. The investments from abroad sustained these carriers and redirected them on a new course, while new blood in the executive suites, from outside the airline industry, brought with it fresh ideas.

Northwest, based in Minneapolis/St. Paul in the Upper Midwest, occupies the high end of the middle sector of the U.S. airline industry, even though it is one of the top five airlines in the world in terms of revenue passenger miles. By 1993 standards, Northwest was ranked fourth in the world, flying 59 billion revenue passenger miles, a figure boosted by its long-range Pacific routes. Northwest's network concentrates at the Twin Cities of Minneapolis and St. Paul, and at Detroit. It serves the northern tier of the United States on a line from Boston through to Seattle, and operates a small hub at Memphis. Northwest's route authority to Japan and the Far East, codified in the U.S.–Japan aviation agreements since 1952, provides it with a valuable franchise.

In the 1980s, when British Airways began its search for a U.S. partner, Northwest was its top choice for investment. British Airways Chairman Sir Colin Marshall sought access both to the domestic U.S. market and to the trans-Pacific market centered in Japan. KLM Royal Dutch Airlines plucked the Northwest plum, as one of the investors in the 1989 Wings Holdings' buyout of Northwest. British Airways later elected to invest in USAir, perhaps its only alternative at the time.

Northwest appeared to fare better than most through the 1980s, owing to its virtually debt-free status. Chief executives in this period, M. J. Lapensky and his successor, Steven G. Rothmeier, avoided much of the work associated with market development, instead merging with Republic Airlines and gaining an instant domestic system. Republic itself was the creature of a merger, the combination of the regional carriers North Central, based in the Twin Cities, Hughes Air West, and Southern Airways. Northwest was still patching together that system when Wings Holdings, now known as NWA Corp., acquired the carrier in a 1989 leveraged buyout. The acquisition was financed with $3.1 billion of secured bank debt and the proceeds of the sale of $683 million of common and preferred stock to the investors. KLM was a primary investor, along with Alfred A. Checchi; Gary L. Wilson; Frederic V. Malek; Fosters Brewing Group Ltd., of Australia; Bankers Trust New York Corp.; Richard C. Blum & Associates–NWA Partners, L.P.

Steve Rothmeier had introduced an easier-going, less confrontational management style during his term, and that, coupled with the fresh approach of the new co-chairmen Checchi and Wilson, became the accepted norm. No one in the unions liked the idea of an LBO, but there was a strong effort under way to make the airline work. Before Congress and Wall Street grew anxious over leveraged buyouts, Wings Holdings had completed the LBO of Northwest just under the wire in June 1989. (For more on leveraged buyouts, see Chapter 10 and Appendix A.)

KLM Royal Dutch Airlines and Northwest have formed the world's most advanced alliance. It involves joint flight operations and purchasing, and a closely connected strategy (see photo). The two carriers have been party to several firsts in the arena of joint operations, and between them they have the makings of the first truly international airline company. As such, NWA–KLM is an anomaly in international civil aviation, where flag carriers of individual nations still predominate. The linkage between the two carriers hasn't been entirely easy, but it is showing signs of becoming a lucrative venture.

## FROM NEAR-DISASTER TO LEADING EDGE
### *Minneapolis/St. Paul:* June 1993

If ever there was a lousy month for Northwest Airlines, it was June of 1993. In the previous three years, the airline had lost more than a half-billion dollars, and it was still losing. Its long-term debt amounted to $4.43 billion. Further, officials of the nation of Australia had been alleging that Northwest was violating the U.S.–Australia aviation agreement by permitting an excessive number of passengers to board Northwest aircraft in Japan for a final flight leg to the continent Down Under. Finally, negotiations with the six Northwest unions had broken down over an $800-million concessionary package and bailout. The company was operating as if it might file for bankruptcy at any time.

Yet by mid-July, the airline's financial crisis was all but over. Agreements with stockholders, lenders, and employees in the months that followed placed the airline on a new track. Employees accepted $886 million in wage and benefits cuts over three years. Employees and Northwest management set in motion a stock pur-

**Joining Together.**   The joint logo of KLM Royal Dutch Airlines and Northwest Airlines literally tells the story of their alliance. They are two companies that operate as one. The close relationship, unique in commercial aviation, has been approved by the U.S. and the Netherlands governments, the world's top proponents of free trade in aviation. (*Illustration provided by KLM/Northwest*)

chase plan that has brought 33.4 percent of the total voting shares to the employees and managers. Lenders cooperated, deferring $1.8 billion in Northwest obligations to 1997 and later years. The choices for labor and management had been limited to two: bankruptcy, or an employee buyout agreement.

The breakthrough in labor-management negotiations in latter June came about largely owing to a new attitude on the part of labor. Union officials had studied the project and knew the risks, but they were willing to proceed. In later balloting, the rank-and-file approved the program by wide margins. The responses at Northwest differed radically from the death-wish reactions displayed a few years earlier by their East Coast counterparts at Eastern Airlines and Pan American. Northwest's employees had learned lessons from what had occurred at those doomed carriers where labor and management had dragged each other down. Job preservation became the underlying issue at Northwest, and labor accepted wage cuts and changes in work rules so as to accomplish their goal. The contribution of Northwest's employees was substantial: $755 million in wage savings, $23 million in reduced vacation benefits, and $60 million in work-rule changes. These commitments were traded for an ownership stake and three seats on the Northwest board of directors.

Northwest Airlines and the International Association of Machinists and Aerospace Workers (IAM) took another step that today is having a positive effect on the industry's labor-management relations. They eliminated an entire classification of maintenance employees, numbering more than 100. The position, "foreman" at Northwest, is known generically as "first-line supervisor." If this cut is any indication, one of the more unproductive management staffing ideas of the 1970s appears to be on its way out. Foremen had been given supervisory responsibilities, but no authority. Their job classification was wedged between management and the crews comprising a dozen mechanics already headed by a lead mechanic, known as a "crew chief" at Northwest. In the reorganization, some foremen returned to the line as mechanics or crew chiefs, others were absorbed into management.

Since this restructuring, other carriers have taken a close look at this notion of reducing middle management. United's new

Indianapolis Maintenance Center has dispensed with the foreman classification. Mechanics there work in teams, and elect their own lead mechanic.

The Northwest restructuring has been effective. Though new labor agreements didn't go into effect until August 1, 1993, Northwest saved a total of $130 million in wages and benefits in the last five months of that year. The carrier eliminated small airport hubs at Washington's National Airport and in Milwaukee and in Seoul, Korea, which weren't working for it. Other unprofitable routes were cut, while new, more promising services were added. The overall result of the changes that came about during 1993 was a savings of $270 million in that year. Northwest's market share increased slightly, to 12 percent of the total U.S. market. And as the Japanese economy improved in 1994, the airline and its KLM partner were looking forward to cashing in on their franchise there.

One ominously dark cloud floating over Northwest comes from the direction of Japan. Northwest's franchise provides it with access to Japan and the right to collect passengers in Japan and fly them to other Far East destinations. Accordingly, Northwest has been authorized 316 weekly landing slots at Tokyo's highly restricted airport at Narita. During the recent downturn, Japanese airlines suffered heavy losses. Pressures to restrict Northwest's privilege to fly beyond Japan have intensified. This special right, referred to as "fifth freedom authority," essentially takes business away from the Japanese. It has become a bone of contention for the Japanese, who view it as a prime example of war reparations paid to the United States after World War II.

During the early 1990s, Northwest began to expand its fifth-freedom rights, beginning a flight schedule from Itami Airport at Osaka southward to Sydney, Australia. The Japanese objected to the flights, but their objection wasn't specific. The Australians joined in the objection, which led to an international brouhaha in the summer of 1993. The Aussies complained that Northwest was violating the U.S.–Australian agreement limiting the number of passengers Northwest can board in Japan and fly to Sydney to 50 percent of the total traffic on the Northwest flight that originated in the United States. The Australians claimed that the Osaka-boarding passengers represented as much as 80 percent of the total traffic. The number of passengers was a matter of dispute. Northwest claimed that the ex-Japan traffic never reached 80 percent, and varied considerably from flight to flight.

Tensions grew between the two countries as the Australians threatened to cancel Northwest's landing rights. A full-scale trade war loomed between the United States and Australia. A cartoon in *The Canberra Times* portrayed a red-tailed Northwest 747 heading into a black cloud in the shape of a Japanese Sumo wrestler. As the June 30 deadline approached, the dispute attracted massive press coverage in Australia and moderate attention in U.S. newspapers. Top government officials from both sides entered the dispute, and it was quickly settled by negotiation. Northwest agreed to abide by the letter of the agreement as to the numbers of ex-Japan traffic, and Australia was to keep on counting passengers. The dispute can now be seen as a skirmish in the larger battle over U.S. fifth-freedom rights in Japan.

## In This Marriage, Northwest Does the Talking
### *Minneapolis/St. Paul:* June 1994

The weather was overcast, the temperature in the muggy 80° range, when the Dutch contingent swept into the Twin Cities for the June meeting of the Alliance Committee of Northwest and KLM. Their June 23 session at the headquarters in suburban Eagan started promptly at 8 A.M., and the full agenda would take up most of the day. By the post-lunch break, ashtrays on the boardroom table were brimming with bent and smudged cigarettes. When the doors swung open for the break, tobacco-allergic nonsmokers among the officials welcomed the freedom to breathe as well as a dozen journalists from France and the United States, there to inquire about the alliance.

Northwest's long, paneled boardroom looks out through a wide window onto a living scene of bosky Minnesota. A dense green forest on one side gives way to a village dominated by a white-spired church. The room is sparsely furnished, except for the long boardroom table of rich dark wood and a sidetable of Japanese artifacts—denoting the carrier's long and fruitful ties with the Far East. It was Northwest's franchise to Japan, and its right to serve other Asian countries from Japan, that had attracted the interest of European partners in the first place.

The alliance committee cochairmen, one from each airline, were broad-faced, heavyset men who exuded an air of resolve. Michael E. Levine, Northwest's Executive Vice President, Marketing, is a prominent figure in air transport in the United States. He gained fame in the airline community in the early years of deregulation as the primary implementer of the government's pro-competition policy at the Civil Aeronautics Board (CAB). In 1979, a leaked memo of his, which spoke in no uncertain terms of a strong-handed negotiating strategy, caused an international ruckus. After his CAB days, Levine gained practical experience as president of New York Air, the Frank Lorenzo–owned East Coast air shuttle, and returned to academe as a professor and later a dean at Yale University.

His Dutch counterpart, Jos Kamp, had an equally diverse background for the challenging task. After college he was commissioned a Navy officer in 1959. He served in the Netherlands Antilles and in the former Netherlands New Guinea, before an assignment with the Ministry of War at the Hague. He joined KLM in 1965 and specialized in passenger handling, sales, and marketing. His first sales assignments took him to Central and South America. He did a stint in the cargo specialty at KLM, and in 1989 he was placed on special assignment for KLM to build a new airline, (SWA) Sabena World Airlines, as part of a joint initiative of British Airways, KLM, and Belgium's Sabena. A decision of the European Commission ended that initiative, and Kamp was returned to the Netherlands and put in charge of the coordination between Northwest and KLM.

The alliance committee meets monthly, and rotates the site between Minneapolis and Amsterdam. Members speak to one another daily by telephone, coordinating the promotion and sale of tickets, the handling of thousands of passengers, the paying of bills, and the splitting of profits or losses between them.

John Dasburg, the affable president and chief executive officer of Northwest, attributes the success of the alliance to two factors. First, the mercantile traditions and trade acumen of the Dutch are in harmony with the U.S. version of capitalism. The fluency in the English language of the Dutch representatives eases discussions and helps to avoid breakdowns in communication.

Yet whenever the two groups get together, there is much more to be overcome than culture and language barriers. Members of the committee liken this business alliance to a marriage. There are many areas of agreement, but differences must be accommodated. Committee members agree that they must be tolerant at some times, firm at others, and understanding always. Little things, such as personal style, can be a source of aggravation or found to be jarring.

The Dutch are, for instance, a conservative lot. They are tolerant, but they have a strong appreciation of their own ways and are firm in their commitment to maintaining their own status quo. Precisely because of that conservativism in KLM, Northwest, at first glance, appears to be an ideal partner. It has its own conservative history, growing out of its Upper Midwest regional base. A work ethic prevails there, that prizes innovation and consistency, thrift and modesty. But Northwest is a changed company. It has restructured thoroughly in recent years, and it has been readied for a fight as only that company can be which, once rich, secure, and proud, has found itself cashless after a leveraged buyout. Now Northwest can't help but act like an aggressive modern company, one that, in the words of a KLM official, "turns out press releases by the hour."

When pressed for examples of how the alliance is working, Dasburg avoids any mention of earnings. He claims that the two airlines have saved $10 million in purchases as of June 1994, through joint purchases of fuel, in-flight supplies such as liquor, amenity kits, and blankets, and technical equipment. Another 85 items have been identified that could save another $16 million. To illustrate his point, he relates the phenomonal growth of the joint-venture route between Minneapolis/St. Paul and Amsterdam. The service began with 900 seats per week and grew in two years to 3100 seats per week. The combined transatlantic operation has increased from 2015 to 8558 seats per week.

This growth has been possible under the special U.S. authority that allows the two airlines to appear as one in computer-based reservations systems, which predominate in the industry and provide basic flight information for ticket reservations and sales. In the industry, this is referred to as "code-sharing." Northwest and KLM share each other's computer codes, NW for Northwest and KL for KLM. When an agent seeks a routing for a client—Cincinnati to Moscow, for example—Northwest flights are joined with KLM flights under Northwest flight numbers through to Moscow. The code-sharing system works as follows.

The Cincinnati passenger is ticketed by Northwest through to Moscow on NW Flight 1540, a DC-9 to Detroit Metropolitan Airport. There he boards a KLM Boeing 747 bound for Amsterdam. Our passenger's ticket reads as NW Flight 8616, even though the flight may be known to others on board as KLM Flight 616. The KLM aircraft flies to Amsterdam. There the Northwest passenger boards a KLM flight known as NW 8289 for the final leg to Moscow. The passenger was given boarding passes at Cincinnati for each flight leg. His baggage was checked through each stop to the final destination.

Northwest effectively uses the KLM system to increase its market reach from the American heartland all the way to Moscow. The process is reversed when a passenger approaches KLM in Moscow for a ticket to Cincinnati. KLM will issue tickets and boarding passes for the passenger on the KLM flight to Detroit, and thence on a Northwest flight to Cincinnati.

Code-sharing authority is authorized on a market-by-market basis. The U.S. Transportation Department has approved Northwest for 60 code-sharing destinations beyond Amsterdam. Some European governments have approved Northwest for code-sharing destinations. The governments of Germany and France thus far have been the most reluctant. In 1994, France rejected KLM–Northwest code-sharing to Lyons, Marseille, Nice, Strasbourg, and Toulouse. A court case was holding up the spread of code-sharing flights to German cities.

Dasburg observes: "We've had what I would label an uneven reaction. In some cases, the third countries honor their treaties and welcome the additional commercial air service of the alliance. On the other hand, there are some countries that are jealously protecting their international-flag carriers. They are less welcome." Dasburg's counterpart at the Twin Cities session, A. B. van Luyk, Executive Vice President of Passenger Sales and Services for KLM, expresses the view that times are changing even for the protectionists. "Indeed, in the beginning you had some jealous reaction. But in the end, even those countries realize that this is the way to go, especially for the future."

Northwest and KLM are prepared for the future like few other airlines. Because of their own roles as national carriers, they have access to the United States and Europe, the world's two largest markets, through the European Union. The Northwest franchise to the Far East provides access to the world's fastest-growing markets.

Ironically, the system of international aviation created by governments in 1944, at what was known as the Chicago Convention, does not provide for a truly international airline company. Air services are negotiated by diplomats from the various nations and secured in bilateral agreements. Under the current regime of international aviation, Northwest and KLM must obtain access to other countries with the aid of their respective nations. Their partnership is designed for the future world of free trade in the air. Until that day arrives, KLM and Northwest's alliance committee members are laboring to achieve a mutual vision of a single global airline.

Over the last two years, Northwest and KLM have developed their first joint global product, a world-business-class service common to each carrier. They are coordinating flight schedules for passengers and cargo, cooperating on ticket sales and promotions. They have merged frequent flier programs and computer reservations systems. Each linkage between the airlines helps to seal a partnership first secured by a $400-million KLM investment, and motivated by KLM's yearning for that presence in the trans-Pacific market that Northwest could provide.

## CONTINENTAL GOES FROM DISASTER TO DISASTER TO EXPERIMENT
### *Houston:* May 1994

Continental Airlines, another occupant of "the great middle," also is allied with a non-U.S. carrier, Air Canada, which owns near the maximum 24 percent of voting common shares that U.S. law allows. Air Partners, which joined with Air Canada in the 1992 bid to acquire the airline, owns the majority, 41 percent. Continental has courted and been courted by many foreign carriers, prompting *USA Today* to dub it "the Scarlett O'Hara of airlines."

In 1994, Continental joined with AmWest Partners and Mesa Airlines to acquire a substantial interest in America West, the Phoenix-based airline, prior to its return from bankruptcy. Continental's own shaky financial status in the early 1990s worked against an international linkage with the ever-hovering British Airways and Lufthansa German Airlines. Northwest also was a rumored suitor. Scandinavian Airlines System (SAS), which owned a minority investment in Continental during the eighties, lost it in the restructuring during Continental's second bankruptcy of 1991–1993.

In 1993, when Continental completed its reorganization under the bankruptcy laws, it emerged trim and tough-sounding. Directed by experienced, innovative executives, it was manned by a beaten-down work force hardened by years of labor under difficult financial conditions. Its Continental Lite became the first satellite airline sponsored by a larger U.S. carrier, a low-cost airline-within-an-airline that was to become a flawed new tool to combat the expansion of the competing low-cost airlines.

The last decade has been hard on Continental, a pioneer carrier that Frank Lorenzo tried to remold to meet the new competition of the deregulation era. Difficulties started almost right away.

## The First Fight

From May to September of 1983, the summer after Braniff's demise in 1982 at Dallas, the new managers of Continental Airlines, downstate in Houston, had their hands full. They were attempting to fashion a new, cost-efficient airline for the new competitive environment. The effort was about to make international headlines.

Only in that fall of 1982, Frank Lorenzo had merged Texas International Inc. with Continental, moving the headquarters from Los Angeles to Houston. Under new ownership, Continental was seeking an identity for itself in deregulation's marketing environment, after the loss by suicide of its well-liked and highly regarded president, Bob Feldman. Lorenzo tapped Stephen M. Wolf, later of

United, to serve as president of Continental. Wolf had had success as a cargo manager for American Airlines and had spent a brief time at Pan American, but this was his first experience of the higher reaches of management. He and all at Continental were put to a stern personal and career test that summer of 1983. Labor-management relations at the Houston carrier were about to be shattered.

Wolf served as the airline's chief spokesman when about half of Continental's mechanics struck the carrier that summer. Continental hired some replacement workers to increase staff and maintain a viable flight schedule. Work rules were so restrictive at Continental that even with strikers walking the picket line, the carrier was able to perform with only the nonstriking employees and a few new hires. The walkout had hurt, but it wasn't debilitating. Lorenzo and his managers devised a plan and a backup plan, each with the objective of returning Continental to profitability and streamlining it into a hot, competitive airline. But this was the early 1980s, not the early 1990s when some hard lessons had been learned. The time difference, and the people concerned made all the difference in the world.

Under Plan A, Continental offered its 12,000 employees a package of stock bonuses, options, and a profit-sharing program, in exchange for pay cuts and new labor contracts. Lorenzo was counting on an annual savings of $150 million under the program. Alternative Plan B called for substantial cutbacks and downsizing.

As August passed and September drew to a close, the key unions, the Air Line Pilots Association (ALPA), and the flight attendants failed to support the plan. The pilots and flight attendants threatened a walkout. A street fight was brewing.

In the next few weeks, with Plan A under attack, Continental's managers rejected the option of downsizing the carrier. This decision followed an unsuccessful attempt by Lorenzo to sell the Continental hub at Denver's Stapleton Airport. One of the potential buyers, American Airlines, was interested, but balked at the last minute. Analysts at American evaluated the Continental aircraft, which were included among the Denver assets, and found them sorely in need of rehabilitation. They recommended against the acquisition. The inability of Continental to sell the Denver assets heightened the pressure on executives. Time was running out for Continental and for Lorenzo's grand plan.

Managers in Houston began to worry that cutbacks would reduce Continental to the scope of a regional airline, and that the near-cashless company would be plunged into deeper jeopardy. The risk of downsizing, in their minds, was at least equal to the hazard of bankruptcy. The decision lay with Lorenzo, who, characteristically, fired first in this labor-management street fight, beating the unions to the draw. The company sought protection under Chapter 11 of the bankruptcy code, abrogated the labor contracts, and dismissed 12,000 employees. It was the first and, to this day, the boldest move by carrier management to restructure costs under airline deregulation.

The bankruptcy papers were filed without Wolf's signature. He left the company a week before the filing, citing personal reasons. According to the story told by old Continental hands, Lorenzo and Continental's staff devised a covering story for Wolf: that Wolf had resigned because of his personal distaste for the abrogation of labor contracts. A controversy exists to this day over the real reasons for Wolf's withdrawal. Henry Duffy, the ALPA president during much of the 1980s and an adversary of Wolf's over many bargaining tables, detected in Wolf an uncanny instinct for knowing when to leave a company. It had served him well when he left American, then Pan American World Airways, Republic, Flying Tigers, and finally United. "We dealt with him closely," Duffy said. "He was really very cautious before making a move. He would talk to us a long time about what he was considering and he always wanted to know the lay of the land with the pilots. He was a careful checker."

Whatever his motives, Wolf became a champion to some in labor. Duffy wasn't convinced that the executive had suddenly became protective of labor. "When he went back [to the causes of his departure from Continental], he colored the leaving to be more moralistic," Duffy said.

With the focus on the labor strife at Continental, the precarious state of Continental's finances was obscured, and the focus of media attention fell heavily on the airline's difficulties with labor. Still, Continental was broke, and management had fears that if the true sorry state of Continental's finances was made known to travel agents, the airline would suffer the same fate that Braniff had only a year earlier. Everyone at Continental remembers when Braniff's problems became daily headlines, and travel agents gave up on the carrier and booked passengers on rivals of hapless Braniff. A weak carrier became even weaker. Continental chiefs had other plans for the remains of old Continental than that of a regional carrier crossing and recrossing the hot and competitive Texas plains.

In the next few years, Continental emerged from its first bankruptcy and began to look like a long-term survivor. Lorenzo was everywhere in those days, talking to employees, holding impromptu meetings, answering questions, sometimes dueling with malcontents and outspoken critics at public sessions with employees. Sometimes the sessions grew heated. John Adams, who directed personnel for Continental in this period, recalls the presence of a few fed-up employees who tried to rile Lorenzo with a "zinger" comment or query. "You could see them standing around with a smirk on their faces." Frequently, Adams said, Lorenzo would fire back, and gain the cheering support of the crowd.

Lorenzo was a hands-on executive, a tireless campaigner defending his company who bypassed the VIP lounges to gain greater contact with employees. One day at Houston Intercontinental Airport, an irate passenger at first verbally and then physically attacked a Continental gate agent, in Lorenzo's presence. Former Lorenzo associates remember the passenger grabbing the agent around the neck or pulling at his tie. Lorenzo heard the ruckus, grabbed the passenger, and wrestled him to the floor. He and several Continental agents held the man until airline security and airport police took over.

"That was not at all out of character," one of Lorenzo's former associates says. "Part of his problem was that he was always like Don Quixote, when dealing with economics or whatever, always wanting to take on somebody."

### First Out of the Gate for a Long, Hard Ride Ahead

It's May 16, 1994. Eleven years have passed since the first bankruptcy, and Continental has had a second visit to U.S. court over insolvency. No airline undergoes upheavals of that proportion within a single decade and emerges without scars. A crew bus shambling through Dallas/Fort Worth International Airport symbolized the damage. The bus displayed the broad scrapes and deep line scratches of a hard sideswiping. Such shoddiness could also be seen years earlier, in 1988, on a flight on a DC-9 that still wore the faded apple-red livery of New York Air, a sister carrier under the Texas Air Corporation umbrella. The flight attendants on that flight acted as if they were tormented by some unseen galley monster. The flight itself was a study in cabin sloppiness. The seats felt as old and gritty as antique furniture. Everyone except the passengers seemed harried. The overweight pilot hurried through the gate area, looking as if he wanted to pick a fight with someone.

Six years have passed since that depressing trip. One wonders how a company changes those kinds of conditions. Airline executives have debated since deregulation whether it is better to try to reform an old company or start anew with fresh policies and people. Strong arguments prevail on both sides. Some carriers simply weren't reformable. Continental is a living example of the difficulty of reform, but it is still trying. The long line of new entrant carriers, now defunct, attests to the hardships of starting anew, even with the most enthusiastic employees. A general criticism of Continental executives under Lorenzo was that they exuded a personal frigidity. It was as if the hard economic facts of running a deregulated airline were all that was needed in labor-management dealings. But reports have trickled in in more recent times of an improved situation for employees.

Long-time Continental employees who endured the storms deserve congratulations and a financially easy retirement. They served under nine chief executives between 1983 and 1993, not counting the several occasions when Chairman Frank Lorenzo served as temporary president. No executive, with experience or not, was able to unlock the door to a successful operation in the 1980s and early 1990s. In hindsight, the prevailing Continental vision in the post-deregulation period appears to have been flawed for more than a decade. Executives cast the carrier in the role of a full-service U.S. major airline, flying trunk routes to domestic and overseas destinations. It wanted only the big-time. The domestic niche into which its Texas rival, Southwest, so easily nestled was merely an after-thought. Continental had the right idea—low fares—but it was inconsistent in applying its fares strategy, and its timing was off. American, United, and Delta beat Continental to the gate, firming up their positions as the Big Three in the middle of the decade while Continental was still struggling out of bankruptcy.

The mid-1980s approach to conquering the world, offered in Houston, was the same as that at most carriers: merger. Lorenzo tried to merge with Trans World Airlines. But Trans World's unions pre-ferred Carl Icahn, then an unknown and later their archenemy, over the known factor of Lorenzo. But nothing would stop Lorenzo. By 1987, his Texas Air Corporation had brought together Continental, New York Air, and the failing People Express Airlines, along with the assets of the bankrupt Frontier Airlines of Denver. Operating separately under the Texas Air Corporation umbrella was the doomed Eastern Airlines, a company about ready to explode with labor tensions. Lorenzo tried to breathe life into dead or near-dying companies, an arduous task for anyone, and it proved to be Continental's undoing. Managing alien company cultures at the bloated Continental, a former senior officer said, was like "finding yourself in Medusa's hair" everywhere one turned.

Continental simply couldn't cobble the disparate elements together. Operational performance suffered, and high-yield business passengers left the airline in droves. Whenever an airline encounters problems, management frequently turns to marketing and public relations for answers. An attempt was under way in 1990 to recover the grand image of the old Continental. As a surprise part of that image restoration came the sudden departure of the chairman, Frank Lorenzo, who had gained himself a permanent place on organized labor's hate list. Preceding Lorenzo's departure, an internal report had been generated within Continental management, suggesting that Lorenzo's continued presence wasn't serving the overall good of the company. Finally, Lorenzo agreed to step down and pave the way for new management.

Lorenzo sold his shares to Scandinavian Airlines System (SAS), whose $17 million interest boosted Continental's chances and spread SAS's influence into North America. But as hard as Continental officers tried, the heavy debt resulting from Eastern's demise in 1990 and the recession, higher fuel prices, and the evaporation of passenger traffic hammered Continental into bankruptcy that same year. Chairman Robert Ferguson put the airline on an austerity program, cutting back wages by 10 percent and grounding aircraft. In 1991, 1992, and part of 1993, Continental was practically static, as it regrouped for an uncertain future.

The airline was down but not out. Early in 1993, Ferguson named top staff members to a special team to find an answer for Continental. The team members were charged with blueprinting a domestic short-haul carrier to function in tandem with the full-service, long-haul Continental. The Ferguson team was set up on its own, away from the high-rise headquarters on 2929 Allen Parkway. Team members were instructed, in jest, to come back with an idea to revamp the airline or not to return to work.

The product, Continental Lite or CALite as it was dubbed by the team, was born several weeks later. One of the chief architects was Donald Valentine, who had worked under Herb Kelleher as vice president for marketing at Southwest Airlines. He serves as the senior marketing vice president at Continental. Ferguson scored another coup in hiring Gordon Bethune, an operations veteran who had earned a solid reputation at Piedmont Airlines prior to the USAir takeover. Ferguson had both a new team in place and a fresh idea. With Continental Lite, Continental became the first major carrier to develop a new competitive weapon for the nineties.

Continental executives based their new strategy on the notion that an airline seat should be sold as if it were a commodity. Travelers planning a short-haul flight (750 miles or less), are looking for basic transportation and little else. They may prefer an airline to operate several flights a day in a city pair, but the prerequisite is a low fare. It's important, Continental executives believe, to define and offer a good product in basic air transportation, yet still offer a low price.

Thus, Continental has cloned the operations at Southwest Airlines and spread their version quickly into the eastern half of the United States. This follows a scheme that Southwest had been contemplating but couldn't carry out for lack of aircraft. Continental blanketed the East with point-to-point flights from Atlanta, Baltimore, Fort

Lauderdale, Jacksonville, Tampa, New Orleans, and Norfolk. Continental executives were spending money on computer and printer time—no small amount, we're told—to provide passengers with seat assignments. In a small way, Continental had begun to define its new service. Everyone on top at the airline insisted that their passengers wanted it no other way.

But Continental Lite was still in its formative stage, and more changes were coming. The operation had taken off with the energy of a new start-up carrier, and unfortunately, with more delays and cancellations than could be tolerated. Some of the Continental Lite aircraft were too large, had too many seats, and were too costly to operate in the markets they were serving. With communications lacking and maintenance people scarce and always in the wrong place, the flight completion rate of Continental Lite suffered. Flying squads of mechanics were formed to quickly respond to problem airplanes.

As the U.S. economy slowly improved in 1994, Continental Lite appeared to be catching on. But the new service encountered tough competition from short-haul operations by other carriers, including USAir. "That's the great thing about deregulation: It gives our customers a choice," John Luth, Senior Vice President, Continental Lite, told *Aviation Daily*. Continental will be flexible, he added, and adopt any new idea that works. "It's a tough business if you don't have a sense of humor and a little humility."

In the fall of 1994, Ferguson resigned as Continental president and chief executive officer, signaling that problems still existed in carrier operations. He retained his position as a member of the board of directors, but the chore of running the company fell to Gordon Bethune, the operations expert. As 1995 began, Bethune announced a 10 percent cut in aircraft capacity and, subsequently, a furlough of 4000 Continental employees, which was scheduled to take place in 1995. Deliveries of Boeing aircraft scheduled for 1995 have been delayed.

Operating costs at Continental are the lowest of all the full-service major airlines'. In 1993 its average cost per available seat mile fell below 8 cents, closing in on Southwest's. Continental is using that low unit cost to wield leverage in the new markets. Continental's executives have been dedicated to stripping away all unnecessary expenses from the operation to keep them comparable with the lowest in the market. Being first in the market might have been helpful if Continental had defined itself and gained acceptance from passengers. But Continental failed in this task. Many new markets in the eastern United States were unprofitable. Luth was reassigned, and any distinction between flights of regular Continental and Continental Lite began in 1995 to blur. The executives had enough trouble defining one carrier. Two airlines within the same company was one too many.

The biggest challenge for Continental lies in upgrading its poor image, which stretches back to the time of the first bankruptcy in September 1983, and the sometimes vicious labor campaign against it. Continental was second only to its former affiliated carrier, Eastern Airlines, in the intense criticism leveled by labor at both management and operations.

Continental's level of safety has been challenged several times. An FAA manager confides that Continental has been investigated so frequently, owing to the barrage of labor charges, that it has to be the safest airline in the U.S. A sign of fairer weather for the carrier occurred in 1993, when it returned operating profits in the third and fourth quarters. Promptly as promised, employee wages were improved for the first time in several years, in the hope of lifting lagging morale. But clearly, the years of strife have taken a heavy toll.

America West, now aligned with Continental, is one of the airlines that American's Bob Crandall has complained about. Its reorganization under Chapter 11 of the U.S. bankruptcy law ranks as the longest of any bankrupt carrier in modern times, stretching from June 1991 to August 1994. Crandall has rightly criticized the bankruptcy laws for permitting this drawn-out reorganization, during which America West or Continental could play the spoiler in the marketplace. The criticism, often heard at the national airline commission hearings in 1993, may have set the stage for bankruptcy law reform in Congress.

America West turned a corner of sorts in the spring of 1994, after nearly three years in bankruptcy. It reported a $15 million profit, its fifth straight profitable quarter. This represented a sevenfold increase over the first quarter of 1993. The profits rolled in even as America West underwent a management change at the very top. Michael Conway, its president and chief executive officer and one of its cofounders in 1981, had been fired on New Year's Eve after a year-long power struggle with the Chairman, William Franke.

The reorganization was lengthy, as a result of seven 120-day extensions of America West's right to file a reorganization plan, granted by a federal court. The first investment group terminated its agreement, prolonging the process. A second group of investors was turned down in favor of the current owners, AmWest Partners, L.P.; Fidelity Investments, Boston; Lehman Brothers, New York; Continental Airlines; and Mesa Airlines. The AmWest chairman, David Bonderman, a Texas financier, also serves as chairman of Continental Airlines. Under an arrangement worked out in August 1994, America West received a $214.9 million injection from AmWest. Continental's share gives it a 4 percent stake in America West.

## USAir Slowly Responds to a Crisis
### *Arlington, Virginia*

Even a few years ago, top USAir officials were insisting that they could manage even though the airline's operational costs exceeded those at all other majors. USAir was different, they argued. Its costs were high because flying short-haul routes is costly on a per-mile basis. There was a certain logic to those statements, but many old-line hands in the airline business believed that USAir was flying on borrowed time. They were right.

Over the years, many of USAir's short-haul routes have been monopoly routes, where USAir was the only game in town. Prices may have been a little high but the carrier was reliable, and it developed a strong clientele. The loyalty of its customers, and its splendid isolation in the Mid-Atlantic region, boosted USAir's confidence in itself and its network.

Short-haul routes are costly by comparison because costs are focused in a shorter time frame. Fuel-burn is greater on short hauls, on a per-mile basis. The stormy weather of the Mid-Atlantic region, caused by the proximity of the sea coast and the Appalachian mountain chain, can turn an airline schedule into a nightmare and devolve into a cost factor. Landing fees are higher in the expensive East. Therefore, according to USAir management, ticket prices were high because costs were high. Further, the management said, USAir unit costs and ticket prices couldn't be compared with those at other carriers. The officials insisted that short-haul monopoly routes had nothing to do with the high prices.

That old USAir argument collapsed in the summer of 1993, when the word spread that USAir's monopoly days were over. Competition was entering the once-safe markets at a brisk pace. Inside of several months, Southwest Airlines entered the heart of USAir's market at Baltimore/Washington International Airport. Shock and dismay registered on the faces of USAir station managers on the day a cadre of Maryland state officials greeted Herbert Kelleher and spoke gloriously of a new day dawning for BWI airport. USAir's station managers were cordial to inquirers but refused to address the fact of the new competition.

The Mid-Atlantic region represents a unique set of problems for airline management. The region doesn't lend itself to hub operations as well as other areas of the country. Cities in the East are more numerous and are situated closer together than cities in other U.S. regions. The geography has caused other airlines to adopt a strategy of overflying USAir hubs at Baltimore, Charlotte, and Pittsburgh, and of providing point-to-point service in the denser markets. Low-fare airlines had avoided the region in the past because of the difficult weather, busy airports, and high landing costs. But in the changing U.S. market, the new low-fare operators could smell blood along the East Coast.

Even more immediately dangerous for USAir in 1993–1994 than the entry of Southwest, was Continental's low-fare services out of Greensboro/High Point Airport in North Carolina, a USAir strong point since its merger with Piedmont. When Continental expanded in June 1994, into 350 city pairs, most were traditional USAir markets. Management conceded in a report in *Aviation Daily* that USAir generated 36 percent of its annual revenues from secondary markets, many of which Continental was entering with very low fares.

It took USAir five months to show evidence of a competitive strategy. It started up a short-haul, high-frequency, fast-turnaround operation of Boeing 737s, called High Ground, and management began to talk about a wholly new airline product emerging by the end of 1994. As an immediate strategy, USAir slashed fares to match those of its new competition and, with its high cost structure, took a beating. Its net loss in the first quarter, released in the Spring of 1994, reached 196.7 million, by far, the greatest loss among the major carriers. Furman Selz Incorporated, of New York, commented in a first-quarter update on USAir, "The company won traffic back from discount carriers at the expense of yield. It was a very expensive way for the company to protect its market share."

But by early 1995, 18 months after USAir first became aware of new low-fare competition, USAir negotiators still hadn't wrangled any concessions from their unions even though they were desperately needed. A union coalition was studying the carrier's situation, with the intention of proposing its own solution to USAir's problems. One hundred 737s were designated for High Ground markets, and management intensified its search for an all-new kind of airline service, unveiling a frequent-traveler-designed product in the Fall. Basically, USAir refitted the forward part of the cabin with roomier seating for its higher-paying business travelers.

Within hours of this event, on September 8, 1994, at about 7 P.M., a USAir Boeing 737-300 at 6000 ft altitude began a downwind approach to Pittsburgh International Airport. Suddenly the 737 rolled to the left. The angle of bank increased, and the 737's nose pitched downward. Twenty-three seconds later the aircraft, carrying 132 occupants, slammed into the ground at a speed of 260 knots. It was USAir's second fatal crash of 1994, after the loss of a USAir Douglas DC-9 in July at Charlotte, NC. The 737 crash had an eerie similarity to a United Airlines 737-200 crash in 1991 at Colorado Springs. The investigators of the National Transportation Safety Board (NTSB) had been unable to determine the probable cause of the Colorado Springs accident, in which there also had been no survivors.

As 1994 ended, USAir suffered from a huge financial hemorrhage. The parent company, USAir Group Inc., reported that the year's net loss reached $684.9 million including $226.1 million in one-time charges. That was bad enough, but the news got worse with a close check of the operating results. The airline subsidiary reported an operating loss of $516.9 million. The fourth quarter had been a disaster, with the operating loss of $277.5 million.

Against the pressure of low-fare competition, USAir had dropped its ticket prices an average of 9 percent for the year and 10 percent in the last quarter. The airline had taken cost-cutting measures during the year that slashed $400 million of expenses, but the savings were woefully insufficient.

Talks with union groups failed to produce any cost-cutting agreement. The pilots had broken off discussions late in 1994, only to be resumed in 1995. "Everyone acknowledges that lower costs are essential to the future of this airline and the service it provides to hundreds of communities," Seth Schofield, USAir Chairman and Chief Executive Officer, observed after the release of the year's disastrous results. "We are extremely disappointed that we have been unable to reach an agreement with our labor groups."

USAir deferred delivery of eight Boeing 757s scheduled for 1996 delivery, and Schofield said other cost-cutting steps were clearly necessary. The airline has begun a needed downsizing with the sale of 11 Boeing 737 aircraft and a 5 percent capacity cut. This is only the beginning of a "rightsizing" for USAir.

# FOUR

# The Populist
# of the Planes

Imitation is the sincerest form of flattery.

—CHARLES CALEB COLTON
Lacon, 1780–1832

## SOUTHWEST: THE MODEL DOMESTIC AIRLINE
### Dallas, 1992-1994

In 1992, Southwest Airlines found itself under the threat of a lawsuit alleging that one of its slogans, "Just Plane Smart," was the copyrighted property of a Stevens Aviation of Greenville, South Carolina. Herbert J. Kelleher, chairman and president of Southwest, took up this challenge with almost childlike glee. He telephoned Stevens' president, Kurt Herwald, and challenged him to an arm-wrestling duel, winner take all.

The event attracted 1800 mostly Southwest employees, jammed inside a local sports center. Flight attendants donned cheerleading outfits to encourage their hero. Herb, a lighted cigarette dangling from his mouth, flexed his muscles not with barbells but with cartons of cigarettes. Television crews from the major U.S. networks, the British Broadcasting Company, Japanese television, and the Canadian Broadcasting Company filmed the feigned struggle from the first to the last absurdity. When Herb came up second, losing the match to his opponent, it was as if Superman, the man of steel, had lost all of his powers and taken a public drubbing. But the whole drama had been contrived farce. Several days afterward an agreement was announced between the two companies, permitting Southwest, for a fee, to continue to use the slogan, Just Plane Smart. Even in losing, Herb wins. . . .

History will show that Kelleher and the Southwest founders unearthed a goldmine in short-haul flying in the United States. It is a genuine niche that others had ignored for too long. Moreover, Southwest exploited the consumers' desire for low fares and developed a widely acceptable, no-frills style of cabin service.

Another Southwest discovery was the power of a creative work force. Kelleher and fellow executives listen to employees and follow

**Flying Smart.** A Southwest Airlines Boeing 737 cruises above broken puffy clouds on one of its short-haul flights. Southwest operates only 737s in its U.S. network. The management decision to focus on one aircraft type has saved the airline many training and maintenance dollars, and has contributed to the goal of keeping operational costs to a minimum. (*Photo provided by Southwest Airlines*)

up on suggestions. Employees are given an opportunity to transform their work into a challenging and rewarding enterprise. The final key for Southwest, particularly to its low-cost structure, has been the simplicity of its operation.

A remarkable spate of annual profits stretching back to 1973 persuaded the airline industry—big and small, poor and rich—that Herb Kelleher and company at Southwest Airlines were on to something. It took a while for the notion to sink in, simply because Southwest appeared so unlikely a candidate. It has chosen to excel in the unglamorous short-haul market. In this niche, Southwest diverts people from automobiles to fast, convenient airplanes. Southwest doesn't fly to Bali or Puerto Vallarta. It's an aerial bus service operated by an excellent team of employees. It sets fares based on its costs plus an adequate profit, and the costs are among the lowest in the industry. If Southwest enters a market, traffic goes up sharply and fares come down to its level.

### *Dallas:* May 16, 1994

The corporate headquarters of Southwest Airlines occupies a light gray-and-white, three-story building off of Denton Road, paralleling the runways at the municipally owned Love Field. A small sign on Love Field Drive, pointing to the Southwest Airlines Training Center, provides the only direction. Visitors who haven't been given explicit directions may drive extra miles around the airport. Once a visitor is close to the headquarters building, the environs look no different than those around many other office buildings, with the exception of a sand-based volleyball court wedged in a corner of the vast automobile parking lot. The sandy court stands as a symbol of the company's unwritten rule that employees should have some fun in the place where they also work very hard.

A group of eight blue-suited women gathers in the spacious lobby, displaying ample confidence in their demeanor. They chat about mutual friends in aviation. It's obvious after a while that they're pilots, and feel slightly uncomfortable about their sartorial commonality. But they have followed the instructions from the Department of People—not *personnel* mind you, *people*—and each is trying to present herself as a willing candidate for a coveted pilot's job. Two are United States Air Force pilots, one of whom had gotten lost temporarily in her white two-seater car on a headquarters approach road. But here she was minutes later among a group of fine-looking, obviously talented women, awaiting interviews.

Southwest's employees, looking fresh and healthy, paraded through the main lobby in shorts, golf shirts, and other sorts of casual clothing. The freedom to dress in very unbusinesslike attire through the remainder of 1994 was a reward from the Executive Vice President of Customers, Colleen Barrett, in recognition of the employees' contribution to Southwest's sweep in 1994 of the Transportation Department's Triple Crown of performance awards. Southwest was rated as having the best on-time performance, the fewest baggage problems, and the fewest complaints from the department's Office of Consumer Affairs. The Triple Crown is taken seriously by this giant-killer airline, and most employees entering the lobby this morning have taken advantage of Ms. Barrett's offer.

Strolling into the lobby in a business suit, Herbert J. Kelleher, chairman and president of Southwest Airlines, shakes hands with people and kisses a few. He is rangy, like the fabled Texan of the Old West, and he looks taller than his six-foot frame. Silver-toned gray hair is combed up and back in pompadour fashion, with the effect being somewhere between that of a thespian and an executive. Kelleher greets his guests and gallops toward the elevator and his second-floor office.

Visitors have a lot to see at the headquarters. Most impressive is a sculpture by the American Jim Brothers, a gift from General Electric/CFM International to airlines that launched the CFM engine. It depicts a young boy in a 1930s style flying helmet and goggles, perched on a tree stump. His hands are releasing a bird into the air: a wonderful depiction of the freedom that derives from the ability to fly. The sculpture in Southwest's lobby is a miniature of the full-size opus. Herb Kelleher interprets the flight theme in terms of Southwest Airlines. The airline was still a cub among U.S. carriers when the sculpture was presented. But still, the airline has become the instrument of affordable short-haul transportation for thousands of people who otherwise would have taken trips across the spacious Southwest by driving their cars or taking the bus.

The walls of the second-floor hallway leading to the executive offices are lined with photographs, plaques, and framed certificates.

Photographs of aviation heros, Lindbergh and Yeager, hang beside hundreds of photographs of smiling Southwest employees. And then there are pictures of Herb, in Halloween dress as an Arab; Herb, line-dancing; Herb, standing on the wing of an airplane; Herb, doing an Elvis impersonation; mugging, always mugging for the camera, and most everyone around wreathed in smiles. But Herb's pictures are eclipsed, if not in style, certainly in volume, by hundreds of photographs of Southwest employees.

Kelleher opens a pack of cigarettes and lights up the first of 14 he will smoke in the 75 minutes. He observes that the state of Kentucky, which Southwest serves at Louisville, is the biblical land of milk and honey. The state produces Pall Mall cigarettes and Wild Turkey bourbon, "the only true American drink." A stuffed wild turkey occupies a place of honor on the left of his desk, the gift from a friend who has a sense of humor. A serious side of Herb Kelleher also may be seen here. Along the far wall of his office hang a line of like-framed portraits of Presidents Truman and Roosevelt, British Prime Minister Winston Churchill, U.S. Marine Corps ace Pappy Boyington, and a group photograph of United States commanding officers including the Army's George Catlett Marshall. Kelleher willingly explains. An adolescent during World War II, he grew up with a legion of heros. He says he tells his son he's been deprived because today's society has no heros.

An accommodating person, Kelleher leans forward in his large easy chair and inclines toward a small, whirring tape recorder. He answers questions easily and fully, reflecting his lawyer's profession and his knack for dealing with others. He says that the secret to Southwest's success is its people. Now that the carrier has grown to a workforce of 8700 individuals, employee screening is more thorough than ever. The carrier needs hard-working and loyal employees. Herb is serious when he says that a sense of humor in an employee was and remains very important.

## FIRST THE CONCEPT, THEN THE FORMULA
### San Antonio, Texas: 1967

In the 1960s, Herb Kelleher transplanted himself to San Antonio from New York and looked forward to pursuing a legal career in his wife Joan's hometown. One day in 1967, Rollin King, a pilot and entrepreneur, invited him to a meeting at the city's St. Antony Club. King was in process of dismantling a commuter airline that couldn't generate sufficient traffic from its network of small Texas towns. He had another idea for an airline that he wanted to discuss with Kelleher. On a napkin on that St. Antony Club table, King drew a triangle and labeled the three points, San Antonio, Dallas, and Houston, the three major Texas cities.

At first, Kelleher wasn't impressed with the idea. But he did some research on what was already happening in California aviation. California's intrastate flying was, like Texas's, regulated by a state commission rather than the U.S. Civil Aeronautics Board (CAB). The California commission had been open to new ideas and permitted a new carrier, Pacific Southwest Airlines (PSA), to offer low fares and high frequencies in the coastal north-south markets in California. PSA was showing the rest of the industry how to run an airline. Soon, King's idea had entranced Kelleher. He recalls those early days:

When we started, we focused on the fact that the original Braniff was a monopoly carrier among the big cities of Texas. Its corollary was Trans Texas, a subdsidized regional carrier that had a monopoly from the small towns to the big cities. As a consequence of the fact that there really wasn't any competition in Texas in those two different areas, the quality of service was very, very poor. The prices for that time, we thought, were unduly high. And it occurred to us that there was an opportunity to bring to Texas what, in effect, PSA had done in California, and that it would probably be even easier in Texas, since the quality of competition wasn't as good as it was in California.

I think we were right in the sense that the prices were too high, and the quality of service was very poor. But we misjudged the fighting capabilities of our competitors. They tied us up for three and a half years in court before we ever flew an airplane, and assiduously tried to put us out of business thereafter.

Southwest had no difficulty obtaining a certificate from the Texas Aeronautics Commission in February 1968 to serve Dallas, Houston, and San Antonio. But rivals Braniff, Trans Texas, and Continental

Airlines turned to the state courts and won a restraining order pro-
hibiting the delivery of the Southwest certificate. Southwest's fate
hung in the balance for several years. Kelleher lost the case in lower
court and then in the State Court of Civil Appeals. Investors grew
uneasy after the setbacks but risked a extension while Kelleher fash-
ioned a final appeal to the Texas Supreme Court. Their confidence in
him was repaid. He won a series of decisions that permitted the airline to operate three aircraft in "the Texas triangle."

Kelleher learned a valuable lesson when Southwest Airline's competitors tried to stop the carrier from gaining new routes before the
Texas commission:

Much to my surprise, they didn't really believe there was any price
elasticity in the airline business. They had been regulated by the federal government for so long, because they had no real incentive to
keep their costs down since the CAB set fares based on the average
costs of the industry as a whole. The way they attempted to rectify
any financial difficulties they got into was by raising fares. As a consequence of that, that's the way they thought the world was. Only
businesspeople or only wealthy individuals wanted to travel by air.
We said that's not true, that everyone would love to fly for 45 minutes rather than drive for six hours, but they couldn't afford to do so.
We went into city pair markets, doubled and quadrupled them,
within one year, which showed we were right. There was latent
demand for air transportation in the short-haul markets that was not
being satisfied by the incumbent carriers.

Recognizing a weakness in the opposition, Kelleher developed a
penchant for choosing new routes:

That's one of the things that I am deeply involved in in a very personal way, today. I have relinquished other things as we have come
along. I have acted as a sort of troubleshooter. When we didn't have
someone to do the financing, I did the financing. Whatever it might
be. We have excellent people in that area, and it's kind of interesting,
it is to me, because we do it differently than any other airline that I
know of. And I'll tell you why.

First of all, we approach it strategically. We look around and say, gee, USAir is not doing very well in California, and that looks like it might be an opportunity for Southwest Airlines. Then we bring it down to the next level and start looking at city-pair markets. Believe it or not, it is one of the few formulas that Southwest Airlines has. We actually have a formula for evaluating the amount of traffic that our added service and lower fares will develop. It is astoundingly accurate and it is proprietary. We've developed it over the years, refined it and honed it, and it is amazingly accurate. You know, this market has 150,000 passengers in there now, and when we are in [the market for] a year, there will be 500,000 passengers, of which we will carry 250,000. Usually we are not off by 5 percent and usually we are on the low side, which is good and it is conservative."

Kelleher credits John Eichner, the principal partner in Simat, Helleisen & Eichner, New York, for writing the basics of the formula in use today. Kelleher remembers:

I became very familiar with it through the route proceedings. When I came to Southwest, I said "I will do this in ways that are not algebraic, that anyone can understand, and I am going to abide by it." We look at markets; the Midwest responds different than California, so you tweak it for the Midwest. Population alone is not necessarily indicative. You find that you can have a very large city that is primarily industrial, and the amount of flying that it generates in comparison to the population is small. One of the things we look at is [passenger] trips-per-thousand [people] for cities on an equivalent basis. You will find that Dallas is a big progenitor of trips. Detroit is much less so. Market cities tend to generate more traffic than industrial cities.

But the other thing that figures into the strategy as well is that a byword here is that we "manage in good times so we can do well in bad times." Now, how does that affect us? Here in the last four years, Southwest has expanded far faster during the recession than would have otherwise been the case, because we had the financial strength to take advantage of the incapacity of the other carriers.

The formula's author, John Eichner, a founder of the Park Avenue, New York, consultancy, may be the longest running, best-known airline consultant in the business. He knows the airline business from the first crank of the jet engine to the switch-off at night. His role as consultant is comparable to that of a trainer of a thoroughbred horse but also that of advisor to the jockey. He had replaced M. Lamar Muse at American Airlines after Muse departed in January 1971 to run Southwest for Kelleher and King. Eichner later turned to airline consulting, and was hired as a consultant by Southwest. Eichner recalls:

The first route case was the Harlingen case . . . before the Texas Aeronautics Commission in 1974. It ended up that Herb and I and Lamar spent two to three months there in Austin, fighting the TAC hearing. We were saying that there was a large market for O&D [Origin and Destination passengers], because of diversion of the automobile traffic. It was a big number, and nobody believed it.

Southwest encountered formidable opposition to its plan to move into the Rio Grande Valley at Harlingen. One of the opposers was Frank Lorenzo, later chief executive at Continental and Eastern Airlines, then the owner of Trans Texas, predecessor of Texas International Airlines. A strange turn of events at Trans Texas paved the way for Southwest to gain Harlingen. In the first of the series of labor problems at Lorenzo airlines, a labor group struck Trans Texas, bringing down capacity in the state and making Southwest's experiment look more attractive and viable to state authorities. "They allowed them to go there, and it developed even more traffic than forecast. Southwest Airlines really broke the valley wide open, and it turned a little market with a few hundred passengers a day into one with thousands a day, almost instantaneously." Southwest in 1994 was carrying 1000 passengers a day in the Harlingen market. Kelleher observes:

Really, as we went along, what we did was portray to the industry that this was a separate specialty. Because theretofore, the short-haul passenger had always been kind of an addendum to what the carriers were doing on a long-haul basis. And when I say that, I mean: If you

looked at a flight between San Antonio and Dallas, it wasn't scheduled for the San Antonio-to-Dallas passenger, it was scheduled for
the San Antonio–Minneapolis or the San Antonio–New York passenger. If local passengers happened to be on-board that was fine, but
if they were not there, the other carriers were not particularly concerned about them either.

Southwest's niche was the short-haul passenger. As an intrastate
carrier it managed to get an airport niche at its very own Love Field.
This occurred in 1979 through an amendment to the International
Air Transportation Competition Act. Authored by Representative
Jim Wright, a Texas Democrat, the Wright amendment denied new
entry at Love Field to any large, scheduled carrier. The amendment
allowed the commercial carriers already operating at Love Field to
continue to serve the state of Texas and destinations in the four states
contiguous to Texas, namely, Louisiana, Arkansas, Oklahoma, and
New Mexico. The Love Field intrastate carriers could fly to other
destinations, but the passengers from Love would have to get off the
Texas airplane and board another from the contiguous states. The
amendment remains in effect today.

Kelleher addresses the allegation that the Wright amendment
provided Southwest with a franchise at Love Field. "I've always loved
that," he gasps, between spurts of laughter. "Other airlines could
lose tons of money at any other airport across the rest of the United
States, but they consider themselves deprived from making it 'all up
at Love Field . . .' That's got to be the most prosperous little airport,
the corner store," the executive crows. Kelleher predicts that Southwest will perform well at Love Field with or without the Wright
amendment. He illustrates this by pointing to Southwest's record at
Houston's Hobby Airport, the second airport at Houston that has
been revitalized by Southwest's presence. Southwest performed well
when it was the only carrier there. When restrictions were removed,
competing airlines entered one by one until now they number 12.
Still, Southwest has 70 percent of the market and a 7 to 8 percent
growth rate in mature markets.

Southwest became the lovable, formidable upstart. Its fares were
low. People were flying in huge numbers. Old airports away from

congested airspace were being revitalized by Southwest service. To gain attention, Southwest executives slathered the airline operation with glitzy promotions. Flight attendants wore space-girl outfits, scarves and flight blouses, belted hotpants, white-laced go-go boots, big Texas smiles, and lots of comfortable chatter. Drinks aboard the flights became "love potions"; peanuts, "love bites."

The airline gained national media attention just as the writings of academics and economists, critical of the commercially stifling aspects of regulation, began to impact on Congress. Coincidentally, the staff of Senator Edward Kennedy of Massachusetts had been looking for a many-faceted public issue the senator could explore at Judiciary Committee hearings. The airline industry offered great potential. On one side, regulated airlines charged high prices and served the rich. On the other, exemplified by Southwest and Pacific Southwest Airlines (PSA), there was flying at affordable fares. The campaign for airline deregulation began in earnest in Judiciary Committee hearings in 1974. Four years later, on October 25, 1978, the deregulation of airlines became the law of the land.

Growth came to Southwest steadily in the post-deregulation era, then quickly as it dislodged the majors from dominance in California; but Southwest's formula for growth required no change. Kelleher:

Being an intrastate carrier virtually defined the type of carrier you were going to be. "You flew in the State of Texas. Subsequently, after deregulation, we had to make a studied decision whether this [short-haul flying, Southwest-style] was or was not a niche. The decision made at that time was, yes, it was a niche, and that we would pursue the short-haul, high-frequency, low-fare, point-to-point service throughout the United States of America. So that really transpired in an intellectual way subsequent to deregulation, because there was no alternative prior to that.

## OUT OF ADVERSITY, THE 10-MINUTE TURNAROUND
### *Love Field, Dallas:* **June 18, 1971**

Like any other start-up carrier in this capital-intensive business, Southwest lost money in its first 18 months. The first flight got under way from Dallas's Love Field on June 18, 1971, less than six months after Muse took the operational reins. An experienced airline executive, Muse had raised $1.25 million to acquire aircraft, and he rejoiced over Boeing's offer of four Boeing 737-200s backed by 90 percent financing. But the costs of setting up operations, the hiring and training of personnel, and the constant legal battles all took a financial toll. Southwest was forced to sell one of the 737s, leaving only three airplanes for the three-city triangle network. Eichner recalls, "This was the start of the 10-minute turnaround."

Short turnaround of aircraft is important to any airline operation. The shorter the stay on the ground, the more time the aircraft is spending productively moving people through the air. During the turnaround time, the aircraft are fueled and provisioned. The flight dispatcher prepares the pilots for en-route weather and provides other navigational information. The ramp agent oversees the removal of baggage, cargo, and mail from the flight just concluded. He or she is in charge of the boarding of people, their baggage, and new cargo and mail for the next flight. Vital data on the amount of fuel, the number of passengers and bags, and weight and balance information for the aircraft, are recorded. He/she and the pilots are responsible, and must put their signatures on the appropriate lines.

Bill Franklin, a top Southwest executive and one-time president of the affiliated TranStar, devised the 10-minute turnaround for Southwest. When asked by Eichner how he accomplished the turnaround in such a short period, Franklin replied, "We just willed it." The comment is telling. It illustrates that it was sheer determination by Southwest's employees to do their job that made the short turnaround a reality. But as important as enthusiasm is, there are other elements to making turnarounds a success.

### Love Field, Dallas: May 17, 1994

Gate One, the San Antonio gate at Love Field, exudes that anticipatory air of people waiting for a flight. Gate attendants issue recyclable boarding cards to last-minute passengers. The frequent fliers among them are known to the agents who work the San Antonio flight most every day, almost always at the same gate. Large windows open onto the ramp area, where the passenger boarding tunnel extends to receive aircraft. The high-pitched whine of the Pratt &

Whitney JT8D engines announces the arrival of the taxiing Southwest Boeing 737-200, Aircraft Number 86, from Midland-Odessa. As operations manager, Larry Smith, a veteran Southwest employee, is in charge of what will be Flight 159 to San Antonio.

Smith has been informed of the precise timing of the aircraft landing. Crews of people and equipment are in place as the aircraft docks to the jetway. In less than a minute, the cargo door has been opened and a conveyor belt attached. Two tugs, one for the local bags and another for the new baggage and cargo, are wheeled into place. A mechanic is preparing to add fuel. Two provisioning trucks have parked at opened rear and front doors. The second mechanic is conferring with the pilots about any aircraft problems. Finding none, he hooks up a telephone for communications with the cockpit crew during pushback, which is 19 minutes away. The tow bar is locked into the nose landing gear, and the tug stands parked and ready.

Provisioning is speedy; the delivery of snacks and canned beverages takes little time. The refuse from the previous flight is bagged and ready to go. Flight attendants have swept through the aircraft, clearing newspapers and throwaway items even as the passengers filed out the single aisle onto the jetway. The provisioners are helped this day by a class of flight attendant trainees, who have volunteered their time to learn how it feels to be a provisioner. All know what they are doing; the process moves along. A Southwest employee observes, "There is a different perspective when you are standing on that truck looking in, and standing in the airplane looking out. The people in provisioning look to the people in the airplane as their customers."

Keen on developing personal relationships, Southwest has invented a program called The Day in the Field, in which every employee is encouraged to work, once a quarter, for one day or part of a day with another Southwest employee on a different job. Employees aren't obliged to follow up but many do, frequently Kelleher himself. Michael Sand, who heads ramp and operations at Love Field, remembers working as a provisioner shoulder-to-shoulder with Kelleher, who, wearing one of his now-famous jumpsuits kept in his office closet, was dumping refuse and loading sodas onto a Boeing 737 the night before Thanksgiving, 1983.

An experienced Day-in-the-Field employee who knows about a job other than his or her own is able to lend a helping hand at critical times. When an ice storm struck Dallas in the winter of 1993–1994, headquarters personnel volunteered at Love Field, where operations had fallen into slippery chaos. A telephone operator was among the volunteers and her job was taken by Ann Rhoades, head of the Department of People, who pitched in herself to answer the many telephone queries.

But today at Love Field the temperature is above 70°F, and the turnaround of Aircraft No. 86 is going smoothly at the San Antonio gate. Smith is stationed at the end of the jetway, at a small table near the aircraft. His means of communication to the ramp personnel recalls the pneumatic tubes of nineteenth-Century offices, yet the system he has in place is an even older bit of technology. Smith holds a large cannister, in which he encloses a work order and lets it drop down on a rope through a jetway opening to the ramp personnel below. It tells the ramp agent that 90 bags will be removed for the 62 Dallas passengers. They will be removed first, to meet a goal of having them arrive at the baggage pickup station in 10 minutes or less. There are new bags coming in, 23 from transfer bins. Other information is available on the passengers remaining on-board for the San Antonio leg, and how many will be transferring to Tulsa, Little Rock, and Houston.

As operations manager, Smith is responsible for accomplishing the turnaround inside of 20 minutes, the current standard turnaround time. He counts the boarding cards, the number of bags, and the amount of cargo, and makes quick calculations for the weight and balance of the aircraft. The added fuel is recorded and signed off for by the pilots. It's an easy turnaround for the pilots. With the cadre of volunteers and a fully staffed crew, there's no need today for the pilots to lend a hand, push a wheelchair on-board, or unload and load bags, both of which are common practices if staffing suffers or bad weather or other hindrances occur. The pilots relax on the jetway, taking a break before checking the flight dispatch report. Even the weather is cooperating. Scarcely a cloud disturbs the blue sky en route to San Antonio.

Within eight minutes of the Boeing 737's arrival at 10:40 A.M. (CDT), the Dallas passengers have debarked, and only a few of the San Antonio–bound passengers remain in the line at the gate. They're aboard within the next two minutes. The aircraft has been fueled, provisioned, unloaded, and loaded within 10 minutes. Smith is preparing a report on the vital statistics of the new flight, which he will send to San Antonio, where the process will begin anew.

At Love Field, Southwest operates 132 flights similar to Flight 159 every day, Monday through Thursday; 135 flights on Friday; and lesser numbers on weekends. Morning-shift employees start as early as 5 A.M. Evening-shift personnel start as late as 4 P.M. The first flight leaves at 6:30 A.M., the last at 10:10 P.M.

Employees get the job done by cross-utilization, and there's a structure that helps. Ramp and operations manager Michael Sand divides the 13 Love gates into 4 zones. The first zone embraces Gates 1, 2, 4A, and 4B, each of which is assigned a ramp agent who will be on the ground looking after the baggage and coordinating with the operations agent. Each zone also has one tug driver for local bags and another driver for transfer bags. When more than one aircraft docks at any of the four gates, these baggage tug drivers have their hands full.

Southwest employees try to improve on past performance by dissecting the operation. If a flight departs late, the operations agent must file a report and select a coded reason for the delay. A TD70 is a Team Delay, an OP21 is an operational problem. The most common cause of delays: slow passenger boardings, usually complicated by a large number of passengers with heavy baggage that must be checked at the gate. But moving people and baggage, however important, is not the only job at Southwest, although it may seem like it.

### Blocking and Tackling on a Daily Basis

Costs of any kind are put under the microscope at Southwest Airlines. The first-line responsibility for keeping costs in line falls to managers such as Michael Sand. Sand is under a heavy obligation to keep the operation moving and the employees productive. He more than tolerates the job; he wants to *succeed,* and there is something infectious about that.

Southwest's company culture promotes the delegation of responsibility to people like Sand. But "on topside, the senior management is looking at each cost center to see if costs are adequately explained," observes Chief Financial Officer Gary Kelly. It is that close oversight that allows company officials to know what's going on.

Kelly refers to cost control at Southwest as a dynamic, everyday process. "Airline operations have high fixed costs. You cannot slash by 20 percent by a snap of the fingers. You can shave a percent, but even coming up with a 1 to 2 percent cut is difficult. We ask our people to block and tackle on a daily basis."

At his post since 1986, Kelly has amassed historical empirical data on Southwest's total operation, which serves as the basis for comparison of current trends. Passenger traffic is monitored on a daily basis and compared to forecast traffic. It is re-forecast for the month, if unexpected trends make that necessary. Kelly's office produces detailed revenue data on a weekly basis. The revenues are related to passenger traffic, the data on passengers' origins and destinations, and average yield. A new revenue forecast for the month is developed if trends require it.

Kelly's office looks at special cost-reducing projects that promise long-term costs savings. New technology is one avenue; improving employee productivity is another. Kelly provides the example of a finance office plan to reduce costs by improving the productivity of reservation agents. The hours spent by agents correlate directly with the number of ticket sales. A program to introduce new sales techniques that would complete a sale in a shorter period may be undertaken. But such a project, he maintains, would have to be given adequate time to brainstorm the issue, implement changes, and evaluate results, before effective cost reduction could be accomplished.

Three annual budgets are prepared for any year, and these are revised regularly as information on the operation flows in. The first budget, for personnel, is a fixture, except that any addition to the head count must receive top-level approval. The operational budget is revised under the influence of actual revenues, traffic, and costs. Finally, the capital budget allows for a degree of flexibility in the event that some surprises, such as fuel price increases, jolt the financial planners.

When it comes to finance, Southwest operates according to certain rules of thumb. Kelly's office keeps an eye on productivity in terms of each aircraft. The gross figure for pilots is 10 pilots per aircraft, and it is watched carefully. Pilots are paid per trip, and they are the most productive in the country. The 10-pilots-per-aircraft ratio seems the right one: just enough pilots to keep their pay rivaling that of others in the industry while maintaining an appropriate and legal schedule. The overall gross target per aircraft is 80 employees. This number compares to hundreds per aircraft at some European airlines. In the late spring of 1994 the figure grew to 83–84 employees, but that didn't concern Kelly. The figure is high as a result of the unusually heavy training load as Southwest has been growing in aircraft, destinations, and passengers, through the recession and into this recovery period.

"We need to grow faster. Growth is part of who we are," Kelly says. "We are focused on growing the domestic route system. We're still an adolescent, and have a long way to go before we are mature."

A primary reason for Southwest's success is a correct business philosophy centered around its niche in operating short-haul flights. The airline business, according to the boss, Kelleher, is the only business in which a simple procedural change made in one week can cost the airline millions of dollars in the next week.

Southwest is growing throughout its system, and it is growing fastest in new markets in new sections of the country. Kelleher has mulled over the idea of transplanting the concept to other countries. He has been contacted by foreign interests to provide help in establishing similar operations abroad, and he is fascinated by the prospects. Franchising is one possibility. Most other countries don't have the large traffic base that this country does. Growing congestion, bigger and costlier infrastructure, and other limitations such as aeropolitics may form obstacles to franchising.

Southwest has become a symbol of post-deregulation airline success. It is an airline that succeeded when its owners recognized a niche market and exploited it. Southwest has set the standard for short-haul operations and written the book on how a company should work. When it started up in the 1970s, Southwest had four Boeing 737s. Along with USAir during the 1980s, it was a co-launch customer of the 737-300. In this decade, it solely launched the Boeing 737-700.

Several questions relating to its future hang in the air, as dark clouds over the otherwise unblemished distant Texas horizon. Will success lead to carelessness about the product? Will expansion change the company culture? Will the company's many imitators curtail future opportunities? Is Southwest strictly a Herb Kelleher show, which will close down when he leaves the starring role? Kelleher dismisses the last question with a self-effacing hand wave, which translates into the notion that no one individual is indispensable. The corporation has groomed several potential successors who will be required to fill those substantial shoes. As for the other questions, Southwest has shown itself capable of taking the right steps and resisting the tempting wrong ones, compiling an excellent record on which to build a bright future.

One important right step taken by Southwest has been its policy of cost-plus pricing. Owing to its low-cost structure, Southwest is able to offer the lowest fares in the marketplace and still operate profitably. While it has solved the problem of pricing under deregulation, most other airlines in the United States have found pricing to be their nemesis.

## OTHER MONEY MAKERS
### ValuJet Brings Fresh Ideas and Millions to Its Owners
*Atlanta:* **October 26, 1994**

This day of celebration, the one-year anniversary of ValuJet's start-up, brought the carrier's primary owners to Atlanta for a party that extended all day throughout the 17-city route network. Passengers were presented with commemorative Coca-Cola bottles bearing the ValuJet logo, a pop-eyed critter that looks as if it flowed from the same pen that created the Pillsbury doughboy.

It was a gala day. The four principal owners wore birthday hats as they walked through Hartsfield Atlanta International Airport. Back at company headquarters along Phoenix Boulevard, the two antique bells normally used only for company announcements peeled in celebration. Employees dined on birthday cake and cheered the owners, three of whom had invested $1 million each in 1992. By the airline's first birthday, each $1 million investment had paid off 34 times in the value of ValuJet stock.

ValuJet found its place in the market at the right time, in the right city, with the right ideas. The owners chose to fly from Hartsfield Atlanta International Airport, where Delta Air Lines has dominated since the days of the DC-3. The demise of Eastern Airlines in 1991 left an opening that ValuJet filled. It offered low fares, which are welcome anywhere but particularly so in Atlanta, where air fares are high, typical of hubs dominated by one carrier. The Douglas-refurbished DC-9 aircraft fit neatly into the short- to medium-haul route structure ValuJet had in mind. But there was more to why ValuJet was a success in 1994. The owners and managers weren't afraid to innovate, in an industry that had grown rather stale.

ValuJet was a risky investment. Quick-witted owner Timothy Flynn made that clear in one of his standup routines at headquarters that anniversary day. First, he explained, the investors were backing a new airline in an industry suffering an extended downturn. ValuJet would vie against entrenched Delta, a carrier that has represented the pinnacle of employee and customer loyalty. It was going to introduce untried concepts: for one, ValuJet would break with a 60-year tradition and provide no tickets to its passengers. It would propose a personnel policy designed to hire patient, loyal workaholics who exhibited positive attitudes and a willingness to serve people. These untried concepts, radical-sounding the year before, played a big part in ValuJet's success, along with a sprinkling of luck and some business acumen.

The initial investors, 43-year-old Flynn and Maurice J. Gallagher, Jr., 45, who jointly founded the commuter/regional WestAir, and Robert L. Priddy, 47, a veteran of the regional airline business, rewrote the book on airline innovation. Their "coauthor" was Lewis H. Jordan, 49, who invested a half-million dollars and became ValuJet's president and chief operating officer. Jordan brought to the new carrier his experience of operating a large U.S. airline as president of Continental Airlines and of the cargo line Flying Tigers.

Among the new ValuJet approaches to business, the ticketless airline was the most obvious departure from tradition, at least for passengers. Company surveys indicate that the ticketless feature has won passenger approval by a 98 percent margin. ValuJet has kept the process simple. At flight booking time, a passenger is identified by name and then assigned a confirmation number. The information goes into the computer under the flight and day of departure. Passengers are warned that refunds won't be forthcoming if they don't appear on time for the flight. The process is similar to the practice at hotels, which issue a confirmation number to a future guest, certifying that a room has been held in reserve for him or her.

Gate agents have ready access to the ValuJet computer, which contains the list of passengers and confirmation numbers for particular flights. As departure time nears, the passenger goes to the ValuJet gate and gives his or her name and confirmation number to the agent. A plastic boarding pass is issued, and passengers gather at a waiting area until boarding is called. Agents have foiled several attempts to fly for free. For the airline, the ticketless process avoids the cost and involvement of producing, handling, and accounting for paper tickets. Jordan estimates the savings at $3 to $4 per passenger on a $60 to $70 fare.

ValuJet's other major innovation, its personnel policy, is the envy of traditional air carriers. Potential employees are given an opportunity to work as temporaries. They are evaluated by coworkers and managers, and within three months the good candidates are given a chance at a permanent position. The policy rewards those who show enthusiasm and a knack for the airline business with permanent positions and bonuses. In contrast to this kind of flexibility at ValuJet, personnel managers at most large airlines are hamstrung by the customary practice of hiring an employee for a probationary period, which is followed by a union-protected job.

"Almost every company has a probationary period, but it is viewed in many cases as a way to get through 90 days without getting into trouble," Jordan said. "The approach here is that we *evaluate* people during those 90 days."

ValuJet hires mechanics through STS Services, Nashville, and other employees through Jordan Temporaries, a Georgia company owned by Jennifer Jordan, daughter of the ValuJet president. (Jordan distanced himself from negotiations with the personnel companies, which were selected after a competitive bid.) Temporary workers are paid at the lowest wage level in the industry while they are reviewed and evaluated by their peers.

Temporaries must wait 90 days before the review is complete. The offer of a permanent job may come at any time after the 90 days. If there has been no offer after 180 days, this usually means the temporary has not passed muster. But there have been exceptions. In December 1994, ValuJet's work force stood at 1416 employees, 938 of whom were permanent employees. Only permanent employees receive medical benefits and flight passes. Only they are eligible for additional compensation in the form of bonuses, which are paid quarterly to employees, with a supervisor's approval, if ValuJet turns a sufficient profit. Bonuses were paid in three quarters of 1994.

The bonus program is another good example of ValuJet's financial flexibility. If the airline faces a downturn or a sudden increase in costs, quarterly earnings will reflect the change and bonuses are not likely. Employees receive only their normal salaries, keeping labor and operating costs to a minimum, but management will be spared the awful duty of cutting back on the payroll.

Operating costs in ValuJet's first year started out at 7 cents per available seat mile (ASM), the standard industry measurement. As 1994 drew to a close, the ASM cost dropped to 6 cents, as the carrier expanded and grew more productive. This cost level compares to 8 to 10 cents per ASM for the major airlines in the second quarter of 1994.

The million-dollar investments of 1992 each bought 1.5 million shares of ValuJet stock. As the airline took shape and won passenger acceptance, the stock price rose to $4 and then leapt to $12.50 when the company went public. In March 1995 ValuJet shares hovered in the $38 to $39 range before a 2-for-1 stock split, an extraordinary climb for so risky a venture.

### The Slow, Sure Rise of Comair
### *Hebron, Kentucky:* November 1994

From a high point in the steeply rolling hills east of the Cincinnati/ Northern Kentucky International Airport, the starry night sky gleams with the flashing beacons of swiftly moving aircraft. Above the distant western horizon, where air transports are sequencing on approach, their high-beam landing lights form a cluster of bright pearls, intensifying as the aircraft draw near. The transports break from the lineup and turn on the final leg, veering across the city's western suburbs toward the airport. Shawnee Lookout, a hulking land mass at the intersection of the Great Miami River and the broad Ohio, provides a memorable landmark for pilots as the airliners hurtle over the dark river and the high Kentucky bluffs to a pair of north-south runways.

One of every two commercial aircraft arriving at the Greater Cincinnati airport bears the name of the hometown airline, Comair. The name occurred in 1977 to an attorney, the late Joseph Summe, as he and the founders searched for something to identify the airline on the incorporation papers. He knew the airline was meant to be a "commuter airline," therefore he abbreviated the two words into Comair, and it stuck.

No one, not even the Mueller family that financed the two-aircraft operation, imagined that Comair would become what it is today. A successful carrier operating a fleet of 84 modern turboprop and pure-jet transports, it has deftly produced sizable, record-breaking profits in all but one of its 17 years. It flies as many as 600 flights a day to airports in 27 states,and operates hubs in Orlando and Cincinnati. In 1994 Comair opened its own 53-gate terminal at the Cincinnati airport, the largest air terminal in the United States dedicated totally to regional/commuter operations.

If Comair has emerged as the young airline prince in a Midwest aviation renaissance, then Delta Air Lines is its liege lord. Comair serves Delta as a connection carrier, meaning that it feeds passengers to Delta. Comair flies passengers from cities such as Omaha, Columbus, and Cleveland to the Orlando and Cincinnati hubs, where as many as half of its passengers connect to Delta flights. Comair is like a small version of Delta, its aircraft even being painted in Delta's white and blue colors.

The relationship began in 1981, when Comair joined the Delta computerized reservations system. In 1986 Delta acquired a 20 percent interest in Comair's common stock, the year Delta delayed on its pledge to start a hub operation at Cincinnati, which left Comair with an overextended feeder network and a break in the tradition of huge earnings. The two carriers worked closely in the next year, however, to develop the Orlando and Cincinnati hubs, and they have done so ever since.

In the topsy-turvy world of commercial aviation, Comair, on the feeder end of the business, is expanding and earning profits, while Delta, like other majors, is cutting back. Delta is working on the gargantuan task of cutting $6.6 billion from its operations over a period of three years, and Comair is posting large profits. Operating income at Comair reached $47.3 million in fiscal 1994, a performance better than most any airline in the U.S. industry. The performance testifies to the slow, sure development of the carrier, the businesslike decisions of its managers, and the tight rein kept on costs.

Today, Comair's operating costs are coming down by virtue of the pure-jet service in its fleet of new 50-seat Canadair RJs (regional jets): fast, new twin-jet transports, powered by fuel-efficient General Electric CF34-3A1 engines. It is reaping the same kind of harvest the major airlines did in the 1960s, when jets were introduced. Comair is carrying more passengers on longer trips, and the company's costs when measured on the basis of each aircraft seat are dropping fast. In short, it is growing more productive. The 1994 fleet of 20 RJs operated at a cost of below 10 cents in available seat miles. This figure is about half of the average seat-mile cost for the total fleet of 84 aircraft. Comair will add at least 10 RJs in 1995, and probably more of the Canadian aircraft in time.

The RJ experience is the latest example of a series of effective aircraft decisions by Comair managers. Today, many airlines operate aircraft that are not matched to the markets they serve. Most are too large (offer too many seats), and the high operating costs of mismatched, oversized aircraft are damaging to bottom lines. Comair hasn't had that problem. It has bought new-technology aircraft, upgrading in size in small increments. When it wanted to expand its market reach, it became the North American launch customer for the 33-passenger Swedish SAAB 340 in 1984. This aircraft pushed the Comair market outward 400 miles. Thirty-passenger Embraer Brasilias were bought later for their speed.

Comair officials have been careful to size new aircraft to their markets. The RJs are flying 700 miles from Cincinnati to cities such as Montreal, Providence, R.I., and Wichita. The hub at the Cincinnati airport becomes a midwest connection center for one-stop trips from all points of the compass. Comair runs the new-technology aircraft harder than most, getting the most out of their efficiencies. On average, the RJs are operating 10 hours a day, an hour or two more than the average jets of the big carriers.

"We are not an airline trying to figure out how to be a business. We are a business that is in aviation." This comment on Comair comes from Senior Vice President, Marketing, Charles Curran, a Comair employee from its early days. Curran sits at his desk in a corner office of the modern headquarters building on the outskirts of the Cincinnati/Northern Kentucky International Airport. He is an energetic lawyer from Illinois who made the shift easily to the dynamic world of airline marketing.

Curran's convictions about the airline business are clear. Comair is, first and foremost, a business, not a public utility or an interesting plaything for aviators. "A lot of people have started airlines for the glory and the glamour. They have gotten into difficulty when a lot of ego and emotion got involved, rather than business practicality. We have imposed business disciplines on ourselves. We are not going to cities because it will feel good or because they are our favorites. We fly to a city because it is the right business decision," Curran says. New city markets are studied at Comair for at least a year before service is started. Comair gives a route 90 days at the maximum to show its worth.

At times, the relationship between Delta and Comair can be one-sided. A Delta officer occupies a seat on the nine-member Comair board of directors. Delta sets ticket prices for Comair, generally employing a mileage-based formula. Approximately half of Comair's passengers at Cincinnati now connect to Delta flights, and that percentage is expected to grow, perhaps to 70 percent, when Delta completes its restructuring in the coming years.

Because of sheer financial outlay and commitment, the close relationship is expected to continue. In 1994, Delta opened a $375-million flight center at the Cincinnati airport and began to bill it as a rival to Chicago's O'Hare International as a midwestern hub. Comair serves as Delta's closest ally in serving connection cities from the Plains states to the Mid-Atlantic region, from Canada to the Deep South. The relationship between the two airlines has enabled a well-managed, cost-conscious airline to reach the top rank of U.S. regionals.

# FIVE

# Low Fares Forever

Freedom to cut prices is a valuable competitive tool in private businesses, but airline use of this tool in the early years of deregulation has turned into a compulsion.

> —WILLIAM H. GREGORY,
> former Editor-in-Chief, *Aviation Week & Space Technology*

## NO WONDER THEY CAN'T MAKE ANY MONEY*
### *New York City*

IT'S WEDNESDAY AFTERNOON. Herman Jones, chief financial officer of a Manhattan firm, gets the bad news at 4:30 P.M. He's told to be in Chicago at midday Thursday for a final review of an important company transaction. Under normal circumstances, a trip to Chicago would be fine, almost pleasing to Jones. But Herman's ten-year-old daughter is making her debut on Thursday night in a play in Manhattan presented by The School for Unusually Gifted Children. Whatever happens in Chicago, the rising young executive still wants very badly to return home to see his little girl in that play, or at least to be with her at the post-event reception.

Herman departs early from his office and stops at the airline ticket center on Park Avenue and 42nd Street, adjacent to Grand Central

---

* A fictionalized account of a true story.

Station—a place where, incidentally, Herman's railroad trip to Chicago would have begun 40 or 50 years ago. As he walks along, he mentally reviews his options. American Airlines has a lot of flights to Chicago, but there are also a lot of competitors to choose from. The Chicago-based United and a bevy of discount carriers fly to the Windy City. Since the trip is being made on the spur of the moment, Herman is sure he will have to pay top dollar, which he hates to do as CFO. Buying at the last minute, he can't meet advance purchase requirements for a low fare. Since he'll be returning on Thursday afternoon, he doesn't qualify for the discount offered to those who stay over Saturday night at the destination. The company will have to bite the bullet on this one.

The ticket agent at the 42nd Street center is helpful. Flying to Chicago in the morning poses no problem. American has two scheduled return flights in the afternoon, the first at the 5 P.M. peak time and the second at 7 P.M. The price difference between the two is extraordinary: The fare for the 5 P.M. flight, when Chicago O'Hare Field is busiest, is $500, whereas it is $250 for the later one. The agent smilingly advises Herman to reserve a seat on the 7 P.M. flight at the lower fare, and show up for the 5 P.M. flight. Both flights are far from being booked up, she says. The only disadvantage for Herman is the lack of a reservation for the 5 P.M.

Herman was a success in both cities that day. He confirmed a good financial deal in Chicago, got on-board the 5 P.M. flight, and watched with delight as little Millie danced up a storm that night.

## A TYPICAL RESPONSE TO FARES: UNITED
### *Elk Grove Township, Illinois:* Spring 1994

Every Saturday and Sunday, a pricing analyst at United Airlines enters the gate leading to the UAL Corporation's two-story, modernistic complex on East Algonquin Road, parks his car, and makes his way through security to a second-floor office. After tinkering with his personal computer, he begins to monitor the system-change tape that records fares filed the night before by airlines with the Airline Tariff Publishing Co. (ATPCO), Chantilly, Va., the industry-owned fares publishing house.

If a fare war is breaking out, the analyst will know right away. Information comes in summary form, telling him how many markets are affected by a new fare. United operates in 23,000 markets across the world. In order to find out precisely what is happening to United, the analyst uses a software program to sort out the new fares, dollar amounts, effective dates, and rules. The program then displays which United markets are affected. Footnotes to fares are important, because they indicate certain conditions for fare use.

A pricing manager is on duty, in a way, as well. He stands by at his home on weekends, awaiting a telephone call from the analyst. If a major fare war is under way, the pricing manager quickly marshals a team from advertising and marketing, and a counter-strategy is developed. A full-blown campaign can be put in motion right away, but definitely on the following Monday when the sales will actually begin with the new workday. This kind of reaction has been part of United's fare policy since deregulation, and it is replicated at most U.S. airlines. Any fare action, whether it covers 10,000 markets or a handful, is analyzed for its competitive impact. More often than not, United matches the new low fares.

Pricing is not an area in which United has been a leader. It has been happy to concede the crown of pricing leadership to more aggressive folks at American Airlines, Continental Airlines, and the many low-cost carriers. During the 1980s, United, like other carriers, experimented with the new freedom to set prices at levels the market would bear. Discounts were offered for the primary purpose of stimulating travel in periods of low demand. Cut-rate fares were plentiful in off-seasons, but seldom were low fares available in the peak holiday and summer travel periods. Now discounts are more readily available, even, at times, right through the summer.

Over the years, United has attempted to inject some control into the pricing process. More than a decade ago, it adopted a program of yield management, also known as revenue management, which is now common to the industry. It works like this: By paying close attention to the types of passengers and their fares on each flight, United hopes to manage its pricing and produce enough revenues from the mix of passenger fares to make each flight profitable. Actually, airline managers use the term RASM, the acronym of Revenue per Available Seat

Mile. In order to make a profit, the revenue amount must be be sufficient to pay the cost per available seat mile.

Further, United through the 1980s attempted to differentiate its product from that of other airlines. It offered benefits through Mileage Plus, its frequent-flier program, such as new and even sumptuous international cabin services and other amenities like early boarding privileges and special foods and beverages. United adopted a product strategy that emphasized service and flight frequencies in the most populous markets—the antithesis of the usual low-fare approach. United has been seeking out the high-yield, first-class, and full-coach passenger. Its predicament during the recent lengthy worldwide economic downturn had a lot to do with the absence of high-yield passengers.

In the 1980s, United Airlines was like most other carriers. It experimented with the new freedom to set prices at levels the market would bear. On balance, the tendency over the years has been toward steadily declining average fares when compared to such standards as the Consumer Price Index (CPI). But tariff-making was noticeably more reasonable in the early years, as compared to today's environment. The emerging airlines such as Southwest have established their fares based on their lower costs and pounded the opposition with a powerful market presence.

What little control was exercised over fares in the past by the major airlines has passed to this new generation of carriers. In the brief period from 1992 to the spring of 1995, airlines ranked as low-cost carriers grew from representing a fraction of total domestic capacity to more than 10 percent of all domestic operations. The rest of the market fell principally to major airlines that had already restructured or, like American, Delta, United, and USAir, were working out restructuring programs.

## A CYCLE OF UNREASONABLE UNDERCUTTING

Under deregulation, pricing has been a shambles. Any attempt by the full-service airlines to inject rationality into pricing has failed. American Airlines tried twice. For a period in the middle to the later

1980s, airlines developed a pricing pattern in which one carrier—usually American, sometimes Continental—served as price leader. The other carriers then played an unruly version of follow-the-leader, matching fares when they found them competitively prudent. Such behavior has led to a cycle of unreasonable undercutting.

The elasticity of pricing constitutes a special discipline at airlines, as it was at the old Civil Aeronautics Board, the former regulatory body. Standards have been developed to measure the meaning of a rise or fall in prices, as it relates to actual passenger traffic. After a long review of pricing patterns, the CAB formulated an *industry elasticity coefficient*. The standard measure of elasticity was −0.7. If airlines fares rose 1 percent, traffic would fall 0.7 percent. An interesting development under deregulation has been the increased number of passengers flying for personal or pleasure reasons. They tend to be more sensitive to prices than business fliers. An analysis at the Air Transport Association (ATA) has resulted in the adoption of a standard measure of −1 percent. If prices rise by 1 percent, traffic will drop by a full percentage point.

Studies at American Airlines, the academy of the airline industry, have indicated many of the ramifications of pricing elasticity. One conclusion of American's work is that when you're dealing with specific markets, the standard measure of elasticity can be even greater than 1 percent. American also has become aware of the impact of fare reductions in one market on other markets. If fares to Hawaii are reduced, that reduction can have an effect on traffic to Puerto Rico. American's pricing studies have been conducted to support American's fare actions, which have come under fire by competitors and resulted in several civil legal battles over the years.

It is obvious from a review of airline pricing habits that tension exists between the airlines and the U.S. government over pricing. Collusion appears to threaten, particularly in hard financial times. Airline veterans of Washington affairs acknowledge, in moments of candor, that the Justice Department, which routinely monitors pricing habits, issues warnings that tend to discipline airline behavior and demarcate the boundaries of the law. Airlines have tested those legal boundaries many times.

## AMERICAN HAS TRIED EVERYTHING

American's history as a modern price leader stretches back to 1969, when it introduced a fares system based on flight distance. The regulatory body, the Civil Aeronautics Board, when in one of its pro-competition moods, accepted American's plan. But a federal court quashed the CAB order, claiming that the board had violated administrative rules. The CAB found the issue interesting, however, and promptly initiated a study of fares referred to as the Domestic Passenger Fare Investigation. This study resulted in the adoption in 1974 of a distance-based fare formula called the Standard Industry Fare Level (SIFL). The fare level was based on costs and was applied as a standard in all those cases the CAB heard in which the board had to choose between contending parties for a particular air route. The formula is still in existence today. The Transportation Department calculates the SIFL for other federal offices, so as to compare the standard against current airline prices.

Over the years, American has introduced more than its share of fares. The SuperSaver, the most widely adopted fare system of recent decades, originated at American in 1977. The characteristic restrictions on the traveler have varied, as have the levels of discount. American offered the SuperSaver, like any loss leader, to attract customers and to fill seats that otherwise would have been empty.

Innovations continued in 1983 with a retread of the mileage-based system. American reduced the types of fares to four, plus a special one for overseas business travelers. Most competitors copied the American idea. As the year wore on, the mileage base eroded, as seasonal discounts and other fare schemes from rival carriers folded into the system. If there was a hint of a competitive advantage the new fares were matched, and the whole system became a constantly changing patchwork.

American's mileage-based proposal resurfaced only a month after a sensational disclosure that was to mark a new era in airline pricing. The airline's president, the hard-driving Bob Crandall, had been charged by the Justice Department with attempting to engage in an illegal monopoly practice. The government had a tape recording of a conversation that allegedly took place on February 1, 1982, between Crandall and Braniff International president Howard Putnam:

> PUTNAM: Do you have a suggestion for me?
> CRANDALL: Yes. I have a suggestion for you. Raise your [*expletive deleted*] fares 20 percent. I'll raise mine the next morning.
> PUTNAM: Robert, we—
> CRANDALL: You'll make money, and I will too
> PUTNAM: We can't talk about pricing.
> CRANDALL: Oh [*expletive deleted*], Howard. We can talk about any [*expletive deleted*] thing we want to talk about.

Putnam had his gripes against American. In 1982, he had testified before a grand jury in Fort Worth that was investigating allegations that American had used "dirty tricks" against Braniff, and had misled travel agents about Braniff schedules in the American-owned SABRE computer reservations system. American denied the allegations, and eventually the investigation was terminated.

In any case, the exchange between the two executives failed to yield what it had intended. American settled the civil court action in federal court, with no admission of a criminal violation, under a 1985 consent decree. Antitrust lawyers have regarded the American case as delineating the beginning of a new direction by the Justice Department in the investigation of airline pricing practices. By 1990, at least five separate investigations were under way at the Justice Department, each related to allegations of anticompetitive behavior in the industry.

Ironically, for as long as the airlines have experimented with fares, reducing them as often as they have raised them, the industry has not produced an adequate profit margin. Only once in the past 25 years have the airlines achieved the average profit margin for U.S. industry. Basically, the airlines' performance improves when the economy is strong and demand high. When the economy was still stumbling in recession, American Airlines, as a price leader, tried several times to establish an industry pricing policy.

## CRANDALL'S LAST ATTEMPT TO RESTRUCTURE FARES

### *New York:* April 1992

American's latest attempt to reinstitute a mileage-based system and simplify the fare structure occurred in April 1992. Crandall was looking for maximum publicity for his Value Pricing plan. He staged a press conference in New York to garner national media (and particularly TV) attention. He was at his most fearlessly Crandall-esque. Taking front and center stage, he applied his impressive business rationale to a system of airline fares that he called complicated and inequitable. His resonant voice boomed out over the rows of reporters and analysts. Travelers were confused, Crandall said, even angry, over the fares mess.

"We've made our pricing so complex that our customers neither understand it nor think it's fair. When you consider that the deepest discount fare can be as much as 78 percent lower than the full coach fare, it's easy to see why." Crandall asked for simplicity, equity, fairness, and a return of value to airline pricing.

No doubt, American's Value Pricing plan was a bold innovation. Crandall recreated the structure of four fare levels: reduced First Class and Coach fares, and two leisure-type fares. The litter of junk fares and the half-off corporate discounts were to be eliminated. Moreover, in sharply improving the discount for Coach and First Class, the fares were to become more affordable for the vanishing business traveler and augur a boost of higher-yield passengers. Adhering to its standard marketing jargon, the airline dubbed the tickets for leisure travelers PlanAAhead fares.

Crandall predicted a short-term loss, as people who had bought tickets cashed them in for the new lower fares. But if the plan held—he was speaking here more to fellow executives than to travelers—he pledged an increase in returns. On average, fares under this system would increase in price as more high-yield passengers took to the air. Some in the industry agreed with Crandall's notion of imposing a discipline on the fares system, but thought it would be as difficult as imposing discipline on a very unruly child.

In September, at an industry analysts meeting in New York, Crandall pronounced the Value Pricing Plan dead. The child had balked at the proferred discipline. Airline competitors were offended at the way American was trying to serve as a regulatory body, like the old Civil Aeronautics Board, with an in-your-face imposition of discipline. American's reduction of the full coach fare was very deep— *too* deep, according to critics—but no matter how low the full fare was going to be, it still wouldn't induce the white-collar worker to return to the air. The economy had changed too drastically. Further, to some critics, the leisure fare was sure to go up in price and lose its compelling attractiveness for travelers. One thing was certain: Corporations didn't like the increase in their airline fares. Those with special contracts with airlines suddenly saw their discounts drop from 50 to 38 percent off.

Crandall lumped the blame for Value Pricing's demise on "discounting, couponing and give-aways." He singled out independent fare actions by Trans World, America West, USAir, and Northwest as having hastened the demise. When Northwest offered a "Kids Fly Free" promotion, American broadened the offer to include any life partner. In the fare war that followed, American joined with its competitors to set the lowest prices of the decade during the summer of 1992. For a 10-day period, most airlines were selling tickets at 50 percent off normal prices. A disgruntled Crandall predicted that the industry was doomed to a regime of constant undercutting. The inherent economics of the industry required airlines to match any lower-fare initiative.

Then Crandall leveled a cogent criticism at the industry's own inability to price airline tickets to actual costs. Crandall observed that it costs more to carry passengers through a hub, between a starting point and a destination, than to carry them nonstop between the same two points without the hub. Chaotic pricing at U.S. airlines ignored that fact. Value Pricing, in any case, was dead. During the extended pricing debacle of 1992, when passengers were flying at half prices and less, the industry journal, *Aviation Week & Space Technology* had this headlined on its September 28th edition: U.S. FARE WAR PLUNGES TOWARD ARMAGEDDON. Doubtless overstated, the headline did catch the spirit of what was happening in the U.S. industry. Airline pricing was a mess. It was causing a major upheaval that would play a strong role in the restructuring of the industry.

At this time, Frank Mulvey was monitoring the U.S. airlines' pricing behavior, as assistant director of transport of the U.S. General Accounting Office (GAO). The GAO, a persistent industry critic, has identified a booklet-full of transportation issues arising from airline studies done at the request of individual congressmen and committees. Government auditors have observed a system of comparatively high fares in markets where a single airline dominates a hub airport. "The airlines have had more truces than Beirut has had, with about as much success," Mulvey says. "When it seems like the war is over, then someone fires another volley." Average fares in 1992 fell 14 percent from what they had been in 1991, a bonanza for passengers but the last straw for the airlines.

The British Civil Aviation Authority (CAA) upset a hornet's nest in December 1994, with a 234-page analysis of the state of airline competition on long-haul routes to and from Europe. The report pointed fingers at the International Air Transport Association (IATA), the industry group that presides over public tariff coordination meetings covering most regions of the world. "The existence of formal and highly developed fare-fixing machinery works to cement anti-competitive behavior," said the report. Evidence was shown of a leveling of prices even on U.S.–U.K. routes over the previous two years.

IATA has rejected the notion that airlines are holding back-room meetings to collude on pricing. The IATA coordination sessions, which operate under antitrust immunity from the United States, are portrayed as being needed to maintain a worldwide system of interlining under which a passenger may travel using several or more airlines on a single ticket. The interline system permits airlines to sell tickets for travel on other airlines, and a degree of predictability in the value of a ticket has been regarded as necessary. For that reason, the governments have permitted coordination.

The British report clearly allies the U.K. government with the historic position of the U.S., which has barely tolerated IATA.

## A New Experiment to Keep Business Fares Low
### *Lafayette Hill, Pennsylvania:* July 1992

Kevin Mitchell had been in charge of Cigna, Inc.'s $30-million air-line travel budget for nearly a year, when American's Value Pricing program—and responses to it—began to make mincemeat of the company travel plans. Cigna was looking at double-digit increases and several millions of dollars in costs. The Philadelphia–Hartford round-trip flight, a staple for Cigna executives in insurance and financial services, jumped from $220 in January to $540 in September.

"All of the corporate discounts in place were ripped up and thrown in the trash can," Mitchell says. "Deals that Cigna had made with United, USAir, and Delta all had gone with Value Pricing. There was real confusion in the marketplace, and it didn't look like solutions were coming from anywhere."

However damaging that might sound to Value Pricing, Mitchell supported American's concept. What sold him was the simplicity, which he believed the fares system definitely needed. He was critical of some aspects. "The introduction and implementation were not the surest way to gain marketplace support," he says. Because of antitrust laws, "American had no choice but had to work exclusively within its own walls to develop strategy, and then shocked everyone."

Most deeply shocked were managers of travel budgets for compa-nies that, Mitchell points out, became targets for extinction if simplicity did indeed return to the fares system. With the fares so complicated, negotiations have developed into the largest work segment for officials of business travel departments and airline sales personnel—between 60 and 70 percent.

Mitchell persuaded his employers that Cigna should thoroughly review all costs associated with its travel department, and call in other corporations with similar concerns. In September 1992, when Crandall was pronouncing Value Pricing dead, Mitchell was actively recruiting companies. He found 20, including General Motors, Chrysler, Bell Atlantic, Xerox, and Gillette, willing to enter into a joint "problem-solving" effort.

Experts were called in from the airline and travel industries. The primary consultants were Tom Plaskett, the last president of Pan American World Airways; Randall Malin, the former head of marketing at USAir; and Harold Seligman, a travel consultant. Over the next year-and-a-half, Mitchell conducted 125 of what he refers to as "problem-solving" sessions, with heads of travel departments and purchasing and key executives at Cigna's Eagle Lodge, at the international training center at Lafayette Hill in the northwest suburbs of Philadelphia. Further, this collective enterprise hired Jones Day Reavis Pogue, a Washington law firm specializing in antitrust litigation, and Edelman, the New York public relations firm.

Then, in July 1993, a plan of attack was carried out that began, in the utmost secrecy, with the top officials of major airline companies and travel agencies. "We always met with the top one or two officers, and there was a pledge of strict confidentiality," Mitchell says. "They agreed not to share the concept within their organizations, and we pledged not to enter their organizations through the side door. This is an industry that cannot keep a secret, and if there was a leak, then access to senior-level executives would then be cut off."

Mitchell won't discuss the cost of this joint effort, or describe the responses he received, other than to say, "We were encouraged to continue our work." He and his colleagues visited a total of 15 airline executives and travel agency heads to share their ideas. They were looking for an alternate way to purchase airline tickets for corporate travelers that would eliminate the present complex, costly, and involved process. The cost of distribution for corporate travel—the travel agent commissions, overrides, credits, fees for computer reservations system (CRS) services, and frequent-flier programs—were estimated at 20 percent of airline costs. Mitchell and company hit the executives with three ideas. They wanted an across-the-board discount, applicable to all of their flying; a new process to reduce reservations and ticketing costs; and a means to eliminate airline–corporate negotiations and costly internal audits of their own expenses.

These ideas must have come as a shock. Airlines grant discounts to large corporations, but those discounts don't apply to every route and every situation. Therefore airlines have depended on business fliers, who usually fly on short notice, to pay most of the full fares, whether in first, business, or coach cabins. Business fliers are those "high-yield" passengers that most airlines covet, for they pay the higher fares that contribute the most toward a profitable flight. In theory, the airlines had been keeping open seats for last-minute fliers, and for that service had charged them full prices. A simplified system would wreck the airlines' formula.

Further, a simplified fares system might allow corporations to use new technologies to make a reservation and acquire a ticket. Mitchell offers a concrete example. A corporate travel manager has a contract with Airline A for a certain percentage of his company's flying. But in a particular market, Airlines B and C compete with Airline A with frequent-flier programs and commission overrides to travel agents. Mitchell cites studies which estimate that frequent-flier programs cost corporate America as much as $7 billion and inflate travel and entertainment expenses between 11 and 15 percent. Much of this cost comes from travelers taking unnecessary trips, circuitous routings to gain mileage benefits, and avoiding company rules to fly only on the airlines of company choice.

The Mitchell-led study has turned into a career. With the backing of 18 of the large corporations, Mitchell founded the Business Travel Contractors Corporation of King of Prussia, Pennsylvania. He is no longer connected with Cigna, but the company supports his effort.

Whether the Mitchell concept lives or not, the executive has pin-pointed a host of real and costly problems that exist in the current ticket-distribution system.

Long-established practices in airline ticketing and distribution are yielding to new ways for U.S. airlines to sell seat space. The trend toward "ticketless travel," started by ValuJet and copied by United Airlines, is disturbing the status quo of airline ticket sales. When no ticket is required, passengers are less inclined to call a travel agent whose traditional service package has extended to both issuing a ticket and delivering it to a passenger. A second change taking place relates to consumers using personal computers and new on-line products. They are gaining access to information on airline schedules and fares that once was the exclusive domain of travel agents. Under these influences, direct sales between airlines and passengers are expected to increase over time, skirting the travel agent middleman.

One estimate, from Frank Dinovo, president of Travel & Transport Inc., an Omaha travel management company, projects that, in five years, one-third of all passengers in the United States will be booking their own reservations. He expects that the percentage of tickets sold by travel agents will drop from the current 80 to 70 percent, very possibly a conservative estimate. He predicts that the pressures on travel agents will force a restructuring of the business. He expects a new round of mergers to shrink the number of agencies, and he believes the surviving companies will begin acquiring reservations centers for airlines, hotels, and automobiles.

Airlines in the United States quietly welcome the direct contact with consumers. A direct sale that sidesteps the agent saves the airlines from paying a commission. Agent commissions reached a 1993 peak of $7.49 billion and are the third highest operating expense for U.S. airlines, behind wages and fuel. In 1994, Delta Air Lines took a large risk and reduced the rate of commissions it paid travel agents. The rate was reduced from the standard of 10 percent of the value of the ticket to 8 percent. The reduction applies only to full-fare Coach, Business, and First-Class tickets on international flights. These tickets are typically high-priced, and their sale still would furnish an adequate commission.

Delta's action miffed many travel agents, but the Atlanta carrier was not deterred. In February 1995, Delta amended its system of commissions and proposed a fee-based reward system to complement it. Delta set the maximum payment at $50 for a travel agent who sells a round-trip ticket valued at $500 or more. The old commission rate applies to tickets sold that are valued below $500. In short order, three other majors—American, Northwest, and United—matched Delta's proposal. The carriers projected that these changes could pare commission costs by $400 million a year.

## A FINAL WORD ON PRICING FROM THE JUSTICE DEPARTMENT
### *Washington, D.C.:* **March 17, 1994**

All of the U.S. airlines operate in a leading-edge electronic marketplace, where the ticket price charged by a competitor can be revealed by a click on a PC mouse. Beginning in the summer of 1989, the Justice Department took an interest in the information that was exchanged between the carriers through the ATPCO computers. Civil Investigative Demands (CIDS) were filed with the airlines in the summer of 1990, requesting information on those exchanges. Academic lawyers predicted a long and laborious investigation. Two years later, just prior to Christmas of 1992, the Justice Department filed a civil antitrust action against eight U.S. carriers and ATPCO.

The Justice Department alleged that between 1987 and 1990 the airlines had been communicating with one another through ATPCO, which allowed them to propose fare increases, counterpropose fares, and even reach consensus on dollar amounts and other aspects of pricing. The government's key gripe had to do with the airline practice of proposing a "first ticket date" on which the fares were first to be offered for sale. This time-lag permitted airlines to negotiate a consensus on what fares to charge, according to the Justice Department.

United Airlines and USAir entered into a consent decree on the day the Justice Department filed its suit in 1992. But six others— Alaska, American, Delta, Northwest, Continental, and Trans World—and ATPCO, fought the allegations. But in less than a year-and-a-half, on March 17, 1994, the six carriers settled the case with the Justice Department. In the consent decrees, the eight airlines agreed that all fares listed in ATPCO would be available for immediate purchase. No first ticket dates would be listed. Notice would be given only for the end of the fares sale. This is the procedure followed by the airlines today.

The Clinton Administration, battered daily in the spring of 1994 by revelations in the Whitewater investigation, made the most of its own unveiling of scandal. At a press conference in the Justice Department's headquarters on Constitution Avenue, Attorney General Janet Reno commented, "The Department is determined to challenge price-fixing or other anti-competitive conduct, no matter how sophisticated the tools or technology employed." Investigators said they had found more than 50 separate price-fixing agreements over hundreds of routes. A government economist tried to make the scandal look even richer by claiming that consumers might have paid more than $1 billion more for airline tickets between 1988 and 1992. The airlines had been caught, but nobody went to jail and no penalties were assigned.

*    *    *

In pricing, the full-service U.S. airlines have met their nemesis. Since deregulation, these airlines have been unable to set fares at levels that achieved consistent profits. Consumer demand for discounts has foiled many grand plans based on "superior" service at a premium price. Instead, the marketplace has accepted the concept of safe transportation at the lowest price possible.

Advocates of deregulation correctly predicted that increased airline competition would bring about low average fares. Airline fares have compared favorably with consumer prices as reflected by the Consumer Price Index (CPI). Since 1983, when the CPI and average fares equaled $100, consumer prices have climbed steadily to a 1993 high of more than $140. In contrast, average airline fares have climbed a crooked course to a peak of $115 in 1993. Low-fare competition in 1994 caused the average fare to drop by 4 percent.

While the pressures were predicted, no one understood the consequences of the low-fare trend: the inability of airlines to price profitably, the damaging fare wars, the bitter rivalry among the carriers, or the forced restructuring of the airlines now taking place.

# SIX

# The Odd Couple: Government and the Airlines

Government policies, legislative initiatives, and regulatory actions have also contributed to the deterioration of the airlines' financial condition.

—The National Commission to Ensure a Strong Competitive Airline Industry, August 1993, A Report to the President and Congress from *Change, Challenge and Competition*

## THE FLYING SENATOR: MOVE OVER FOR THE MIGHTY
### *Washington, D.C.: 1974-78\**

IT'S A COMMON occurrence on flights going in and out of the nation's capital for a flight attendant to announce, "Today we have on board the Honorable Seymour Spending, the United States representative from the Fourth District. Transtates Airlines welcomes him, and wishes him well."

Representatives and senators are truly frequent fliers, and they rely on air services to maintain personal contact with their con-

* Before deregulation.

stituents. In the early days of his Senate career, Senator Edward M. (Ted) Kennedy, Democrat of Massachusetts, was no exception. He regularly took a Friday flight from Washington's National Airport to Boston's Logan Airport on American Airlines. Those were the days of hot debate in Kennedy's Judiciary Committee over whether the nation should deregulate its airlines.

Kennedy flew so often that he grew familiar with many of the cabin crews. He was then and is now probably one of the most recognizable politicians in the country. According to flight attendants routinely assigned to the Boston flight, Kennedy would come on board with a Coach ticket and sit in Coach while keeping an eye on the First-Class cabin. If First Class didn't fill up, which it usually didn't in those days, he would go up front and take a seat. Knowing who he was, the flight attendants made no objection. This occurred time and again with various cabin crews, and eventually it became a matter of talk among crew members. One of them decided to bring up the matter with her superiors. What was the right thing to do? She was told that the flight attendants were handling the matter properly. If seats were available in First Class, by all means, let the senator have a seat there.

For a time, then, Senator Kennedy bought Coach and rode First Class. Then the congressional debate in Washington became concentrated on deregulation, and Kennedy became known as a leading advocate. By this time, fearing the unknown, most airlines including American Airlines were dubious about deregulation, and they began to show their opposition.

As the airline lobbyists trotted out all the arguments they could muster against deregulation, the flight attendants received new instructions regarding Senator Kennedy. He was about to lose his perquisites at American Airlines. On the next Friday night, as scheduled, the senator came aboard with his Coach ticket and at the convenient time headed up to First Class and took an empty seat. The questioning flight attendant went over to him and asked to see his seat assignment. It was a Coach seat, of course, and she escorted him to it.

The loss of the perk wasn't permanent, however. Some flight attendants continued to allow the senator to upgrade on his own. He wasn't the only member of Congress who could get a better seat if he or she wished. But the American flight attendant followed her orders to the letter. Whenever she was on duty, Senator Kennedy apparently recognized her and never attempted to go up to the First Class cabin.

## FLAWS IN FEDERAL SUPPORT
### *Washington, D.C.:* October 1994

A strong symbol of the longstanding ties between aviation and the U.S. government sits just to the north of the Art Deco main terminal building at Washington's National Airport. It is a parking lot whose spaces are conveniently reserved for government officials: Supreme Court justices, Cabinet officers, and congressmen. Usually quite well filled with automobiles, the reserved lot is a relic of the days when the Federal Aviation Administration operated the facility. The current owners, the Metropolitan Washington Airports Authority, continued the special accommodation without a second thought. Critics occasionally inveigh against the practice as anti-egalitarian and un-American. But the lot probably will remain in place for as long as there is a downtown airport in Washington. It sits there serving the high and the mighty, a symbol of the long and strong ties between aviation and the government.

The tradition of government–industry ties has paid off for both sides. Bipartisan support for aviation came early from Congress. Fears that the United States had fallen behind Europe in the number and quality of its aircraft drove Congress in 1915 to create the National Advisory Committee for Aeronautics (NACA), the predecessor of the National Aeronautics & Space Administration (NASA). Without NACA's research leading the way to technological innovation, U.S. aviation would never have gained its preeminent place in the decades that followed. The government research paved the way for efficiencies that reduced costs and maximized performance of aircraft. Studies in drag reduction, lightweight materials, structures, and engines resulted in improved lift and made faster aircraft possible.

A pragmatic rationale prevailed in Congress, which clearly was looking for ways to expand an industry with both economic and military benefits. In 1926, Congress ordered the creation of the Bureau of Air Commerce to support airline technical operations, with the underlying purpose of improving the margin of safety—the very duties of the FAA today. Eventually, this mission evolved into providing for airways and the air-traffic-control system, and administering the federal funding of locally operated airports.

Airport funding by the government has been substantial. Between fiscal 1982 and fiscal 1994, the FAA was authorized to grant $16.1 billion to local airports for capital projects ranging from the purchase of fire safety equipment to construction of new runways. While there has been expansion of local airports and FAA encouragement, few airports have been built. The new Denver International Airport, opening in 1995, is the first since the Ft. Myers, Florida, airport was constructed in the early 1980s. Each was made possible in part by federal aid.

Money is the cement that keeps the government and airlines stuck together in a constantly contentious relationship. Each benefits from the other. Besides paying income and property taxes just as any business, the airlines collect taxes and fees for the government. In a recent fiscal year, the airlines collected nearly $7 billion from a domestic airline ticket tax and from fees charged passengers for international departure, for the services of the U.S. Customs Service and the Immigration and Naturalization Service. Much of the $7 billion goes to the Aviation Trust Fund, which pays for improvements to the air-traffic-control and airway system and a large portion of the FAA budget. In return, the airlines welcome every cent spent by the government on research and development for aircraft at the FAA or at the National Aeronautics & Space Administration (NASA).

The airlines–government relationship has been tested by two obvious government blunders. First, the government has failed to modernize the air-traffic-control system as was promised after the air-traffic controllers' strike in 1981. Billions have been spent improving radars at FAA stations, but key elements of automation of the system may not be in place until after the year 2000. Besides, the cost of the system overhaul has risen nearly three times from the original estimate of $12 billion. The bureaucratic FAA is responsible for this failure.

Secondly, the government has fallen down in its attempts to bring free trade to international skies. U.S. airlines have expanded internationally, but many other nations haven't accepted the U.S. version of free trade in the air. Many foreign governments have remained protectionist, limiting entry of U.S. and other carriers, and restricting flights and operations under bilateral aviation agreements between the United States and the other nations. While there has been a certain degree of liberalization, the shift away from total government control of world airlines has only just begun. Executives at the U.S. carriers feel that the lack of success of government efforts has put a deep crimp in their broad international expansion plans.

The concerns of members of Congress for the economic viability of the airline industry was the primary driver of the National Commission to Ensure a Strong Competitive Airline Industry, which convened in 1993. The commission members, serving under former Virginia governor Gerald L. Baliles, performed like yeomen in relaying the story of the heavily indebted, overtaxed airlines. The report of the National Commission largely adopted the views articulated by the airline representatives. Recommendations were more detailed and probing than those offered by the Air Transport Association, but the influence of that group was obvious. (See Appendix A.) Further, the commission refrained an old ATA anthem: "The FAA needs to reform, badly!" As the industry now enters the mid-nineties, FAA reform will be much in vogue in Washington. A part of that reform package is likely to be either a privatized air-traffic-control system or a federal corporation to run ATC. In any case it probably will be removed from the bureaucracy, in time, as another step in the long-term trend toward privatization that began with the deregulation of the airlines.

A standard joke frequently heard at commercial aviation gatherings alludes to an FAA employee who walks onto an airline's property. "I'm from the FAA," he says. "I'm here to help." The remark raises howls of laughter from the audience, even a chuckle from some good-humored FAA personnel who understand the use of irony. They know that the FAA can perform very well—it is by no means a joke as a federal agency, and to many around the world it is the model civil aviation agency—but as a bureaucracy it seems to have a life of its own. Now for an inside story about it.

## BUREAUCRACY THAT SOMETIMES DOESN'T LISTEN
### *Rogers Dry Lake, Edwards Air Force Base,*
### *California:* Fall 1984

A federal agency that has made as many expensive public mistakes as the FAA must be endowed with some inner strength that keeps it going. The agency has been criticized for its dual purpose: keeping aviation safe while promoting it. But most in aviation see no conflict in the dual role. Safety is a sine qua non in aviation that few outside it can comprehend. No one, particularly the people who fly the airplanes, perceives any gain in shaving maintenance expenses at the risk of an airplane. When one is flying at near Mach 1 at 41,000 ft, this becomes a heartfelt axiom.

As for the promotion of aviation, there are no greater boosters of aviation than the people who wear wings. The FAA is, in a real sense, part of the brotherhood. But once it acts officially, the agency is regarded by aviation as the final word, the legal authority, she who must be obeyed. The agency is held in the highest esteem as a trendsetter by the aviation authorities of other nations, a fact that always comes as a shock to many in America.

The FAA blundered onto national television screens in late fall of 1984, during what became a colorfully humiliating disaster for the agency. The government project, cosponsored with the National Aeronautics and Space Administration (NASA), sounded simple enough. Britain's Imperial Chemical Industries and the Royal Aircraft Establishment had devised a fuel modifier termed FM-9, a long-chain polymer that prevents fuel from misting into a haze of droplets, a condition that sets it up for a friction-sparked fire. The FAA had spent five years and more than $11 million on a program to improve the crash-worthiness and fire safety of jet airliners, especially in the fuel fires that can follow violent crashes. Laboratory testing showed the workability of FM-9. A controlled-impact demonstration with an FAA-owned and -operated, 75-seat Boeing 720, fueled by anti-misting kerosene in its four engines, was to be the culminating test in the program. A test site, complete with ground-based steel prongs, "wing-openers," and a field of approach lights, was established on the bombing range at Rogers Dry Lake near the Edwards AFB main runway.

The project had a secondary purpose of testing the effect of the crash on an aircraft structure, the passenger and cockpit seats, as well as testing the survivability of airline passengers in the controlled crash. Most of the 75 seats were occupied by instrumented test dummies, to gain data on crash impact. The Boeing 720 had been flown by remote control, with pilots on-board, on 20 previous test flights. All the bugs had been worked out, and the FAA/NASA team was nearly ready for the November 10 flight. White canvas-covered dummies were installed in the 720's seats, starting with the first rows near the cockpit door. The company that produces the dummies exhausted their supply after installing about 50 dummies. An additional order for dummies was placed for the back of the airplane.

When the installation of dummies was resumed, an FAA official stood at the cockpit door to survey the workmanship. He found not an airplane prepared for a scientific experiment but an example of social inequality. All of the black dummies were confined to the back of the airplane! Concerned that people might get the wrong idea, he ordered an integration of the dummies. Dumbfounded workmen had to remove some white canvas dummies from their installed places and reinstall them at the back, to achieve a balanced mix of black and white canvas. A report on the overly sensitive FAA official and his concern for social equality appeared in *Aviation Week & Space Technology* in its November 5, 1984, issue, prompting a reader to write:

All America must be proud of the Federal Aviation Administration. Its actions to protect the civil rights of the 75 instrumented dummies who will sacrifice themselves in the interests of air safety ranks as a high point in the long and arduous struggle for the equality of dummies. The next test should be less costly, since there will be no need to contract for crash dummies. The FAA has demonstrated that it has an adequate supply within its ranks.

The test was postponed in any case until December 1, and it caused more red faces at the FAA when it actually occurred. The agency had planned on a descent rate for the test aircraft of 15 to 17 feet per second. The agency had disregarded a warning from the manufacturers represented by the Aerospace Industries Association

(AIA) that the descent rate was too fast and the crash impact would be too severe. Confident of a publicity bonanza, the FAA invited Transportation Secretary Elizabeth Hanford Dole to appear at the press conference following the test.

On the test day, FAA personnel remotely controlled the Boeing 720 on the takeoff. It was empty of real people but loaded with instrumentation and the integrated dummies. After the takeoff and a left turn crossing south of the target area, the aircraft climbed to 2300 ft. It was turned left again to align with the runway, and the Boeing 720 began a smooth descent. But when it reached an altitude of 150 ft, the nose dropped slightly and the aircraft began to roll. The left wing was low when the Boeing 720 touched down 281 ft from the target point at a descent rate of 20 to 22 ft per second. The right wing was penetrated by the wing openers, and a fireball engulfed the airplane. Before a host of television cameras and members of the news media, the fire burned for more than an hour.

The FAA held the press conference as scheduled. Not surprisingly, Mrs. Dole was nowhere to be found. As the fire burned brightly, sending waves of billowing smoke into the air, a government jet lifted off and disappeared into the eastern sky. Astonishingly, much test data was recovered from the blackened hull, but the FAA's plans for an anti-misting additive went up in smoke over the California desert.

*   *   *

Fiascos apply to public policy matters as well. A key issue of recent years has centered on the operation of the FAA's air-traffic-control system. The debate over its ownership, whether by private sources, a quasi-public corporation, or the FAA, illustrates the roundabout ways of politics in the nation's capital.

The most recent efforts to relieve the FAA of responsibility for ATC started early in 1985. Most major airlines of the mid-1980s were fairly robust. They based strategies on route expansion largely through new hub-and-spoke flight networks, which concentrated operations at key airports at certain hours of the day. The FAA's ATC system, damaged by the 1981 strike of the Professional Air Traffic

Controllers Organization (PATCO), lacked experienced controllers and the new systems and equipment that had been promised in the post-strike reconstruction.

Flight delays in the mid-1980s began to be a problem. (The FAA counted a delay if an aircraft departed more than 15 minutes after the scheduled departure.) The FAA figures did not include delays that aircraft encountered as they moved through the system. In any case, the number 1000 had served as an old FAA benchmark for the maximum permissible. Delays kept climbing during summer periods and began to levy unnecessary costs on the airlines. Aircraft wasted expensive fuel as they lined up awaiting departure clearances in FAA-ordered "ground holds" of aircraft. The situation soon became untenable.

Probably no government agency was organized to grow with the fluid, dynamic operation that the airline business had become. In the regulated past, the government had monitored the airlines' every move. They moved slowly, and the FAA had ample time to plan and address the technical requirements of new airline services. Aviation business was conducted at a much slower pace. New complications set in as the airlines expanded in the post-deregulation era.

PATCO's shutdown of the ATC system and the subsequent firing of 11,000 striking controllers by President Reagan was both a blessing and a curse. Many controllers had been hoodwinked by PATCO officers into violating the no-strike clause in the labor contract. By walking off the job, the strikers forced the hand of President Reagan, and they should have known better. He gave them a chance to return to work, set a date for their return, and took action against the violators who remained off the job. The mass firing, however appropriate, dealt a serious blow to the ATC system.

Controllers who could function at full performance levels—that is, those who were qualified by experience to perform virtually all of the numerous tasks at an ATC facility—were far harder to come by. The shakeup gave the agency an opportunity to upgrade the ATC system to meet the needs of the post-deregulation period. Thus, the National Airspace System Plan (NASP) that got under way in 1982, under Transporation Secretary Drew Lewis and FAA Administrator J. Lynn Helms, was a $12-billion modernization plan. It was to

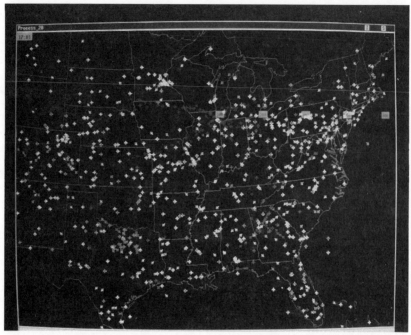

**Busy U.S. Airways.**    Radar targets, each indicating a high-altitude commercial aircraft, dot this pictorial from the Aviation Situation Display (ASD) at National Headquarters of the Federal Aviation Administration (FAA) in Washington, D.C. The ASD system, which collects radar information from around the nation, provides visual pictures of air traffic on a wide scale, as shown. A controller may telescope the display to the air traffic in each of the 20 air route traffic control centers in the continental U.S., or to the 700 sectors in the U.S. air traffic control system. (*FAA Display*)

transform ATC and make it even more the envy of the world. Yet delays were plaguing the system.

By the mid-1980s Lewis and Helms had left their posts, and the ATC system was under heavy strain from congestion and delays. The Air Transport Association of America, the industry association comprising the major airlines in the United States, searched for solutions to the delays and a way to jump start the lagging NAS Plan. At one of the ATA board of directors' meetings, American's Robert L. Crandall suggested that the problems might be solved if a new way for the FAA to do business could be found.

## THE AIRLINE PLAN THAT SHOCKED THE FAA
### *Washington, D.C.:* **Spring 1985**

Mary Downs began work as staff counsel at the Air Transport Association (ATA) in February 1985, following a brief stint as a lawyer in private practice. Earlier, Ms. Downs had acquired a solid grounding in aviation law as a counsel to the Civil Aeronautics Board. The ATA assigned her a challenging task: work out a way to extricate the airlines from the gridlocked air-traffic-control system.

Her study soon brought her to the conclusion that the problem lay neither with new technology nor with the plans of the Reagan Administration for rebuilding the system, but with the FAA itself. "The ATC situation was not improving very quickly. The number of full-performance-level controllers was a major problem in many different places. We felt that the FAA was not situated to move people and assets around to address congestion and capacity issues."

Funding was in 1985, and still is to this day, a large part of the problem. The FAA receives 70 percent of its budget from the Aviation Trust Fund. This fund, created by Congress, receives excise taxes paid by airline passengers and other users of the aviation system. The dollar amount reaches astonishing levels, and at times the fund has ranged into the double-digit billions. In most years, this resource is used sparingly as part of a slow and cumbersome process.

"One of the things we looked at was an analysis of the ATC system from 20 years before," Downs recalls. "The criticism was the same. These were hardy perennials: problems with procurement, the financing stream, and the inflexibility of the FAA. The FAA couldn't move people around without going through hoops, couldn't pay people differently in different locales."

The airlines were free to operate domestically like any ordinary business; the inadequacies of the air-traffic-control system were becoming a major hindrance. When coupled with capacity restrictions at congested airports, the system's inadequacies might even have been considered a threat to free enterprise.

Downs' ATA study reviewed, among a number of alternatives, the complete privatization of ATC. That option was dismissed at this stage largely due to the expectation of military resistance. The military, in the throes of the Cold War with the Soviet Union in 1985, foresaw a possible breach of security if individuals of a privately held company had full access to radar information. The ATA decided to propose a federal corporation to govern air traffic control.

"All of the federal corporations are different from one another. There is no requirement that one do any particular thing. They can be flexible," Downs says. The consensus of the ATA board of directors was that a new federal corporation should control funding and guide the development of a new ATC system under a new set of rules. While some members of Congress were fascinated, on the whole the response was hostile. The bureaucrats in the FAA, which stood to lose 37,500 employees to the new corporation, were reluctant and critical. Many in Congress, serving on key subcommittees, were dubious.

The proposal was ahead of its time.

## COLLAPSE OF THE TRANSPORTATION DEPARTMENT CORPORATION PLAN
### *Washington, D.C.:* July, 1994

After deeper analysis by the airlines and "fine-tuning" by a heavy-handed Transportation Department, the promise held out by the proposed federal corporation for air-traffic control began to fade. Critical examinations of the proposed corporation began early in 1994. Concerns emerged at the May meeting of the Regional Airline Association (RAA), a trade association for regional and commuter air carriers based in Washington—the same month the Transportation Department's study and report favoring the corporation was released.

By raising those concerns at the RAA meeting, Gary Church, president of Aviation Management Associates, Inc. of Springfield, Va., an FAA contractor and specialist in ATC management, became one of the first public critics outside of Congress. The Administration had misunderstood the problem, according to Church. In his view, the real problem was mismanagement within the FAA, stemming from a committee mentality, the lack of direction and incentive, and a bureaucratic approach to all issues. Further, Church offered the opinion that the Administration had leapt to the federal corporation idea without investigating alternatives. If the corporation was to be established, and nearly two-thirds of the FAA's employees and resources diverted to it, the residue FAA would remain untouched and still be badly in need of reform. Sectioning out the ATC division would not, in and of itself, solve all problems associated with the agency.

Critics found a flaw in the government calculations. Cost estimates had been based on projections of new benefits and on additional revenues expected, a "best-case" scenario. The costs of the current system at the FAA, an agency that has never been audited outside the government, actually are unclear, and can't be used to project what may be ahead for a federal corporation. Accounting rules differ, for instance, on a small but important expense: funding of annual leave for employees, quite a sum when the number of employees is more than 30,000. Such backup funding isn't an issue in government, but in a federal corporation, means must be found to fund vacations and sick leave. Further, the Transportation Department's vision of the federal corporation became encumbered by the initiation of special FAA veto authority over fees and regulations.

As of this writing, the fate of the FAA's air-traffic-control operation, now known as the United States Air Traffic Services Corporation (USATS), has been placed in the hands of the Republican-dominated Congress. The November 1994 election stripped the Democrats of power in both the House and the Senate. Republicans are discussing the merits of full privatization and the establishment of a quasi-public federal corporation, but no action on this transfer is likely to be taken until the new committees are prepared to conduct full hearings and explore many questions.

In the late fall of 1994, Michael Durham, the chief financial officer of American Airlines, endorsed full privatization of the ATC system at a meeting with airline analysts. He raised an indisputable point: The ATC system would function more efficiently if it were totally outside of the government's control. If the drive for privatization were to fail, he told a group of airline analysts that Fall, a shift to a quasi-public federal corporation would not be acceptable. Government rules for the procurement and personnel that have stifled the FAA would stifle progress of a federal corporation as well.

# SEVEN

# Liberalization Unfolding

International air transport is playing an increasingly important role in the world economy. There is considerable concern, however, about the ability of the airline industry to provide efficient air transport services in the future, and to meet the expanding needs of actual and potential users.

—Report of the Organization for Economic Cooperation and Development (OECD), Paris, 1993

## DEREGULATION, LIBERALIZATION, AND WHAT HAVE YOU
### *Washington, D.C.:* October 1978-February 1995

AIRLINE DEREGULATION has yielded a mixed bag for the United States: low fares, more flights, and industry upheaval. The impact of this change has been felt around the world. Deregulation has accelerated a slow transformation of the airlines from being an expensive means of travel for the elite to a system of mass transportation. Consumer interests are demanding low fares and improved services all across the globe.

From an inter-government standpoint, the United States had a free-trading soul mate in the Netherlands. Aviation agreements between these two countries have reflected commonly accepted views. After 1978, only a few dozen nations have followed the U.S. lead. Canada and Australia have deregulated, and Europe has headed down its own path to liberalization of airline regulations under the European Union. Protectionist nations are in a bind. They seek out and willingly accept increased air service for business and tourism development but maintain strict controls, in large part to keep their inflexible and inefficient flag airlines intact.

The European Union followed the same path as the U.S. government in formally studying the causes of the ongoing air-transport crisis. In a series of meetings, the European Wise Men Committee, formed in July 1993, (also known as "the Comité des Sages") listened to testimony from free-trade advocates, protectionists, and consumer groups. A report issued in February 1994 criticized the air carriers' slow response to the changing air-transport market.

"There is no way back to the previous era of nationalistic protectionism," the report stated. Wise Men Committee Chairman Herman De Croo traced the source of the crisis to the government protection of nationalized carriers. This produced, he said, a fragmented European market and inefficient airlines dependent on state aid. Uses of state funds for bailing out airlines has distorted the European market. In any case, government bailouts have permitted bloated airlines to continue to exist. Bailouts have thwarted efforts by airlines to reduce the size of their fleets in Europe. That would have led to cost-cutting and efficiencies.

As the European Union inches toward liberalization, free-trade advocates battle with protectionists over state aid, political intervention, and regulatory issues. Europe's fragmented and backward air-traffic-control system is a target of all airlines. Swissair's chief executive Otto Loepfe has estimated that 50 to 60 aircraft are flying in European skies at any given time, awaiting clearances from ATC, as a direct result of inefficiencies in European air-traffic control. Free-trade advocates are pressing for privatization of EuroControl, the organization jointly operated by European governments, which still lacks authority to provide complete ATC services.

The Wise Men Committee examining Europe's needs recommended a unified air-traffic-control system, the removal of monopolies, and an end to state aid, among a host of free-trade-inspired suggestions.

Another battleground for aviation diplomats has been the U.S.–Japan bilateral aviation agreement. As Americans try to obtain additional rights for U.S. carriers, the Japanese offer stout resistance and seek a rewrite of the unbalanced 1952 accord. Japan has been stymied in its attempts to increase capacity at Narita airport outside of Tokyo. The airport is restricted to the operation of a single runway. Completion of a second runway has been delayed for years by the successful protests of Narita-area farmers.

During the 1980s, clashes between farmers, aided by activitists, and police authorities have frequently been violent. The perimeter of Narita airport resembles a modernized version of a feudal castle, rimmed as it is by walls and electrified fences. In its thoroughness, security at Narita rivals that to be found anywhere in the world. It isn't uncommon for a passenger to undergo two, perhaps even three body searches.

As the deregulation trend picked up speed in some nations during the 1980s, interest quickened in the privatization of nationalized airlines. Government-bloated payrolls and inefficiencies had made the national carriers easy targets for the more efficient deregulated airlines, particularly those from the United States. Governments began to sell their financial interests, or reduced their shares significantly. The Netherlands and Switzerland were among the first European governments to bring share levels below 50 percent, in KLM Royal Dutch Airlines and in Swissair, respectively. Great Britain's total release of ownership in British Airways started a new world trend. Afterward, Japan shed its interests in Japan Airlines, Canada in Air Canada, and Australia in Qantas.

In the span of a few recent years, Latin American commercial aviation has shifted from a highly regulated industry of national flag carriers to a more competitive marketplace of largely private airlines. Spain's government-controlled Iberia has embarked on an acquisition binge, recreating in a modern version the Spanish Main. In 1994 it acquired a majority interest in Aerolineas Argentinas, the flag carrier of Argentina, raising the question in international circles of whose nation should represent the Buenos Aires–based airline. Earlier, Iberia had taken a substantial share of Ladeco of Chile and Viasa of Venezuela.

The tide seems to have turned in the nineties, however. More than 30 government-owned airlines targeted for privatization early in the decade were still under government control in 1994. The slowing of

the privatization pace has been a reflection, perhaps, of the new caution resulting from the string of disastrous financial reports around
the globe.

An overriding trend has been toward alliances or partnerships
among the world's airlines. New marketing agreements between the
carriers have replaced the old system of inter-airline coordination
referred to as *interlining.* Travelers interlined when they flew on two
or more airlines to reach their final destination. In the days of high-
technology communications and co-marketing agreements, the
movement between allied airlines has become nearly as easy as if
the passenger stayed on the same carrier. A July 1994 survey of the
world's airlines in *Airline Business* revealed that there are 280 various
alliances at 136 air carriers, ranging from marketing agreements to
joint catering services. The trend keeps growing, in part as a defense
mechanism employed by smaller airlines against the rising world
influence of the large airlines, mostly American, that are known as
the *megacarriers.*

United Airlines and Lufthansa Airlines of Germany allied in 1994,
as the German carrier was beginning a long-awaited restructuring.
Lufthansa has since taken the remarkable steps of slashing labor costs
and reducing the work force while increasing flights. The result is a
healthy 8 percent growth of traffic in 1994, which has pushed
Lufthansa into the number-two position in Europe, behind British
Airways. A European bank analyst says that transforming Lufthansa
was analogous to turning the once-ugly duckling into a swan.

The alliance between KLM Royal Dutch Airlnes and Northwest
Airlines is an example of how closely two separate companies can
operate. It is the strongest partnership to emerge from the deregulation era, an example of the spread of airlines beyond the limits fore-
seen by world governments.

## THE U.S.-DUTCH AIRLINES FORGE AN UNBEATABLE ALLIANCE
### *Amstelveen, The Netherlands:* June 1994

KLM Royal Dutch Airlines and Northwest Airlines are merging in
every way but name. Northwest remains a U.S.-based airline and

KLM a Dutch carrier. A free-trade agreement between the United States and the Netherlands, the first ever in the world, has permitted the development of a global carrier, part Dutch, part American, and part hybrid.

Officials of the two airlines refer to their joining of operations as a "marriage," one that looks positively toward the future. The machinery of this common effort is oiled by a grant of antitrust immunity from the U.S. Justice Department, the only one granted to a joint operation. It was granted largely as a favor to the Netherlands, which, on September 4, 1992, signed the precedent-breaking Open Skies agreement with the United States. Airline officials are immunized from prosecution under the U.S. law, and may discuss joint fares and promotions and cooperate in ways that airlines in other, restricted alliances can only dream about.

The United States now regards the issuance of antitrust immunity as an incentive for other nations to join the few that favor free trade in the air. The Netherlands has been the most ardent seeker of the freedom to operate.

\*   \*   \*

In the peak summer season, a Boeing 747 wearing the sky-blue colors of KLM Royal Dutch Airlines crosses the Netherlands coast, coming in from America, 69 times a week. From 10,000 ft, the frontier is seen to be demarcated by a thin strip of sandy beach bordered by the white foaming waves of the North Sea. The green land beneath, looking much like Japan from the air, exhibits the handiwork of man. Its geometry is linear and and neat. In spring, the Dutch tulips bloom en masse in long, thin rectangles of bold reds and yellows. The coastal plain on the approach taken by the 747s en route to Amsterdam's Airport Schiphol has served as a gateway to the world for nearly five centuries. If history serves as a grounding for the future of this nation of 13 million people, the aerial gateway will be open and busy for many years to come.

Recent developments in Netherlands aviation give ample reason for optimism. The Dutch are the spearhead of world aeropolitics, and the masters of the new trend of globalization of the airline business.

In navigating a course toward free trade in the air, they are duplicating the seminal work of their ancestors. Dutch seafarers opened the way to global trade in the late sixteenth and seventeenth centuries. Hugo Grotius, the Dutch jurist and codifier of international law, proclaimed the doctrine of the freedom of the seas, which became the international standard under which trading fleets sailed around the world. As the Dutch extended trade to the East and West Indies and to North America, principally New York, the British adopted the freedom-of-the-seas principle and joined in establishing world markets. The sea lanes established by these bold and courageous captains transformed the Netherlands into a world trade center and Britain into a world power. The Dutch emphasis fell more on trade rather than force of arms, but each nation was catapulted to the first rank. The Dutch burghers, so honestly recreated in Amsterdam's lifelike Rijksmuseum paintings, speak across the centuries of the determination and straightforwardness of the Dutch people.

In 1919, commercial aviation began in the skies over the Netherlands. KLM was among a handful of pioneer airlines that launched commercial services in the months after the Allies and Germany officially ended World War I with the signing on June 28, 1919, of the Versailles Peace Treaty. British and French aircraft manufacturers may have been first in the air, but from among those pioneers only KLM, formed in October 1919, remains a working airline. KLM looks back to the same man, Dr. Albert Plesman, as having been the driving force behind the start-up of the carrier in 1919 and its renaissance in the ruins of World War II. Soon after the Allied liberation of the Netherlands early in 1945, Dr. Plesman traveled to the United States where he obtained 14 C54As, the military version of the DC-4, and 22 C-47s, the military version of the DC-3, under a lease-purchase arrangement. Since that rebirth, the contemporary Dutch have built an aerial network in KLM that connects to some 87 countries.

## FREE-TRADERS WORK CAUTIOUSLY IN A PROTECTED WORLD

Diplomats have a penchant for using the name of a productive meeting place when designating their ground-breaking accords. The

Geneva Convention refers to the well-known accord on the treatment of prisoners of war, signed in 1864 in the Swiss city. International aviation has its equivalents. The Chicago Convention takes its name from the assembly of 54 nations in Chicago in 1944, when the framework of standards and regulations for postwar civil aviation was erected.

The Chicago Convention marks the first effort by the United States to instill free-trade principles into international aviation, and its first defeat. The U.S. delegation proposed a multilateral international-air-transport agreement. It authorized all nations the right to transit, technical stops, and, with the exception of cabotage, the right to fly commercial traffic. Ultimately, 25 nations signed the agreement, and later a few denounced it. Among the major nations, only the Netherlands and Sweden joined with the United States in signing. The United Kingdom led the substantial opposing forces concerned at the prospect of U.S. dominance in civil aviation. This seemed sure to result from the number of U.S. air bases then existing around the world, the number of available transports, and the capability of the American manufacturing sector. Therefore the International Civil Aviation Organization (ICAO), which sits in Montreal and establishes regulations and standards for world civil aviation, was deprived of a specific role related to the framework for commercial aviation agreements that now linked nations and their airlines. Instead, the nations adopted a general agreement and later a bilateral system of aviation agreements, negotiated by representatives of one nation with those of another nation. Today the system of bilateral aviation agreements—there are more than 3000 of them—embraces flights to every corner of the globe. In fact, the agreements ban all flights not covered in their documents.

In the world of diplomacy, the United States has earned a reputation as a hard-driving negotiator, lacking at times the appropriate finesse required for international negotiations. There is a common criticism of heavy-handedness in pursuing some of our country's objectives. One example is the abrupt policy change in the early days of deregulation, when the United States threatened to take antitrust immunity off the table during discussions of fares by the International Air Transport Association (IATA), the world industry group. Later the United States permitted an accommodation, but the application of U.S. antitrust law to the international arena was widely criticized. Then, too, frequent changes of administrations and top officials have made a hash of U.S. policy initiatives. The United States has been accused of inconsistency and a lack of style. One diplomat associated with the ICAO has spoken of the lack of preparation by U.S. negotiators, and the common use of styrofoam cups for coffee during negotiations!

## The Free-trading Dutch Set the Pace for Liberalization

The Netherlands' government enthusiastically supports free trade. Its diplomats and KLM's managers have taken advantage of opportunities brought on by deregulation. In 1984, the Dutch negotiated with the United Kingdom the most liberal free-trade air-service agreement of the decade. It opened the skies of both countries to new airline entry, permitting airlines to fly to any point in either country with no restrictions on the volume of seats in the airplanes. Moreover, fares could be stopped only if the aviation authorities of each nation agreed on disapproval.

London was KLM's first international destination. The Netherlands–United Kingdom route remains one of the world's busiest, with traffic between the United Kingdom and the Netherlands having averaged approximately three million passengers annually in recent years. The routes between the two countries rank in size among the top 20 cross-border routes. Until the signing of the landmark U.S. Open Skies bilateral air-service agreement with the Dutch in the summer of 1992, the Netherlands–U.K. agreement served as the model free-trade pact.

The road to U.S.–Dutch Open Skies has been bumpy and difficult and it has had its share of odd twists and turns, but the two nations have always been able to thrash out their differences. While the Dutch pursued Open Skies through the 1980s, the United States, though committed ideologically, remained unsure in some quarters of the Transportation Department. The chief roadblock was U.S. law, which stood in the way of a full-scale shift to liberalization in international aviation. Foreign investment in a U.S. airline was limited to less than 25 percent of voting stock. Cabotage was outlawed—no foreign airline could be authorized to serve in domestic markets.

In contrast, the Reagan White House supported free trade everywhere and urged the adoption of liberal trade views, especially in executive departments such as the Transportation Department. Its hands tied by the law, the Transportation Department pursued a pragmatic approach to the negotiations. They sought progress toward Open Skies, but gains were slow in coming. The brouhaha that ensued in 1987 with the United States–Netherlands negotiations was the result of a sharp contrast between theoretical support at high levels of the Administration and the everyday practice of government under the wing of Congress.

Whatever the root cause, the April 1987 talks between the United States and the Netherlands failed to produce an agreement. The issue centered around an innovation proposed by the Dutch to serve Orlando and six other U.S. cities under special agreements with one or more regional U.S. carriers to act as feeders of passengers for KLM. The U.S. negotiators rejected the Dutch proposal. Shortly thereafter, on April 22, Dutch Transport Minister Neelie Smit-Kroes met with her U.S. counterpart, Transportation Secretary Elizabeth Hanford Dole. In that private session, Mrs. Dole discussed the Dutch proposal with Ms. Smit-Kroes, then asked the U.S. negotiators at DOT to develop a counterproposal.

Some in the career staff at the Transportation Department who were not among Mrs. Dole's admirers were shocked at what they considered to be a breach of traditional practice. The U.S. airlines condemned the KLM proposal. They foresaw a huge imbalance of benefits—valuable rights in the U.S. going to KLM—with the expectation of little or nothing to be gained in return from the tiny Netherlands.

The stories leaked to the press portrayed Mrs. Dole as giving away lucrative rights to the clever Ms. Smit-Kroes over a friendly chat and a handshake. The final deal hadn't been cut, however. It came months later, in a thinned-down version of the original proposal. Mrs. Dole signed a memorandum of understanding on July 16, designating Orlando as KLM's seventh U.S. gateway. KLM gained "beyond rights," which enabled the carrier to pick up stopover traffic but not local traffic at Orlando, and carry it on to Mexico. A traffic-feed system for KLM with a U.S. regional carrier was ignored in the final agreement. Thus, the U.S. government put off a dispute over whether a foreign carrier could directly tap into domestic U.S. passenger traffic.

KLM's Orlando service from Europe reflected a new role for cities in the negotiating process. Officials at Orlando, the home of Disney World, had campaigned for four years for direct flights from Europe. Orlando participated in the new organization, USA–Better International Air Service (USA-BIAS). The organization comprised more than a dozen U.S. cities and airport authorities eager to attract international air service. It had become an important new force in the negotiating process.

## PRELUDE TO THE U.S.-DUTCH ACCORD
### *Washington, D.C.:* **October 1989**

A second public flap over the U.S.–Netherlands accord occurred on October 5, 1989, and was related to the drive of the cities for new services. President Bush named a new transportation secretary, Samuel K. Skinner, a lawyer and former IBM executive who later became the President's Chief of Staff. Skinner was an active secretary, highly regarded for his political judgment, intense interest in the industry, and sound decision making. Under the President's directive, he conducted public hearings on air services in major U.S. cities including Baltimore, New Orleans, and his hometown of Chicago.

KLM officials made appearances at several of the hearings, offering to serve the communities. Skinner was looking for a way to permit new services to this country by foreign airlines without disturbing the U.S. carriers—a difficult task. He decided on the Cities Program, under which the United States would authorize service by foreign carriers to any city that was not served by a U.S. airline with either nonstop or one-stop flights.

"We were looking for creative ways to open the market," Skinner recalls, "and this was one we thought might work. We were trying to send a message and get some incentives."

An opportunity to launch the Cities Program came about that fall. Skinner was invited to speak at an aviation symposium sponsored by the Air Transport Association and the School of Foreign

Service at Georgetown University in Washington, D.C. Staff members of the Transportation Department prepared the major part of Skinner's presentation. Concerned that the Dutch would too aggressively seek new services to the U.S., which would irritate the U.S. airlines, the DOT staffers inserted a provision in the otherwise liberal document aimed directly at restricting the Dutch.

Skinner had conflicting appointments that day and chose in the end to attend a U.S. Coast Guard function. His absence was filled that day, October 5, 1989, by Jeffrey N. Shane, then Assistant Transportation Secretary for Policy and International Affairs and now counsel to Wilmer, Cutler & Pickering, the Washington law firm. The Dutch consider the events of October 5 as being a prelude to the new era in U.S.–Netherlands relations. As expected, the proposal offered foreign airlines the right to fly to any U.S. city that was not served by a U.S. carrier with either nonstop or one-stop flights. But it added that no foreign airline need apply if it relied unduly on passengers who had passed through Amsterdam to come to the United States. The Dutch were appalled by U.S. intransigence in writing a liberal policy that still restricted the major Dutch carrier. In contrast, most people in the audience welcomed the announcement of the Cities Program as a U.S. policy breakthrough.

After the Assistant Secretary's presentation, Dr. Henri Wassenbergh, the Dutch representative, stood up in the Georgetown auditorium and made a comment that caused the audience of 250 people to fidget nervously in their seats and fall silent. "With all due respect, Jeff, this is a hollow gesture." In the civil exchange between the two which followed, Shane acknowledged that the provision against "sixth-freedom" traffic would torpedo KLM's ability to serve any city under the program. It appeared that U.S. policy was becoming more liberal, but not enough to include the Dutch or any other sixth-freedom carrier. Shane later said that the document was drawn up so as to take a bold but careful step toward liberalizing international aviation. At that point in time, the United States was negotiating with Italy to allow nonstop services by U.S. carriers. Negotiators were concerned that by funneling traffic from Italy and other European points through Amsterdam, the Dutch might damage the opportunities of U.S. carriers in Europe. Still, in time, much as the Dutch diplomats managed to obtain Orlando service after the earlier flap, they also were given a break under the Cities Program. Officials of several other U.S. cities supported KLM's appeals to the U.S. government, and while the final U.S. order on the Cities Program retained the restrictive language, KLM was allowed to serve under the program, subject to a review of the traffic patterns after one year. KLM won authority to serve Baltimore, Minneapolis, and Detroit. And if a U.S. review ever occurred, no one knows about it. The Netherlands and the United States were on the road to Open Skies.

## THE ANTITRUST IMMUNITY CLINCHED THE DEAL
### *Washington, D.C.:* September 1992

The final U.S.–Netherlands agreement on Open Skies, signed on September 4, 1992, was the first of its kind. It will remain unique unless and until another nation accepts the Open Skies concept as unreservedly as the Dutch.

Exemption from the antitrust laws seemed out of reach earlier that summer. The Dutch negotiators had pressed for Open Skies including rights of cabotage, which, if granted, would allow foreign airlines to operate within the borders of the United States. The Dutch sought rights similar to those granted to Britain in the 1991 amendment to the Bermuda agreement, which allowed the airlines to share airline codes used in computer reservations systems. This sharing allows airline personnel to write tickets for passengers from the point of pickup to destination, even though there may be a transfer of aircraft and even air carriers. Though at first glance such rights appear promising, they never have been exercised by British Airways. The United Kingdom has been unable to obtain from the U.S. landing rights in third countries, thus thwarting their full use of these extensive rights. The Dutch gave up on pursuing rights of cabotage (the right of KLM to operate in the U.S. domestic market), given the impossibility of obtaining congressional approval for such a controversial change in the law on short notice.

Elliott M. Seiden, the Washington representative of Northwest Airlines, remembers everything about the summer of 1992. U.S. and

Dutch negotiators were eager to begin discussions, but annoying scheduling conflicts kept deferring formal bilateral talks. Northwest and KLM were in the third year of their alliance, and problems beyond sheer cultural differences were becoming everyday conflicts. The Dutch carrier was the dominant player, having sealed the relationship with investments of more than $400 million.

Managers of each airline had been searching for ways to make the alliance workable. The phrase "seamless travel experience" had crept into airline lingo at that time. Northwest and KLM officials were looking for this experience for their passengers. They wanted to be one airline, but there was no certitude on how this could be accomplished.

The delays in scheduling the negotiations gave Seiden and his Northwest colleagues time to review the workings of the alliance and to explore a strategy to obtain an Open Skies agreement. Joint services had been operating for a year under the Cities Program. Flying KLM 747s, KLM and Northwest had inaugurated flights from Minneapolis and Detroit to Amsterdam. Under the arrangement, Northwest had signed contracts with KLM to fill half the seats in the 747s, with KLM responsible for the other half. Under the Sherman Antitrust Act, officials of the airlines were prohibited from discussing anything related to fares even though they were selling, separately, seats on the same airplane. The restriction, though unnatural, was required under the law. Seiden says that problems cropped up "from day one." Sales officials became rivals rather than coworkers.

Northwest sales officials inadvertently infuriated KLM's salespeople when Northwest offered triple-frequent-flier miles on the inaugural flights from Minneapolis. KLM officials, who hadn't been informed of the promotion, were put to a sales disadvantage on their own airplane. "We didn't consult because we couldn't, and the promotion eventually went away," Seiden says. "But [the lack of coordination] was always a problem. We were required to compete, and the more successfuly we competed with KLM, the more likely the partnership might fail."

Seiden knew the answer. An antitrust expert, he had worked from 1977 in the U.S. Department of Justice and ended his government career in 1985 as head of the transport section. If Northwest and KLM could win a grant of antitrust immunity, the pricing and scheduling officials could sit at the same table and talk about whatever they wanted to. Seiden believes that his Justice Department experience helped him to frame arguments that government officials could understand.

First, if KLM were an American carrier and met U.S. citizenship requirements, it could merge with Northwest under Justice Department guidelines. It would easily pass the Justice Dept.'s primary test of market power, the Hirschman Herfindahl Index (HHI), which produces values between 0 and 10,000. The combination of KLM and Northwest would produce a value of less than 1000, too small to be considered even for a critical review. Thus, only the citizenship issue debarred the merger alternative for Northwest and KLM.

Second, Seiden argued that although the U.S. Supreme Court had found on June 19, 1984, in the Copperweld Corporation case, that a parent company and a subsidiary were not conspiring to set prices, decided the decision hadn't applied to minority interests, such as those which KLM held in Northwest. Thus the law did not prohibit the airlines from merging, yet it would not protect the new bigger company from antitrust prosecution.

Seiden's final point won favor with staff at the Transportation Department. He said, grant the antitrust immunity, and the Dutch will sign the first Open Skies agreement with the United States. The chief U.S. negotiator, Jeffrey Shane, had predicted in the June 29, 1992, issue of *Aviation Week & Space Technology* that the Netherlands would break precedent and sign an Open Skies agreement in coming weeks. Representatives of the two nations put signatures on the documents on September 4, 1992.

U.S. and British diplomats now claim to seek an agreement similar to the U.S.–Dutch accord, but, in spite of the encouraging words, an Open Skies agreement has eluded them.

## BRITISH PERSPICACITY PROTECTS LONDON

Unlike the Britain that endorsed freedom of the seas nearly four centuries ago, twentieth-century Britain, for reasons of security, adopted restrictions on freedoms of the air. Even before World War I, British leadership foresaw a powerful role for military aviation in warfare. Never lacking in insight when it comes to its relations with other countries, Britain advocated the concept of national sovereignty for aviation, which would effectively create aerial borders around all nations. National sovereignty in the air has indeed predominated throughout this century, and the airlines of most nations have been publicly endowed as instruments of the national purpose. To this day, most airlines outside of the United States are owned, wholly or in part, by the governments of the nations that they serve.

In the years following World War II, Britain adopted civil aviation policies that had as a primary goal the strong support of British interests abroad. The policy seems to be an outgrowth of Britain's mercantile history, with its home industries supplying finished goods to its vast colonial empire in exchange for raw materials. Weakened by the war as the United States had been strengthened, British leaders were intimidated by the prodigious resources of their American allies in transport aircraft and trained personnel. U.K. officials feared the spread of U.S. aviation interests over the U.S.-financed network of military bases in the territories of the British Commonwealth.

When the Americans pushed their free-trade ideas at the Chicago Convention, advocating a wide-scale multilateral system of agreements, only the Netherlands, Sweden, and a handful of other nations supported them. Britain gained the allegiance of other nations that shared its concern over U.S. aerial dominance. The bilateral system of nation-to-nation agreements became the rule. The system was sealed with a protectionist guarantee when the nations adopted for bilateral agreements a guiding philosophy termed a *balance of benefits.* Consequently, airlines and nations, regardless of size, power, or significance, became saddled with a system designed for an equal exchange of trade rights between unequal partners. Accordingly, bilaterals have exchanged rights to serve, but also have traded restrictions on those services. Seldom has the bilateral system been the means to meet the actual demand of markets, or even to prepare for market growth. When the United States and United Kingdom convened to negotiate a bilateral agreement at the Atlantic island of Bermuda in the postwar years, the negotiators mutually permitted market access and restricted airline capacity in each other's markets. This gave birth in 1946 to the first "Bermuda" agreement.

### In Aviation Dealings with the British, No Bunker Hill

In the ensuing years, British civil servants, the consummate artists of bilateral negotiations, have held their counterparts from other nations at bay, particularly those from the United States. Access to London's Heathrow Airport has been open to many airlines of many nations, but it remains under tight British control. The key market in Britain, London, is the steppingstone to Europe and, conversely, serves as the major link between the United Kingdom and the United States, where it represents one-third of the entire transatlantic market. London is one of the top five hubs of world travel, across air lanes of the old empire to the ends of the globe.

British Airways, a private company for more than a decade now, is still treated by Her Majesty's Government as the national flag carrier. It owns 38 percent of the slots at the preferred London Heathrow airport, and the airline's representatives sit alongside British negotiators during official sessions with other governments—a priviledge not accorded to U.S. airline representatives by the State Department. The importance of British Airways to domestic aviation was underscored in a 1983 paper issued by the British Civil Aviation Authority (CAA). It stated:

In the United States, the typical method for dealing with a dominant enterprise under the antitrust laws is to break it up into smaller units. In the United Kingdom, this solution has to be weighed against the many advantages to the U.K. in having a large, strong, and highly competitive major flag carrier. British Airways has the muscle to take on the most able and aggressive of the world's largest airlines, some of which have even greater access to highly profitable markets than does British Airways. There is also something to be said for doing nothing to weaken a national airline that has the strength to weather the worst extremes of the economic cycle. British Airways' Heathrow hub draws much valuable interline traffic into the U.K., and on to British airlines' services worldwide. Any attempt to reduce British Airways' dominance or significantly to reduce its operation at Heathrow would be bound to affect its ability to retain such traffic in competition with efficient continental inter-line hubs such as Amsterdam, Paris, and Frankfurt. British Airways' Heathrow system enables it to counter the great advantages of U.S. competitors, which amass passengers through their domestic networks.

Access to London will be the chief issue in any negotiation. British negotiators brought their U.S. counterparts to their knees early in 1991, over the proposed replacement at Heathrow of the ailing Trans World Airlines and Pan American World Airways by American and United Airlines. American was buying Trans World's route authority, and United was acquiring Pan Am's slots and facilities. A hitch developed when a keen-eyed Whitehall diplomat spotted a legalism in a 1980 amendment to the U.S.–U.K. bilateral agreement. It assigned rights of service to Pan American and Trans World or their "corporate successors."

Knowing that the U.S. negotiators were being pressured by United and American to secure the two carriers as replacements, the British argued that United and American could not be construed as legal corporate successors if Pan American and Trans World continued to exist. The British used this leverage to gain unprecedented access to the U.S. market and beyond for British Airways and Richard Branson's Virgin Atlantic. Most of the rights were unspecified, but the United States did grant the unprecedented right for a British carrier to link in a special way with a U.S. carrier to tap directly into the domestic U.S. market. British Airways has direct access, in cooperation with its investment partner USAir. The two carriers share computer reservations system (CRS) codes that allow travel agents to sell tickets from USAir markets, via USAir and British Airways, to potentially thousands of cities around the world.

"We think code-sharing is truly deceptive," Robert L. Crandall, American's outspoken Chairman, said in 1994.

After all, labeling something incorrectly wouldn't be acceptable in most other businesses. Deceptive or not, however, the thing that really makes us cross is that the arrangement allows B.A. to sell lots of products—that is, lots of markets—in which we are not allowed to compete. While not offering Syracuse to Nairobi may not seem an overwhelming disadvantage, there are more than 20,000 such combinations served by B.A.–USAir from which American is excluded.

Malcolm Rifkind served as Britain's transport secretary in Prime Minister's John Major's government during this period. At a London press conference after the bilateral was amended, Rifkind observed that Britain had achieved "an unprecedented wide range of new opportunities to compete in U.S. markets." When asked the benefits for the United States, other than replacement rights for United and American, Rifkind responded, "That is it." The journal *Aviation Week* suggested in an editorial that the United States should consider hiring the British negotiating team.

## THE NEVER-ENDING TALE OF U.S.–U.K. OPEN SKIES
### *Washington, D.C.:* March 1994

The winter storms of 1993–1994 that racked the eastern half of this nation will be remembered for generations. Winds swept down from the Arctic in successive, massive waves. Temperatures plunged to $-30°$ F and snow piled up to record depths, closing airports and interstate highways from New England to Kentucky. The nation's capital was locked in an icy shroud for weeks.

But the winter will be remembered in Washington aviation circles for other reasons. It was a period of intense negotiations between the United States and the United Kingdom over amendment of the Bermuda bilateral agreement. Each U.S. airline had an agenda regarding amendments. Most U.S. airlines wanted improved access to London's Heathrow airport; USAir, now British Airways' partner, wanted an expansion of markets for code-sharing. The U.S. wanted Open Skies, to duplicate with the British our success with the Dutch.

U.S. policy was in new hands in 1993. The presidency of William Jefferson Clinton had begun that January. One of his first appointments was the former Denver mayor and political architect of the

Denver International Airport, Federico Fabian Pena, as Secretary of Transportation. In one of his first acts, Pena approved the British Airways minority investment in USAir. He authorized an order approving code-sharing by B.A. and USAir to 34 U.S. destinations, but he held out expansion of investment and code-sharing as a carrot to induce a more liberal agreement with the British. Then, all through 1993, U.S. negotiators talked tough. As the months passed and little progress was reported, the tone of the negotiations grew more somber. Airline officials and consultants who were close to the talks began to hear that U.S. negotiators were issuing threats; specifically: If the United States and the United Kingdom could not agree on an Open Skies agreement, Britain would risk the abrogation of the aviation agreement. Further, the British could expect the U.S. government to be negative on expansion of code-sharing points and on approving any additional investment by B.A. in USAir.

Long-time international consultants believe that Pena made a mistake when he placed an artificial time limit of one year on the achieving of Open Skies. No one could have known, however, how poorly the Clinton Administration would guide the transfer of power in the nation's capital. Public flaps over appointments in the Justice, Defense, and Transportation Departments, and to membership on the National Transportation Safety Board, were the rule for months after the Administration took office.

Pena lacked a full complement of high-level support staff well into 1994. He further aggravated policy development, and caused morale problems for the department's career staff, by rejecting their ideas. A final showdown came about in January 1994, when the year's limit for a new U.S.–U.K. agreement fell due. Pena gained time by extending the status quo through March, but he infuriated many airline executives by granting a year's extension of the old agreement to March 1995. British Airways eased the pressures in any case, by withdrawing plans to increase the level of investment in the ailing USAir, alleviating concerns in Congress over an issue of crucial interest to Capitol Hill: the level of foreign ownership of a U.S. carrier.

The lack of decisive action by Pena has cast gloom over the future of U.S. airlines and their services to Britain. United and American have a foothold at Heathrow, and don't anticipate much change. Delta Air Lines cleverly arranged a code-sharing agreement with Britain's Virgin Atlantic in 1994 to improve each carrier's competitive presence in the major markets. The U.S. Transportation Department waited nearly a year before approving the Delta–Virgin agreement, putting a damper on the airlines' plans. Approval came in late January 1995, giving the two carriers time to implement a program for the summer schedule.

## THE BOTTLENECK IN THE ISLAND EMPIRE
### *Airborne, bound for Tokyo/Osaka:* November 1993

The Northwest Boeing 747-400 takes to the sky over Detroit's Metro Wayne County Airport and heads north and westward, carrying a full load of passengers and cargo to Tokyo. The aircraft follows the Great Circle route flown in a 1931 survey flight for Pan American World Airways by the Lone Eagle, Charles Lindbergh, and his wife Anne Morrow Lindbergh. Trained as a wireless operator for the flight, Mrs. Lindbergh has described the daring exploit in her book *North to the Orient.* The Lindberghs flew the Great Circle in a Lockheed Sirius, a single-engined, low-wing monoplane, across the northern reaches to the Far East. In 1994 this Boeing 747 flight to Japan, the gateway, is routine. It is one of 600 flights each week by four scheduled U.S. carriers and Japan Airlines. All flights in the 1994 market carried an average of 12,000 passengers each day between the United States and Japan.

Many flights heading westward depart at a time of day that allows for a long period of light. If the flight originates on the East Coast of America, a passenger can depend on spectacular views of forests and mountains, glaciers and tundra over Canada and Alaska. More than halfway there, heading on the downward stretch to Japan, the aircraft will catch up with the night. The North Pacific down below looks cold and forbidding.

· The aircraft follows Air Route 20, passing the Siberian Kamchatka Peninsula to the west. In the quiet of the cockpit in the early morning hours, crews can remember one of the most callous acts of modern times. Korean Air's Flight 007, a Boeing 747 carrying 269 passengers and crew, had strayed into Soviet airspace due to a navigation error early on September 1, 1983. A Soviet Sukhoi Su-15 Flagon interceptor stalked the commercial transport as it flew southward, its strobe lights blinking. The pilot, under orders from air-defense authorities on the ground, fired two missiles that disabled the aircraft. It crashed in the ocean, with all 269 aboard lost.

Thoughts of war are remote in Japan, the economic marvel of the post-World War II era and the most protectionist nation among the great powers. As the Boeing 747 approaches Japan, day is breaking, revealing the geometric shapes of shoreline reclaimed from the ocean. This aircraft is destined for Narita airport north of Tokyo, the principal entry to Japan for Tokyo-bound international passengers. It is unique among the world's great airports because it is served by only one runway.

Narita has been a battleground for well over a decade between Japanese authorities and the local farmers, who have allied themselves with radical opponents of airport expansion. The consequences of this fight are visible from the air. White concrete pavements dominate the aerial view of Narita, as they do anywhere. The difference is to be seen in the midst of the idle, unfinished, and unusable second runway and in a tiny rectangle in the mass of nearby concrete. In that small rectangular space of approximately an acre, there is a working farm. The farmer-owner would not give up the space and has successfully defended his position in the courts. Narita has grown up around it.

Anti-expansion demonstrations have been violent on occasion. Armor-clad police carrying batons and shields have clashed with the farmers and younger radicals. Security at Narita is among the most visibly stringent in the world. In periods of high threat, it isn't unusual for a passenger to undergo two electronic searches before entering the main terminal. The perimeter of the airport has the look of a medieval city. A wall secures the airport, and an electric fence/barricade keeps intruders out.

Narita's efficiency has been curtailed drastically by the unresolved issues between the authorities and the farmer/radical element. Japan's Ministry of Transport regularly allocates funds for Narita expansion, a plan always foiled by the political opposition. Passengers facilities have expanded to a point where Narita can be styled as "accommo-dating," but it remains very busy, with hordes of travelers.

The Narita experience in land-scarce Japan has given impetus to the adapting of land-reclamation projects for airport use. The major beneficiaries have been two airports: Tokyo's downtown facility, Haneda, and the new Kansai airport in Osaka Bay. Haneda runways now occupy land reclaimed from Tokyo Bay. Kansai is a new man-made island created in Osaka bay to the south, where it will eventu-ally serve as a 24-hour airport.

Kansai opened its terminal and one runway to operations in 1994. Conceived in the heyday of Japan's economic rise, the project was estimated to cost 1 trillion yen, approximately $7.7 billion. It was begun in January 1987 and hailed as a solution to Japan's severe noise and environmental problems. Additional construction was required to reinforce the island's foundation. Heavy interest charges—200 million yen a day—sent project prices soaring. In 1994, estimates rose to $14 billion, rivaling the projected cost of the new airport in the Hong Kong region.

Japan has permitted entry of foreign airlines to Kansai, increasing its status as gateway to the East. Permitting aircraft to fly to other Asian points would assure the airlines of profitability, but few rights to serve beyond Kansai have been granted. Kansai was a welcome technological development, but its high landing costs are a burden to any airline. A Boeing 747 landing at Kansai in 1994 may be charged fees up to $10,000, and the burden falls hardest on Japan's own carriers.

Japan Airlines, the principal flag carrier, was privatized in the late 1980s before the worldwide downturn occurred. In the last three years it has lost more than $800 million. It is a high-cost carrier in a part of the world known for low costs. Passenger traffic for JAL wilted in the downturn, and the carrier faced the additional chore of battling stiff competition from low-cost Far East operators such as Korean Air, Singapore, Cathay Pacific, and Thai. The rising U.S. international carriers have become fierce foes as well. United and Northwest, which own special rights to fly beyond-Japan traffic and cargoes, are competing with Japan in its own market. The shock of heavy and consistent losses was great for Japan Airlines, because (a) it was for the first time as a private operator, and (b) the scale of losses was unprecedented.

Until 1994, Japan Airlines was fighting a losing battle. The tradition of no employee layoffs damaged it financially as traffic volumes declined, costs rose, and low-cost competition increased. The restructuring program that got under way will succeed, if only gradually. In the meantime, the airline lost face when Japanese officials publically criticized the carrier for hiring foreign nationals as flight attendants. The officials sided with Japan Airlines flight attendants, who accused JAL of failing to train the foreign nationals properly in safety matters. The criticism stung deeply at JAL. Officials there were attempting to reduce costs, and followed the growing practice of hiring flight attendants from the nations the airline serves. They were offended by the government's public criticism, especially over a political issue.

Japan's government officials have spoken of a financial bailout for JAL, and there were rumors in 1994 of possible intervention by the government.

Japan Airlines must deal with the reality of a high-value yen. Travelers from all over the Far East regularly buy one-way tickets on Japan Airlines, and once outside the country buy a return ticket in currencies of other nations, including U.S. dollars. This practice has deprived the airlines of true revenue in its own currency denomination. That problem will persist until there is some major reform in currency exchange.

All Nippon Airways suffered as well, in Japan's recession. Its near-monopoly of domestic markets insulated it from the harsh blows sustained by Japan Airlines. ANA reported a fiscal 1993-94 loss of $28 million. Its strengths are apparent in the huge numbers of people it transports every year; in the 1993–1994 fiscal year, the figure was 32.1 million passengers.

## LATIN AMERICA: RARE SIGNS OF AIRLINE UNITY
### *Orlando:* May 1994

Latin American airline executives fill the grand ballroom at the Orlando Hyatt Regency near the international airport, for the second annual International Airline CEO Conference. They discuss their usual concerns: competition with the U.S. carriers; the sometimes intrusive oversight of the U.S.'s FAA; and the new trend toward airline alliances. But there's an obvious new air of confidence about the executives. For the first time in these Latin Americans' lifetimes, a rare unity is being displayed.

Civil aviation in the region to the south of the U.S. border has changed radically, and with uncharacteristic speed, under the influence of U.S. deregulation. In the span of a few years, it has shifted from being a highly regulated industry to a competitive marketplace comprising mostly private airlines. The new industry that is emerging contrasts sharply with the historical image of the region.

The deregulation-spawned international marketing drives of U.S. carriers have caused the Latin carriers to unify. At this May 1994 meeting, sponsored by Aviation Management Services, Miami, the executives of 17 airlines put final touches on the Multi-Carrier Frequent Travel (MCFT) program, known as The Latin Pass. It is their latest marketing tool to counter the inroads of American carriers. The joint program offers an entire region of destinations where passengers can cash in their mileage points, rather than the limited number of destinations that a single carrier can offer. The program has become a symbol of what the Latin carriers can do together, and it has come at a time when U.S. airlines are losing some of their faith in frequent-flier programs.

There is much to talk about, as the more than 100 executives and their representatives review the past and try to anticipate the future. Deregulation has stimulated vast changes. In Mexico, it has provided a seedbed for expansion. The privatized AeroMexico has acquired its long-time rival Mexicana, and 85 percent of AeroPeru. There are other examples of expansion and consolidation. In 1993 alone, 47 new airlines were formed in Latin America. Of 23 carriers fully owned by their governments in 1989, only 7 remain completely in government hands and 3 of the 23 have shut down.

The Taca Group in El Salvador provides a model that Latin Americans find heartening. Taca has been a driving force in Central America. It has equity stakes and management control in Sansa, Lacsa, Nica, and Aviateca, and a management and marketing agreement with Copa of Panama. Taca oversees the operation of 170 flights each week from Central America to the United States. It is viewed by many Latin executives as being a model for the future of aviation in the region.

Latin America is growing in its dependency on aviation. The region generates approximately 28,000 commercial flights a week. This flight-total comprises 25,000 domestic and cross-border operations, and 3000 flights per week to and from North America. U.S. airlines have been profitable in the region, taking advantage of generally high yields. American Airlines has the greatest presence and is the most feared. Its future has been assured by a 47-gate complex at Miami International Airport, which is the key hub for the region.

## FOR THE REST OF THE WORLD, THE PACE OF LIBERALIZATION IS SLOW
### *Montreal:* November 1994

Montreal, in Canada's Province of Quebec, has been the Mecca of commercial aviation for 50 years. The International Civil Aviation Organization (ICAO), the administrative and technical body affiliated with the United Nations and founded in 1944, is headquartered on Sherbrooke Street West. The 27-story, gray-concrete-slab structure stands among a mix of office buildings and an assortment of shops, small cafés, and restaurants.

A large contingent of technocrats occupies the ICAO building. Diplomats from 183 countries meet there in an Assembly Hall, built as a footlike extension off the high-rise base. It is a scaled-down version of the U.N. Assembly Hall in New York, and considerably more austere. Above the head table, the ICAO symbol—wings and a laurel wreath fastened to a globe, above the acronym in English, French, and Russian—suggests the strong presence of state authority. Translation booths hang over the mezzanine of the hall, enclosing the interpreters on a staff of 20 who translate verbal exchanges into English, French, Spanish, Russian, and Arabic, and other languages on request. Delegates slump at desks wearing listening devices that cover the whole ear. Official documents in five languages, translated by another staff of 35, are spread across the desks.

Outside on the streets, businesspeople mingle with the diplomats. Students from nearby McGill University look more European— wearing dark clothes and a determined manner—than the average U.S. college student. They blend into the crowds when classes are out. McGill broadens the aerospace nexus of Montreal, offering studies in aviation and aerospace law. In an office building on Peel Street a block away from Sherbrooke is the headquarters of the airline industry group, the International Air Transport Association (IATA), known in the pre-deregulation years as the cartel that fixed international airline prices. Thus government, business, and academe, each marked by a strong aviation bias, share a square-mile area in downtown Montreal.

Because of its size, the United States over the years has contributed more than any other nation to ICAO, under a formula based on each nation's gross national product. In 1994, the U.S. was assessed $11.95 million. The U.S. delegate to ICAO (in 1994, Carol Carmody, former aid to the Senate aviation subcomittee) serves on the ICAO Council, along with the representatives of 32 other nations. The Council represents the primary aviation nations, and it decides on standards and recommended practices directed toward the safe and efficient operation of aircraft.

The United States has strongly supported ICAO's technical programs, but over the years its representatives have grown uneasy with the organization's concern with economics. This uneasiness stems from the early days of airline deregulation, when the United States began to question its own practice of granting antitrust immunity for pricing discussions among international airlines. Opponents from the many government-owned airlines made use of opportunities at ICAO sessions to bash the United States. These denouncements by the protectionist nations in Montreal were echoed in the anti-U.S. complaints of Third World and Communist nations in the United Nations.

Under President Reagan, the United States threatened to withhold funding from U.N. organizations. It did so for a time, but its continued participation in ICAO was never really in jeopardy, for the it understands the need for an international technical body to oversee world aviation. In 1991, James Buchanan Busey IV, administrator of the U.S. Federal Aviation Administration (FAA), issued the invitation for all nations to freely use for 10 years the U.S.'s global positioning system (GPS)—a constellation of 24 satellites—for air-navigation purposes and to improve search-and-rescue programs. Many nations and carriers now are experimenting with GPS-aided navigation that the International Air Transport Association has estimated may save them as much as $5 billion a year in fuel bills alone—money they could use.

Differences between nations and peoples are readily apparent at ICAO. Of course, delegates and technocrats reflecting diverse cultures are united as aviation enthusiasts, and, officially at least, they generally are respectful and tolerant of one another. The noise of anti-U.S. complaints over the antitrust issue has long since died down. But the latest split surrounds the trend toward Open Skies and all that comes with it: bilateralism vs. multilateralism in national aviation agreements; ownership and control of airlines; cross-border relationships; foreign investment; competition laws; doing-business issues; access and constraints. The first meeting on the issue "Exploring the Future of International Air Transport Regulation," held between April 6 and 10 in 1992, attracted to Montreal 500 delegates from 100 nations and a host of aviation organizations. At a follow-on conference held in the fall of 1994, ICAO representatives reviewed the mandates for change in international aviation agreements.

It has become clear that any changes will come about slowly. Aviation officials agree that bilateral and multilateral agreements could coexist. At the 1992 session, the defense of the bilateral system fell to Susumu Yamaji, chairman of Japan Airlines, and Bernard Attali, chairman of Air France. Each argued that the current bilateral system was a workable arrangement. They feared domination by U.S. airlines if a liberal, multilateral system were adopted. The most piercing criticism came from Aruna Mascarenhas, Deputy Director, Planning and International Relations, for Air-India. She said that while multilateralism "is packaged as pro-consumer and pro-competition, in reality it would create an oligopolistic situation. Besides, it has nothing to offer smaller countries, whose airlines may not withstand the free-for-all."

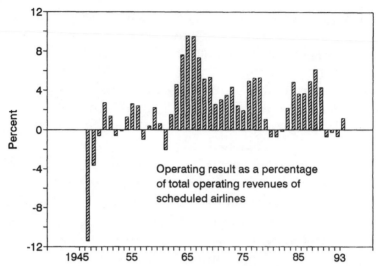

**A Poor Operating Margin.**    The world's scheduled airlines have performed below the average of most other industries in terms of operating margins. The air carriers enjoyed a boom with the introduction of the jet-powered transport in the 1960s and moderate success in several other periods. Their vitality is linked to the state of the economy in regions of the globe. Economic recessions in the first years of the last two decades have been disastrous to earnings. *{From the International Civil Aviation Organization (ICAO)}*

A group of a dozen experts, representing the whole spectrum of views on the regulatory future, has developed working papers outlining options for free-trade agreements. These are being examined as nations decide on one agreement type or another, or even a combination of types. The trend toward liberal agreements may have been given some impetus by the recent adoption of the General Agreement on Trade in Services (GATS), which has penetrated the air-services sector, specifically aircraft repair and maintenance and other areas, including selling and marketing, and computer reservations systems. A dual system of regulation may develop if nations apply existing rules or choose to adopt the GATS system. In any case, in 1999 GATS will review its option of broadening the air-transport-services category.

In the meantime, British reserve seems called for in this slowly developing situation. "History has taught ICAO that multilateralism in the economic regulation of air transport is by no means readily achievable," observes Chris Lyle, the chief of ICAO's Economics and Statistics Branch.

On the Continent, the European Union, formerly the European Community (EC), has been making slow progress. Airline executives are overjoyed by the snail's pace, and the frequent bickering that takes place at Brussels. Rather than an expediter of progress, the Union is perceived as just another layer of government.

But even the slow pace of liberalism is bringing about change. Fares competition for nation members was introduced in 1993. European carriers have duplicated America's post-deregulation experience by flying more people at lower average fares and producing marginal profits. On an annual basis, in 1993, passenger traffic in the Union nations rose 8 percent, average fares declined, and revenues were flat.

Complete deregulation is scheduled to occur in April 1997, when the airlines of any member nation will be permitted to fly to any destination in the Union where they can obtain landing rights, and to set their own fares. Most of Europe will become one economy under a single set of trade rules, in essence the first multinational liberal aviation agreement. For the remainder of the world it might just as well be 1946, in terms of aviation agreements. There are exceptions, but bilateralism remains a way of life.

## IN THE MEANTIME, IT'S A WORLD OF PARTNERSHIPS
### *Washington/Amstelveen:* **May 1991**

What you should expect is that some carriers will have great difficulties surviving. If you see consolidation in Europe as well as on the North Atlantic as an outgrowth of Liberalization, an airline with a market share of less than 10% is not likely to survive.

—L. M. VAN WIJK,
    Managing Director, KLM Royal Dutch Airlines;
    May 1991

Partnerships among airlines have become the means for airlines to gain entry into new markets and to control the level of competition. Partnerships are not new. Air France invested in the airlines of some of its colonies in the immediate post–World War II period, and even penetrated the Iron Curtain in 1978 to form an alliance with Hungary's Malev. Air France and Lufthansa German Airlines lead the world's airlines in establishing and maintaining partnerships. Each carrier operates under 25 separate inter-airline alliances, ranging from joint marketing programs and promotions to catering services and access to frequent-flier programs.

Most partnerships have developed in recent years, partly as a defense mechanism against the growing influence of the megacarriers. These alliances have provided airlines, working togther and connecting passengers on their flights, with a means to broaden market reach and to prepare for a competitive future. Airline partnerships are pursuing common objectives in such areas as purchasing. In 1994, British Airways, Australia's Qantas, and USAir jointly acquired a standardized ticket stock, differentiated only by a cover, and saved for them a total of approximately $500,000.

Areas of the world where partnerships have been scarce are the former Soviet Union and the People's Republic of China. The struggles of these new Russian and Chinese airlines are the subject of Chapter 8.

# EIGHT

# China and Russia

My prescription is straightforward: We need Western government–supported private investment throughout the formerly Communist and Socialist world, to help provide basic services and improve productivity, generate hope, and persuade by example that democratic, market economies work, and work effectively.

—GEORGE DAVID,
   President and Chief Executive Officer,
   United Technologies Corp., in an address to the
   Wings Club; New York City, May 1994

## NEAR THE SINO-RUSSIAN BORDER
### *Shenyang:* December 1993

THE AIRBUS A300 TRANSPORT lands at Shenyang airfield without incident, as night falls across northeastern China. The pilots taxi the aircraft to a parking area, taking care to avoid a pair of young cyclists, bundled up against the arctic winds, as they peddle placidly across the tarmac as if it were a safe sidewalk. Inside the aircraft cabin, passengers gather up their belongings and prepare to disembark. They line up in the aisles, and the few Americans among them are surprised by the cluster of garbage bags jamming the main exit. The bags had been piled there well before the landing. When the mobile stairs are pushed into place and the exit door opened, the garbage is first to go. This unusual kind of efficiency comes first—safety follows.

Passengers crouch down against the cold wind and dash for the terminal. One of the Americans is an aerospace engineer. He is mildly excited about his visit to Shenyang, a city of two million. The proximity to Russia is evidenced by the Russian language overheard in the streets, the menus in Russian, and dishes from that northern neighbor served in the restaurants. Marxist-Leninist thinking took hold in northern China in a way it never did in the south. Even today there is less of an outgoing business sense in the people one deals with, more suspicion of foreigners and a doctrinaire loyalty to the Party.

As the engineer waits for his Chinese contact from a local company, he watches the ground crew prepare the A300 for the night. The temperature is heading toward 0°F. "Cold kits" are standard equipment for airplanes in northerly climes. Designed by the airplane manufacturers, the equipment hooks up easily to the aircraft and drains lavatories and galleys of water that would otherwise freeze in the unheated, parked aircraft.

Clearly, this airline is not equipped with an Airbus cold kit. Several ground crewmen are pushing a large container across the apron. It appears to have been forged at a junk yard. Hoses from it are hooked to the aircraft, and it appears that the water is flowing from the aircraft. The aerospace engineer describes the Chinese cold kit as "a Rube Goldberg," after the cartoon strip that featured complicated machinery. He learned later that not even Airbus knew what the Chinese were deploying that day to perform a necessary maintenance on the aircraft. But it is commonplace to jury-rig a Chinese solution to an aircraft problem. It happens there every day.

Across the border, the situation is different. Western aircraft are being introduced, but most of what is flying commercially today in Russia was produced there under the Soviet regime. The Russians won't jury-rig a solution to a repair problem, as the Chinese will. Their answer will reflect a system of aircraft maintenance that is changing under Western influence. In fact, both nations are undergoing tremendous change in their air-transport sectors.

## ANOTHER KIND OF DEREGULATION
### *Moscow/Beijing:* **1992–1993**

The breakup of the old Soviet Union in the early 1990s, and the introduction of free enterprise over the last decade in Communist-ruled China, have revolutionized air transport across more than a fifth of the world's land mass. The assets of the government-owned airline monopolies—Russia's Aeroflot and China's CAAC—have been radically rearranged. Each nation has taken similar steps in dismantling their air-transport monopolies, but their overall approaches have differed markedly.

The pace of change has been rapid, and filled with upheaval and heightened concern for aviation safety. In the summer of 1994, after several crashes in the Commonwealth of Independent States, as the former Soviet Union is called, the United States prohibited travel by federal employees on Russian airlines unless it was absolutely necessary. The FAA launched an evaluation of Russian safety conditions, and late in 1994 dispatched a team to advise their counterparts in the C.I.S.

The old Aeroflot has split into new airlines, along seams imprinted by the borders of the various Soviet republics, yet there are subsets of other Aeroflot partitions; for example, by aircraft type. Aeroflot still exists as Aeroflot Russian International Airlines (ARIA). The entire organization that shifted from the central directorate of the old international division of the Soviet-run carrier. ARIA has three domestic subsidiaries, based on aircraft type. Golden Star operates the Tupolev Tu-154, Moscow Airways the Ilyushin Il-62s, Russky Vityzaz, the freighter versions of the Ilyshin Il-76 and Tu-154.

Aeroflot formerly consisted of up to 30 distinct directorates. The organizational chart listed hundreds of regional operations across the Soviet Union that embraced airlines, airports, and air-traffic control. All operations were under the authority of the Ministry of Civil Aviation. All aircraft in those days, numbering as many as 8000, bore Aeroflot markings. Among them were transports for civilians and for government officials, and aircraft used in agriculture. The employee roster may have reached the phenomenal figure of 400,000!

Growth in the number of airlines has been astonishing, for a vast nation that functioned under a stilted and repressive Communist regime for more than 70 years. Authorities have certificated some 300 carriers to operate in the C.I.S. A few new start-up airlines are privately owned. Transaero, formed in 1990, has introduced the Boeing 737-300 to domestic flying, and has set a high new standard for cabin service and operational efficiency.

In China, still under Communist rule, the reorganization of air transport has been conducted on similar lines, but the gradual change in orientation from a centralized, controlled system began earlier there. Until 1980, the Civil Aviation Administration of China (CAAC) operated under the supervision of the Air Force of the Chinese People's Liberation Army. By 1986, the CAAC was operating 288 domestic and international routes. Government proclamations related to the seventh five-year plan (1986–1990) laid the groundwork for the gradual swing toward a "socialist free-market system." In time, the monolithic CAAC spun off its CAAC airline into a set of regional airlines, basing each at a primary CAAC airport hub. The number of CAAC inheritors has been restricted. While there is some autonomy at the management level of the new airlines, Beijing controls key operational areas such as fares, routes, and aircraft acquisitions. CAAC has maintained its authority to certificate airlines and aircraft.

Unlike the former Soviet Union, which dramatically transformed its politics first and pursued business restructuring afterward, China has taken the path of gradual liberalization of its business structures first, while maintaining the centralized controls in effect since the Commununist takeover of the mainland in 1949. While China has fallen behind in reforming its state-owned enterprises, small-scale business has flourished. Demand for air travel has soared along with the growth of business, far outpacing infrastructure and aircraft capacity.

Each nation has entered a period of transition from the old ways to the new. Western-built aircraft are preferred for their efficiencies, customer support, and quality construction. Western-influenced practices are being adopted. Concerns for safety have been valid, and are worthy of world attention and personal caution.

In 1993, the Interstate Aviation Committee in the C.I.S., the Russian equivalent of the Federal Aviation Administration, chided the domestic airlines for disregarding flight safety and proper operational procedures in a headlong rush to gain revenues. The report, after investigation of several accidents, criticized airlines on two grounds. IAC found a pattern of airlines failing to divert to alternate airports, even if bad weather or low fuel warranted the diversion. The airlines took the risks, rather than pay the high costs of landing fees and ground services at alternate airports where services must be paid for in cash. Charter operators flying to points outside of the CIS were singled out for harsh criticism. They pushed weather and fuel limits to reach distant airports. Pilots frequently were unfamiliar with the airports. A dozen accidents occurred in charter flights in 1993, killing 132 persons. In 1994 the IAC asked the FAA to act as advisors on the issue of restoring the margin of safety, and the U.S. agency acquiesced. In the same year, the IAC adopted strict policies on airline certification. To show off its new harder line, it rejected 40 applications by individuals and companies to start airlines.

In China, authorities fear a derogation of safety margins, largely stemming from the growth of air transport, which has outstripped its weak capacity for managing flights through air-traffic control. A U.S.–China task force to improve air safety and capacity has been operating in China since mid-1994. The task force comprises the CAAC, the Chinese civil aviation authority, Boeing Commercial Airplane Group, Harris Air Traffic Control Systems Div., and the Washington Consulting Group. A $2 billion market is foreseen for new radar equipment for China. What follows are two stories of Chinese aviation: a tale of air-traffic control as it has been for years, and an unusual incident in the air.

## STORIES ABOUND IN CHINESE AVIATION

Aviators are storytellers by nature. Even the quiet sorts among them will regale an audience with tales of stooges and fools, the bright and the brave, and the curious developments that occur when aircraft carry people through the air. A pair of tales of flying in China has been told by the new China hands. They have an adventurous flavor all of their own.

The first story deals with air-traffic control. ATC in China is antiquated, more like the system in effect in the United States before World War II. Radar does operate, but mostly in the airport terminal areas, and radar information comes via telephone lines. Frequent power outages have rendered the radars unreliable. As a precaution, the Chinese have practiced the dated prewar system of plotting the flights by time and altitude. That is, aircraft are dispatched on a course to a destination and cleared for an altitude. The progress of the flight is followed by the pilot and the dispatcher communicating on high-frequency radio. Its arrival time is estimated. Under this system, aircraft are separated by 10 minutes or 8 miles in terminal arrival and departure sequences. There is little or no positive radar identification of an aircraft in the en-route portion of the flight. If an aircraft strays off course it is in danger of arriving late or, worse, of being shot down by the military.

## The Comrades Down Below

A U.S. businessman boarded a flight in Shanghai for an interior city. The aircraft was the prop-jet Y-7, a 50-passenger commuter transport, the Chinese version of the Antonov An-12. The Chinese and Russian aircraft look very much like the Fokker F-27 and its high-wing derivative the Fokker 50. This Y-7's takeoff was smooth and the aircraft gained altitude—auspicious beginnings for a dangerously wild ride.

The Y-7 proceeded to its destination. The flight was without incident, but as the aircraft approached the destination, thick billowing clouds turned black. The aircraft bounced up and down, and a flight attendant told the passengers, first in Chinese and then in English, that the destination was weathered-in and the aircraft was returning to Shanghai. The pilot had no choice, as no alternate airport was available. His aircraft had been approved for the original destination and was cleared to operate only in that corridor.

Once it had turned around, the Y-7 was buffeted by unstable air all the way back to Shanghai. A major storm front was passing through, and the weather seemed to be getting worse rather than better. Passengers didn't know the exact whereabouts of their aircraft, but after flying for a while they knew it should be close to Shanghai. The flight attendant came back on the public-address system to announce that Shanghai, too, was socked in, and that the aircraft would try once again to reach its original destination!

The U.S. businessman who related this story was the only westerner on-board the Y-7. The flying seemed endless; the aircraft had
been in the air for several hours. Then the flight attendant came
down the aisle distributing paper tags and safety pins to passengers.
She instructed that all should write their names and addresses and
pin the tags to their clothing. She advised them to gather valuables,
their identification cards, passports, and billfolds, and secure them
in the recesses of their clothing. The aircraft, she said, was low on
fuel, and it was uncertain whether the Y-7 would reach its destination.

But why the tags? the businessman asked anxiously. "For the com-
rades on the ground," she said. "For simplified identification."

The storm front was passing as the Y-7 made its second visit to the
destination that afternoon. The pilot found a break in the clouds and
lowered into the gray miasma to make a safe landing on fumes. The
passengers discarded their name tags.

## The Reluctant Cockpit Door

This story was told by a Chinese-speaking Westerner who sat in a
bulkhead seat of a Boeing 737, just behind the front galley. The first
officer of the transport operating at 30,000 ft came out of the cockpit, apparently on his way to the lavatory. After several minutes, he
returned and tugged at the cockpit door. It wouldn't open even after
several tries, and a loud conversation ensued between the first officer
and the captain through the metal door.

The captain gave instructions: Turn the handle to the left, and
push. But the door still wouldn't budge. The captain gave more
muffled advice. Nothing seemed to work. The captain got agitated,
and a shouting match was started within earshot of the passengers.
Suddenly the cockpit door flew open, and the passengers watched as
the captain slammed the door shut. Here's how you do it, he said dis-
gustedly to the first officer, and he began to turn the door handle and
push. The door didn't open. The 737, on autopilot apparently, was
flying at Mach 0.8 with the crew locked outside the cockpit.

The crewmen tried the door and tried again, growing visibly more
upset with each passing second. After a few excited words between
them, the flight attendant pulled the curtain across the aisleway,

shutting off the passengers' view. A terrific banging reverberated through the airplane, and then the clanking, swinging sound of a door opening. Passengers looked at one another with alarm, and the flight attendant came through the curtain to assure everyone that the situation was now under control.

The curtain was reopened, revealing a mutilated door and the backs of the two pilots flying the airplane. The captain had smashed the door handle with the fire ax. The Boeing Co., it is said, some time later received its one and only request for parts for a cockpit door.

## A CHINESE PROBLEM WITH MAINTENANCE MANUALS
### *Chengdu:* 1994

In recent years, Donald H. Lang has spent more than half of each month in China, where his company, the engine manufacturer Pratt & Whitney of Hartford, Connecticut, operates several joint programs. Lang is president of the Chinese division of Pratt & Whitney, a subsidiary of United Technologies Corp., which in 1994 operated 10 joint-stock companies in China. New, late-model versions of Pratt & Whitney JT8D engines are powering the McDonnell Douglas MD-82 aircraft being produced in China under a special license. The aircraft are put together at the Shanghai Aviation Industrial Corp. from airplane kits produced by the Douglas Aircraft Co. More recently, the Shanghai copartner has begun to produce some parts for the aircraft.

After two years, Lang has developed an understanding of working in China. He finds the nation and the people fascinating. He holds to the belief that seeing is believing, and that personal contact is an absolute prerequisite for gaining an understanding of how China works. He also believes that Confucianism, the ethical system based on the teachings of Confucius (551–479 B.C.), has contributed to the restoration of China, and may explain the critical difference between China and Russia in their responses to the post–Cold War era. "Confucianism is the common denominator that keeps society going in a rough period," Lang said. "It's a way of life, and it basically bonds families together and focuses on virtues of work. It keeps the Chinese people structured and focused."

Lang admires the Chinese people and is impressed by their industry. On his first visit to Beijing, he rode into town in an automobile on a 20-kilometer two-lane road, dodging bicycles and horse-drawn carts. He noticed across a barren stretch of land that a new superhighway from the airport was being built. On each return visit, he watched with amazement the progress of the construction. The once-vast, barren land along the road had become a young forest of trees. Tens of thousands of Army troops, armed with shovels, hoes, rakes, and pick-axes, had planted thousands of trees, and in no time at all a young forest was budding under a spring sun.

In his first two years in China, Lang has made an important discovery related to aerospace. The Chinese don't like to use the elaborate manuals that Western companies produce for aircraft overhaul and repair. It took him a while to learn this; he found out through personal contact with mechanics. They weren't accustomed to manuals that provide so much direction. Further, the Chinese were unused to a civil aviation authority, such as the FAA, actually certifying that a repair should be accomplished in a certain way, approved by the part or component manufacturers, as is the case in much of the world.

The experience of the Chinese mechanics was limited to Russian manuals. These are considerably less detailed, perhaps 10 percent the size of western manuals, and they don't specify a fix. For generations, mechanics in China have been left to their own devices to solve problems, which therefore explains the jury-rigged water-drainage system we saw earlier for that A300. Western aerospace officials have found bogus, locally produced washers in some critical components, and they are stressing the critical importance of certificated repairs.

## FLYING THE OLD RED LINE
### *Moscow: 1992*

Arriving at Moscow's Sheremetyevo airport at the time of the breakup of the Soviet Union, visitors are introduced to a new universe, the other side of the looking glass. On one side of the airfield, a large assortment of Soviet-manufactured commercial transports stand idle. The aircraft aren't parked temporarily in anticipation of assignment to gate positions. Rather, their engines capped, they represent a huge parked backlog of airplanes awaiting replacement engines or maintenance—a long and laborious process in Soviet-ruled Russia.

At first glance, the Aeroflot aircraft closely resemble Western transports. A Tupolev Tu-154 nearby could pass for the trijet Boeing 727 in which the traveler had arrived. It has a 1960s-design *t*-shaped tail, and three engines mounted aft. But closer examination reveals subtle structural differences in the Russian aircraft. The Soviet design gives a more rigid look to the aircraft than the Western versions. An even greater contrast lies in the liveries. The Delta Air Lines Boeing 727 on the in-bound flight proclaims DELTA proudly on a white and dark-blue-striped fuselage, and the famous triangle "widget" is painted on the tail. The Russian transports all display scant markings, not much more than a military transport.

A new universe opens up with disembarkation. The Delta transport halts and parks. Mobile stairs are pushed into place, and passengers walk down the steps to the apron and across to the terminal. U.S. diplomats and high-ranking military officers are among the business passengers and the handful of tourists. Once they are inside the terminal, the government visitors receive a hearty welcome from their Russian colleagues. They are joyfully herded together and accommodated through customs, while the other passengers form lines in front of a customs official. A Russian Army colonel bearhugs his American counterpart, a welcome sign of the warming of the Cold War.

Passing through customs takes longer in Russia than it does elsewhere. Refecting perhaps the age-old Russian distrust of foreigners, young and eager customs agents peruse passports carefully, their heads bobbing as they compare passport photographs with the live subjects before them. Once through the gate, visitors face an ordeal of, first, retrieving their luggage and, second, maneuvering with the luggage through crowds as thick as rush-hour traffic on New York's Lexington Avenue IRT subway line. As the visitor groaningly hauls his luggage, he looks around to find a shabby, dark terminal whose lifeless design is alleviated, ironically, only by wall advertisements for Western auto-rental agencies.

Flying to the interior of the C.I.S. entails a new adventure. It begins at Moscow's Domodedovo Airport, which serves Soviet Central Asia. It is dark and forbidding, in much worse condition than the international terminal. In the days of Soviet rule, one saw only Aeroflot-marked aircraft on international and domestic flights. Aeroflot liveries still dominate the apron, but dotted among them are several colorful and freshly painted aircraft of the new Common-wealth of Independent States (C.I.S.) airlines. The terminal is packed with travelers, some sitting, others stretched out on the ground looking as if they have been stranded there for days. The men's room is a buzzing horror straight out of *Lord of the Flies.* Inside the lavatory, men are paying a fee to a female attendant for the privilege of bathing in filthy sinks.

A Russian peasant woman mistakes a blue-suited American for a government official. She asks a question in Russian. The American doesn't understand the language, and shrugs. She tries a second time, fails to get an answer, and goes off muttering. As she leaves, a passerby translates for the American. The woman had wanted to know if she could board the bus parked nearby. When she got no answer, she muttered, "Nothing ever works here, especially the bureaucrats."

The trip to the interior, Siberia, begins with a called gathering of foreigners to the aircraft gate. The foreigners are boarded first, bypassing a large group of bemused Russians. They are instructed to take the seats indicated on boarding cards and warned not to give up their seats under any circumstance. The Russians board the aircraft, and one of them carries a boarding card assigning him to the same seat as one of the visitors. The visitor does not give up his seat, and the Russian native is left to his own devices. Passengers hurl luggage into open, bus-style racks above the passengers' heads, or drop them in the aisle.

Cabin instructions printed in Russian in the Cyrillic alphabet are impossible for most Westerners to decipher. A no-smoking warning was clear to all, but the Russians light cigarettes even as the aircraft is being refueled and the smell of kerosene is filtering through the cabin. They continue to smoke, and are not told to desist.

Compared to those in Western aircraft, passenger seats in the Ilyushin IL86, four-engine, wide-body transport are skeletal and skimpy. If the passenger ahead sits back in the chair, for example, the passenger in the rear can see the spine pressing through the material and could even reach out and touch it with his hand.

Taking off in this Russian version of "the Red Eye" to Siberia comes with its own set of surprises. The roll-out seems endless on the long runways, the lift-off slow, and the engines terrifyingly loud. There is more than the usual sense of relief when the aircraft finally gains altitude. The western traveler thinks to himself, "Thank God for long runways" that aided the takeoff.

The visitor begins to wonder about cabin service in this shift-for-yourself environment. He decides it will be nonexistent on this late-night flight to Siberia, and chooses to nap. Then within minutes, the flight attendants are noisily pushing metal carts down the aisle, offering either fruit juice or champagne—served in wooden bowls! The meal that follows is "Aeroflot hen," the infamous scrawny chicken that has been typical supper fare for years. The visitor really does feel that he is on his way to Siberia. . . .

Cabin attendants on this flight look downright mean, and as tough as dock workers. Their service is performed dutifully, without even the hint of a smile. An *Aviation Week* reporter on another Russian flight overheard a flight attendant snap at a passenger who had not finished a meal as trays were being collected, "Well, are you going to continue eating right through the landing?"

The flight ends at Novosibirsk, an industrial Siberian city of one million inhabitants. As soon as the aircraft is parked, the cockpit door flies open and the crew struggles down the aisle to retrieve their luggage off the racks. Unlike the tradition in the West, where crew personnel gather at the door to bid passengers farewell, here the crew joins in the general exodus from the airplane and in fact always seem to be the first off.

What transpired on this four-hour flight, we are told, was entirely typical of the 1.7 million flights in the C.I.S. each year.

# VNUKOVO, A FRESH START FOR AN
# OLD AIRLINE OPERATION
## *Moscow:* Summer 1994

Vnukovo may be a familiar word to foreign visitors, as the name of one of Moscow's five airports. In the old days, the airport operation and the air-transport group at the Vnukovo Airport served as a single unit under the monolithic Aeroflot organization. It was one of the three largest of Aeroflot's divisions. After the breakup of the Soviet Union, under guidelines from the new Russian government for industry restructuring, the 3000 employees of the Vnukovo air transport group split off from the airport in 1993 and formed Vnukovo Airlines.

The new airline is perhaps typical of a fresh-starting carrier. It began its corporate life in May 1993, with 58 Ilyushin Il-86 and Tupolev Tu-154 transports transferred to it by the government. Half of these aircraft were inoperative for the first summer. This sad state of readiness was reflected at most Russian airlines; Vnukovo officials were honest enough to admit to and discuss the situation.

This lack of readiness has been inherited from the old Soviet system. Aircraft are built and operated under government authority that had small concern for economics and efficiency. Engines that show signs of trouble are removed from the wing and sent to an overhaul center, then possibly scrapped. Engines aren't checked as frequently as they are in the West. Nacelle clamps on many Soviet-built engines are poorly constructed, compared to their western counterparts. There is little need for a well-made clamp when it is not opened for on-wing inspections.

In 1994, Vnukovo's grounded aircraft were in need of repairs and lacked spare parts, mostly spare engines. Since that time, some of the carrier's aircraft have been fixed under unusual agreements. Several engine-overhaul shops that now repair Vnukovo's engines receive a share of profits earned from the operation of those aircraft. In another case, Vnukovo's officials received a loan to make engine repairs and are now providing flight services to the company as repayment for the loan and interest.

When Vnukovo was created, it inherited six billion rubles of debt from the old air-transport group, the equivalent at that time of approximately $12 million. In its first year, the carrier reduced the debt to $200,000, even as traffic declined from pre-breakup levels and prices rose under inflationary pressures. Vnukovo flies to 40 destinations. Its longest flight operates from Moscow to the far-east city of Yuzhny-Sakhalinsk, on Sakhalin Island north of Japan. The fare in 1994 was restricted to 270,000 rubles, the equivalent of $180. Officials of the airline said that only a bare profit was possible under such government restrictions. Profits on domestic flights are limited by government decree to no more than 20 percent per flight.

This new airline, a hybrid in 1994, selling shares of stock and still operating under the government's direction, is gearing itself to carry as many as 1.5 to 2 million passengers on an annual basis. It is looking to expand to international destinations, so as to improve its profit margins with hard currencies. Vnukovo sold shares of stock to its employees in 1994, as part of its privatization. Because of its ties to the government, the carrier was required under a subsidy program to provide flight service to remote cities.

## TRANSAERO SEEMED HEAVEN-SENT AT KIEV
### *On the Moscow–Kiev flight:* Spring 1994

The U.S. executive had business that morning in Kiev, the capital of the Ukraine. He completed it and found himself at the airport well in time for his Transaero flight to Moscow. After checking in, he awaited instructions, and in time he joined a mass of people gathered at a security checkpoint. The police were scrutinizing passports, identity cards, and border passes, and had slowed the flow of passengers to the departure gates. Approximately 200 people jammed into the tight funnel, and some began to push and shove in a near-panic.

Caught between knots of people, the executive felt his ribcage being crushed. He had to fight to keep the other bodies from pressing too hard. The tide of people flowed, as if in intense slow motion, toward a single open door. He grasped his briefcase and held it against his chest. People shouted. In time, one by one the people popped through the open door. After the passport check and a stop at customs, the executive entered a waiting area.

A Transaero employee was there, apologizing to the passengers for the problems at the checkpoint. They were guided onto the new Ilyushin Il-86, recently acquired directly from the Voronezh Aircraft Production factory. The wide-body transport was outfitted with 48 seats in Business Class and 207 in Economy, built to Transaero's specifications with furnishings supplied from the West. The executive was flying Business Class. He sat down, relaxed, and was refreshed by a hot towel. He was served a glass of champagne, and looking out over the apron to other parked aircraft, he found Transaero a relief after the trials of his day.

Transaero is rare among the new start-up airlines, for it is all new and has no connection with the old Aeroflot. Moreoever, most of the employees are new to air transport. It has been profitable since its legal start-up date of October 1990. Fares are slightly below the average rates charged, and they are discounted if purchased in advance—an innovation in Russia. Another distinction is its team of Air France–trained flight attendants, and a growing reputation for cabin service.

## CONTRASTS IN THE EMERGING RUSSIAN AND CHINESE MARKETS

### *Voronezh:* **1994**

It is a Socialist idea that making profits is a vice. I consider the real vice is making losses.

—WINSTON SPENCER CHURCHILL

George David, the president and chief executive officer of the United Technologies Corporation, toured the military-industrial complex in the western Russian city of Voronezh in 1994 to witness for himself the progress of several of the corporation's projects. UTC's Pratt & Whitney powerplant division has joined with the American avionics company, Collins, and the Russian airframe manufacturer, Ilyushin, to produce a westernized version of the Il-96-300 known as the Il-96M. At 600,000 lb gross weight, this aircraft is designed to carry 318 passengers more than 6000 nautical miles, a rival of the Airbus Industrie A340 transport. UTC also is the parent company of the Otis Elevator Company, which has 21 branch offices, one in Voronezh. Some 3500 Soviet-designed and -manufactured Otis elevators are operating in Voronezh. Otis's roots in Russia, David is proud to say, go back to 1893, in the days of Czar Nicholas II.

David visited the Voronezh Aircraft Production factory, where the Tupolev 160 is built. This aircraft is better known by its designation in the lingo of NATO: the Blackjack bomber, the equivalent of the U.S. B-1B. The Il-96 production line has taken over from the Tupolev 160; production is slow by Western standards: about five Il-96-300s a year. David had been to Voronezh and other interior Russian cities before. What he has been has been stunning and memorable.

"This is post-industrial poverty: grinding, broken, dispirited, polluted poverty, poverty of the worst form I have seen in 30 years of extensive travel across the world." David advocates government-supported private investment in Russia and throughout all of the former Communist world to help pull them through the rubble of the breakup. In a talk to the Wings Club in New York in May 1994, David chastised world governments for tying too many strings to the billions in aid funds and for the lopsided concentration of debt investment over equity. From that talk:

From this most recent visit to Voronezh . . . the appalling state of housing in Russia, the appalling housekeeping everywhere, and the same expressionless faces are again what I remember. This is beyond poverty; it is mankind victimized by circumstances, helpless to improve its lot, deprived emotionally to the point of annihilation of hope, the analogue to death by starvation. And this is where the alcoholism comes from, with the bottle ready to hand day and night.

We need to put the spike into the heart of an odious regime, and we will do it by example, by persuasion, by partnering, by investing, by showing these people at all levels of society that Western, democratic, market economy priciples work.

**U.S.-Russian Cooperation.** The latest addition to the line of Ilyushin aircraft is the Il-96M, a wide-body transport powered by U.S. Pratt & Whitney PW2000 engines and equipped with avionics from Collins of Cedar Rapids, Iowa. The advanced U.S.-made systems offer a new level of economics and efficiency for Russian-built aircraft. According to designers, the Il-96M is capable of carrying a full passenger load of 318 passengers in three-class configuration on flights of more than 7000 miles. A freighter version is designed to lift 74 tons of cargo. *(Ilyushin/Pratt & Whitney Photo)*

David compares the state of Russia in the 1990s to that of China less than a decade ago, when fears and caution kept private investment in China scarce. He remembers the debate within the corporation as to whether UTC's Otis should return to China. "The GNP per capita then was about $100, the currency was definitely not convertible, and we clashed often with our local Chinese State partners on management issues. . . ."

Yet from this humble beginning, the change in China has been tremendous. The flow of private capital into China has been at a level of about $15 billion a year. In October 1993, the government of China reported 159,000 foreign joint ventures, involving committed capital of $204 billion. UTC has 10 ventures in China, including very successful Carrier plants in Shanghai where air conditioners are produced.

Pratt & Whitney people have made a strong impression on their Chinese partners. Lang's predecessor was James A. Kennedy, a likeable Irish-American who could pass, with his silver-gray coif and easygoing manner, for a kindly big-city mayor of 40 years ago. Visitors to China find his image on photographs everywhere, hanging on the office walls of Chinese officials.

UTC operates four manufacturing facilities and employs 6000 people, predominantly Chinese nationals. Total 1993 sales were of about $400 million, with profits of $50 million. All ten of UTC's joint ventures have been profitable. Hard currency investments have been paid out on average by about the fourth year. Half of UTC's next 10 joint ventures in China are expected to be in aerospace.

In his talk to the Wings Club, David singled out a shop steward in one of the Shanghai Carrier plants as symbolic of the evolving China. He referred to her as "a charismatic, hard-driving woman, and formerly a ranking member of the local Communist Party organization. She brings just as much zeal now to the cause of capitalism as she once brought to an entirely different idealology. I think hope for her own and her family's future alone did this."

In 1994, David was expecting the same phenomenon to catch on in Russia, where two new plants have been built and a third refurbished, with seven joint ventures done. "What I am waiting for in Russia is the development of hope for the future. This casting-aside of cynicism is the fundamental difference between the Chinese and the Russian economies and systems. And the best single thing we can do for a dispirited people, and the greatest lever to move the Russian monolith, is just that: help them hope."

Practical obstacles stand in the way of investment in Russia that differ from those in China today. In 1994, President Boris Yeltsin called for reforms on taxation, particularly for business, so as to ease a significant burden on the airlines. But some means of control over currency inflation is needed, to ensure investors of adequate return on investment, and disarray in the legal system and the securities market have discouraged capital investment.

American companies have invested in China at a greater rate than in the C.I.S., where a wait-and-see attitude prevails. Chinese companies have been aggressive in applying for listings on foreign stock exchanges, and Chinese airlines are visiting the West in search of foreign investment. Russian companies are close on their heels.

# NINE

# Birds of the Future

For major commercial airlines, the new century will bring development of larger wide-body airplanes, as well as improved supersonic transports and, eventually, hypersonic aircraft.

> —The FAA Strategic Plan, December 1991; written after the development of a National Transportation Policy under Transportation Secretary Samuel K. Skinner

## MARKET FRAGMENTATION SHAPES NEW AIRCRAFT
### *Washington, D.C.:* May 2000

AIRLINE PASSENGERS at the turn of the century will board aircraft that have been sized and shaped under the strong influence of the marketplace. The Boeing 737 and the McDonnell Douglas DC-9—and their many derivatives—no doubt will be a large part of the short-haul fleet, along with the Airbus A319; the MD95, if it is built; Boeing's New Small Aircraft (NSA), and the DASA/Fokker 100 or Fokker 70.

The popularity of the Boeing 737 and DC-9, each products of the 1960s and workhorses of recent decades, provides strong evidence of major trends for future aircraft manufacture: the importance of frequent flights in airline schedules and the tendency toward market fragmentation.

To a very large degree, the designers of the Boeing 737 and the DC-9 anticipated the market that emerged in the post-deregulation era. Their two-engine and two-crewmember efficiency won the favor of economy-minded airline executives. The 737 and the DC-9 could stand the punishing schedule of high-frequency flights that airlines offered in the hub-and-spoke networks developed in the 1980s. Airline marketing chiefs blitzed key markets with frequent flights, knowing that the availability of a flight was nearly as important as price in marketing a service.

Further, the 737 and DC-9 proved adaptable to changing needs. Each model has produced many derivatives—so many that, in 1994, the 737 and the DC-9 and their derivatives, numbered more than 4000 aircraft, representing more than 40 percent of the total world jet fleet in the West.

More recent derivatives of the DC-9 and the Boeing 737 have added range and capacity, granting the airlines new flexibility in assigning aircraft for middle- and even long-haul flights. Shuttle-like operations—hourly flights between large metropolitan areas—have become commonplace. More recent derivatives can fly nearly coast-to-coast in the United States.

Manufacturers have taken heed of these airline trends and applied new thinking to long-range transports in international markets. The tendency of recent decades has been toward long-range transports powered by two engines that offer fewer seats than the Boeing 747. First, there was the Airbus Industrie A300, followed by the Boeing 767, and the Airbus A310. In the latter part of the 1980s, the 767 and the A310 became the workhorses for the airlines flying from the heartland of the United States to European cities. These U.S. flights from airline hubs in the United States demonstrated the fragmentation of traditional markets between U.S. cities such as New York, Boston, Miami, Philadelphia, and Washington and the capital cities of Europe. In the space of a few years in the latter part of the 1980s, Atlanta, Chicago, Cincinnati, Detroit, Houston, Pittsburgh, Dallas, St. Louis, Denver, Los Angeles, Minneapolis/St. Paul, Orlando, San Francisco, Portland, and Seattle became truly international airports as the U.S.–Europe market fragmented.

Fifteen years ago, the Boeing 747 wide-body transport flew more than 80 percent of transatlantic flights. Today, they fly less than a quarter of them. In their place are extended-range versions of the 767 and even the narrow-body 757, Airbuses, and MD-11s, the McDonnell Douglas DC-10 derivative. New aircraft on production lines, the Boeing 777, the Airbus A330, and the already flying A340, are made to serve the fragmented markets of the world.

The trend has not ruled out the superjumbo passenger jets, but the market may be limited to certain key routes between large cities across the globe, where populations are large and concentrated, including such areas as Japan, where specially built 747s carrying up to 500 passengers operate today, and, potentially, China.

If the high-volume superjumbo is built, John Sandford, the managing director of the Aerospace Group of Rolls-Royce, believes that there could be no greater greater impetus for the development of a supersonic transport for the near-exclusive use of jet-setters and those elite business fliers who would pay a premium for a fast trip. A new high-speed transport will be developed only when the noise, sonic boom, and engine emission problems have been solved to the satisfaction of government and environmental forces. Studies in these areas are now a decade old in the United States.

## THE ORIENT EXPRESS RESTARTED THE U.S. SST PROGRAM
### *Washington, D.C.:* January 17, 1985

The meeting of the Transportation Research Board drew its usual large crowd of academics and transportation experts. The TRB is a four-day annual meeting in which the latest research on transportation topics may be reviewed in published papers and heard in hundreds of public sessions. Attendance in the thousands in not unusual. The gathering is so large that exhibits and sessions are held in two hotels in the Connecticut Avenue corridor, and attendees are scattered in hotels throughout the city.

In a luncheon speech that day, A. Scott Crossfield, the X-series test pilot and the second man to break the speed of sound, relaunched the United States in the quest for a supersonic transport.

At that time a technical advisor to the House Science and Technology Committee, Crossfield and his cohorts in Washington aerospace circles proposed a Mach 5 transport, capable of carrying 300 to 500 passengers from New York City to the Far East. It would fly so high that "no one would hear it," he told the audience. The United States needed the transport for economic and strategic reasons. He dubbed the proposed aircraft "the Orient Express."

Crossfield's announcement came only a week before the release of a NASA report that outlined a 15-year, billion-dollar research program. President Reagan found the idea intriguing, and mentioned it in his State of the Union address. In short order, the wheels of government began to accelerate with a new aeronautics program. Funds were allocated in the next budget, and aerospace contractors dusted off reports written 15 years earlier. Aerospace contractors welcomed the program, albeit with a few reservations.

The Mach 5 Orient Express sounded magnificent, but it posed some hard challenges. A vehicle of that speed would require a new kind of fuel and therefore a whole new ground infrastructure wherever it flew. New materials would be needed as well, to withstand the heat of more than 1000° F. The powerplants also would be new. In short, the Orient Express represented a huge leap in technology. One airline official asked, "How would you get grandma on that kind of an airplane?" The engineer/economists wondered how the Orient Express could operate as an airline. After a space flight, or a near-space flight, it would land as hot as a comet. They questioned how such a vehicle could be maintained and returned to productive use in the turnaround times an airline would need.

These questions were pithy enough, but on January 28, 1986, the shuttle orbiter Challenger, on launch of Mission 51-L from the Kennedy Space Center, exploded at 47,000 ft, destroying the vehicle and causing the loss of a seven-member crew that included the schoolteacher Christa McAuliffe. The destruction of the shuttle further dampened interest in a space vehicle for commercial passengers. In time, the high-speed program was divided into two. The U.S. Air Force took over the National Aerospace Plane (NASP), the Mach 5–plus program, and NASA and aerospace contractors began their study of a commercial aircraft to fly between Mach 2 and 5.

## THE RESEARCH IN SUPERSONICS NEVER STOPPED
### *Hampton, Virginia:* Fall 1988

A program hardly ever dies in Washington. Researchers, aerospace engineers, and program managers gathered in mid-October to report on the third and final phase of the High-Speed Civil Transport (HSCT) studies that were part of the research program undertaken in 1985. The delegates baked under the southern Virginia sun, which glared off the massive, white-painted wind-tunnel structures and tubular shapes that dot the NASA Langley Research Center.

This is an aerospace center. When a flight of Navy interceptors roars off from the nearby airbase, the strollers at Langley barely notice the noise. The roars to them are a reasonable annoyance, as oven heat is to a baker.

At this NASA meeting and two earlier sessions at Langley, Michael Henderson, head of Boeing's high-speed program, and Donald Graf, his equivalent at Douglas, served as majordomos. They excited the 150 or more representatives of the U.S. aerospace manufacturers with the prospect of an all-new, incredibly fast transport. Over the last two years of study, they had moved from the euphoria of a Mach 5 vehicle—more Douglas's idea than Boeing's—and had settled in on a kerosene-fueled transport capable of Mach 2 to Mach 3.2 speeds, flying into conventional airports. In a technical sense, such a transport would be a close follow-on to the British Aerospace/Aerospatiale Concorde. The range of the transport would be trans-Pacific distances. It would operate efficiently and cleanly, a technological leap definitely within the grasp of U.S. industry.

The program managers envisioned a production airplane, meaning at least 500 to 1000 units, that could begin service sometime between the years 2000 and 2010. Engine makers at General Electric and Pratt & Whitney informed the researchers that an all-new engine would be ready within that time frame. One of them passed the word along to the airframers, as they sat having breakfast that October morning at the Hampton Inn. "About 2005," the G.E. man said. Engineer/researchers spoke as casually about this next big bird as if it were a new and safe application for styrofoam. The fast new aircraft was achievable, but all present knew that they faced a

**Future Bird.**    Aerospace manufacturers are independently and jointly reviewing new aircraft and engines for the future. Faster aircraft (Mach 2 to 3) would reduce travel times by half on transPacific long hauls and offer the opportunity for improved productivity. Manufacturers are fairly positive about the economic viability of a new-technology supersonic transport (SST), a successor to the Anglo–French Concorde. Several companies are reviewing a concept for a 250- to 300-passenger aircraft capable of long range. Research at government levels is focused on minimizing sonic booms, airport noise, and engine emissions.

raft of very real challenges. These lay in three areas: sonic boom, airport noise, and upper-atmosphere engine emissions. No one pulled any punches in private or public meetings as to the possible impacts. A researcher commented that NASA would dump the study program immediately, if it became clear that the high-speed vehicle would be a polluter. The agency had learned a mighty lesson from the last go-round in the early 1970s, when public concern for the sonic boom and engine emissions had caused Congress to pull the plug on the U.S. supersonic commercial airplane program.

But the supersonic research never really ended. NASA and the manufacturers gathering at Langley that October day reviewed the technologies identified in NASA's Supersonic Cruise Research (SCR) program, which succeeded the program Congress killed publicly. The low-profile SCR program was funded at a rate of between $8 and $11.7 million a year and lasted until 1981. Its hallmark was the identification in 1975 of the variable-cycle engine as a powerplant for a supersonic transport (SST). The variable-cycle engine will play an important role in sonic-boom reduction. It will provide power for efficient operation of an SST at subsonic speeds in a subsonic cycle on the overland leg of the flight, avoiding the sonic-boom problem over populated areas.

Researchers have reviewed an SST aircraft body similar to the now-retired Lockheed SR-71: the Mach 3 Blackbird, with its flat and rounded nose that replaced the needle nose of earlier supersonic designs. Researchers have looked into ways of reducing the annoying characteristics of the sonic boom, and have tested human responses to various sounding booms in the hope that a more tolerable one can be devised

Engine researchers have worked on eight possible engine types, and anticipate that all of the eight will meet the current noise standards for contemporary transports. Studies in 1994 indicated that emissions of nitrous oxide—a contributor to ozone depletion in the upper atmosphere—could be reduced by eight times over emissions coming from current powerplants. This study was the result of the $500-million, initial-phase stage of NASA's high-speed-transport technology-development program.

The United States is not alone in this venture. The European manufacturers Aerospatiale, British Aerospace, and Deutsche Aerospace have joined in a European Supersonic Research Program. A companion joint engine-study program is under way between Rolls-Royce and Snecma, which developed the Olympus 593 turbofan engine powering the Concorde. Exploratory studies by the Europeans have focused on a Mach 2 transport seating 250 passengers with a range of 5500 nautical miles, expandable to 6500. Rolls-Royce and Snecma are studying a variable-cycle engine, with the cooperation of Motoren-und-Turbinen-Union and Italy's Fiat Avio.

The United States and the Europeans are taking a consortium approach to the study of the new transport. The actual development and design of an aircraft will be the responsibility of individual airframe manufacturers. The high costs involved, which could reach $20 billion or more for such a project, may require that a consortium be extended to the other phases of aircraft development and production. But much of the brainwork definitely has been done, representing a giant step toward the next new aircraft.

## THE FAT BIRDS: THE AIRBUS A3XX VS. BOEING'S VLCT
### *Chicago:* May 1991

Boeing has thrived on a traditional practice of simultaneously setting up two warring aircraft-design gangs. In the 1960s, one group fought for the SST, while the wide-body group won out with the Boeing 747. Toward the end of May 1991, just prior to the biannual Paris Air Show, Stephen M. Wolf, then chairman, president, and chief executive officer of United Airlines, released information on United's latest requests. He had asked Boeing to review the possibility of a 650-passenger transport that United dubbed "the N650."

The new aircraft would be an all-new successor to the Boeing 747, one that Wolf felt was needed to meet passenger traffic demand in United's key markets of London, Tokyo, and Chicago. Wolf was looking to the future with a jaded eye, not on traffic or airlines, but on the ability to obtain landing rights at congested airports. Operating restrictions are growing at the busy airports serving the huge metropolises. Few new airports have been built to accommodate traffic and noise. Environmental issues have been on the rise rather than abating. The big airplane could be an answer for mass transportation needs between the large and busy centers of population.

In 1993, Boeing and its rival in airframe manufacturing, the European Consortium Airbus Industrie, began a rare joint study of the Very Large Commercial Transport (VLCT). Airbus continued to partner in the study program through 1994, but the chance of a design and production alliance appears to be slim, however. Studies also are being conducted independently at Boeing and Airbus.

Airbus calls its project the A3XX. Late in 1993, at its headquarters in Toulouse, Airbus formed an Integrated Team, comprising engineers from each of its consortium companies and Airbus itself, to select an optimum configuration. By mid-1994 the team had selected a double-deck superjumbo, in part because of the lighter weight over a horizontally extended version. A new jumbo aircraft may be in service by 2003, if all goes well at Toulouse.

In Seattle in the Summer of 1994, Boeing had a VLCT team in place that had identified potential routes by meeting with aerospace investment analysts. The cities on the map represented wealth, power, and passenger volume: London, Paris, Frankfurt, New York, Los Angeles, San Francisco, Honolulu, Tokyo, Hong Kong, and

**A Version of the Fat Bird.**   Airbus Industrie, the consortium of European aircraft manufacturers, has selected a double-deck superjumbo billed the A3XX as its candidate for a high-volume passenger transport. The aircraft shown on these pages is a computer-based simulation superimposed on Alpine backdrop. Airbus and Boeing jointly studied a superjumbo in 1993–1994. Later in 1994, Airbus formed a special team that selected the double-deck A3XX as the optimum configuration. If the Pacific Rim markets develop as fast as forecasts indicate, the Fat Bird could have a place serving the cities of Asia. (*Airbus Industrie Photo*)

Singapore. In Japan alone, Boeing found the potential VLCT markets of Fukuoka, Osaka, Tokyo, and Sapporo.

If the Pacific Rim markets grow as rapidly as forecasts indicate, the high-volume jumbo jet may have a secure future and a place to fly. The China market alone could represent as much as 25 percent of the manufacturer's output in the years following the turn of the century. VLCTs will be under consideration, but the high-capacity aircraft poses old problems in new and forceful ways. Noise could be a factor in so large a vehicle. The boarding and deplaning of large numbers of people will require spacious and perhaps new facilities. In spite of the enviable safety record of civil aviation, considerations of the potential for loss of life in an accident could be a deterrent.

## THE USA'S POST-COLD WAR TECHNOLOGY GIFT TO THE WORLD
### *Montreal:* September 1991

Admiral James Buchanan Busey IV, a retired U.S. Navy three-star admiral, stood on the platform in the ICAO Assembly Hall in Montreal and made the world an offer it could hardly refuse. Representing the United States as the administrator of the Federal Aviation Administration, Busey turned over, for the world's free use for a 10-year period, the U.S.'s Global Positioning System (GPS), a network of 24 orbiting satellites to aid aircraft navigation. It was Busey's idea to make the offer, and he worked under a concordance of the Transportation Department and, after much coaxing, the Defense Department.

The offer for the world's free use of the GPS system had had a precedent, five years earlier. Then, at the Reykjavík summit with former Soviet leader Mikhail S. Gorbachev, President Ronald W. Reagan offered the GPS system as a means for nations of the world to enhance search-and-rescue efforts. Reagan's offer, a real attempt to contribute to air and sea safety, was not widely accepted. Busey, an appointee of President Bush, found an opportunity to broaden the offer:

We began to push it, because we saw that the air carriers were leaping out ahead of the government from the standpoint of our ability to regulate and control uses of GPS. GPS was a fact. We had research and development funds in it. We were working on developing other navigation systems, the microwave landing system [MLS]. A decision had been delayed on MLS. I had doubts that the U.S. would participate in MLS investment. My feeling was, let's get going on GPS.

Busey, a tall, rangy, and alert sailor who looks almost uncomfortable in civilian clothes, cleared the path for the announcement with then Transportation Secretary Samuel K. Skinner. While the previous administration's top officials at the Defense Department had approved President Reagan's offer, officials at DOD under Dick Cheney expressed reservations. They were concerned that the offer would heighten the pressure for even greater, Swiss-watch accuracy from the GPS system for navigation and precision approaches to landing. Busey convinced them that the accuracy was sufficient, and that research was under way to use the GPS for instrument landings in the worst adverse weather—known as Category 3 landings. DOD later agreed to the offer, and Busey took the opportunity to relay it at the 1991 ICAO conference on air navigation.

The FAA administrator may have been disappointed by the audience's lack of enthusiasm, but, if so, he didn't show it. "I would have to say, my initial take on the reaction was, 'There ain't no free lunch. We don't believe you that there would be no cost.' There was concern in the international community that the U.S. only controlled the system and would make the rest of the world vulnerable, that the Defense Department could turn it off." When the delegate of the Russian republics followed Busey to the platform and offered the free use of their Glonast satellite system for 15 years, the delegates, still skeptical about costs, began to see the offers as merely a technical symbol of the end of the Cold War.

Passengers in the future may not know or even care what kind of system is aiding the navigation of their aircraft, but GPS will be, with little doubt, the major portion of the satellite system in future use. The network of 24 satellites—21 operational units and 3 spares—orbits the Earth along 6 orbital planes. The only cost to users is the price of a GPS receiver, which in 1994 was as low as $350 for a hand-held model. The economics of the satellite system has raised optimism that aerospace will increase its use of satellite navigation and communication systems. Dollars-and-sense thinking will prevail over the objections that have persisted as to U.S. sole proprietorship.

Satellite navigation will be the greatest technology advance for air-traffic control since the invention of radar. Current navigation systems depend on a series of ground stations, situated around the globe. Any aircraft navigating through a particular area must pay charges to use those local facilities. More important to airline savings will be the new capability of air-traffic control to approve routings for aircraft that are more direct than those that are currently possible. The International Air Transport Association (IATA), the industry association, has estimated a savings, primarily from reduced fuel use, of $5 billion annually.

In the twenty-first century, the use of satellites will be commonplace for international aviation. Australia is expected to be among the first nations to adopt a satellite system for navigation and communications. Since 1992, trans-Pacific flights have been benefiting from an FAA-sponsored experiment with GPS on the island of Fiji. Northwest Airlines has pioneered tests of dual receivers, connecting to both U.S. and Russian satellites, in its Boeing 747 aircraft crossing the Pacific.

Aviation poses an additional challenge for GPS navigation, in that precision approaches are necessary for safe landings. It is this aspect of satellite navigation that continues to be studied. Experts believe that blind landings in the thickest of fog, known as Category 3 landings, will be certified in the near future. Airborne receivers are being developed that will function with each of the principal instrument landing systems—a sign of a transitional phase in navigational systems.

### What's Next?

It isn't possible to predict the future, but it is possible to map technological trends.

—ARTHUR C. CLARKE;
   an observation made during a speaking tour
   for the film classic, *2001: A Space Odyssey*

A sequence in Stanley Kubrick's 1968 film classic, *2001: A Space Odyssey*—especially to a viewing audience of that period—portrays a Pan American passenger spacecraft hurtling from Earth toward a space station. Viewers watch the Pan Am ship land, and wonder: Will there be commercial space travel in our lifetime?

The space trip as envisioned by Kubrick would humble all other experiences of the airline passenger, from the first experience in a wide-body or a flight in a supersonic jet. The passengers disembark at the mid-point space station and board a second spacecraft for their journey to the Moon. The process is similar to changing planes today at a hub developed under deregulation over a decade after the movie was made. In an artful portrayal of things to come, Kubrick shows the seated passengers watching shows on screens placed in the rear of seats. A scientist uses a telephone to call home. This is fairly commonplace on aircraft today, though the scientist in *2001* can see his partner in conversation.

Breakthroughs of this magnitude are still far off. Willis Player, the U.S. airline executive and consultant, a former aide to American's pioneer C. R. Smith, has questioned why a "spaceline" doesn't exist and has found Congress to be responsible. "A decade after Orville Wright flew, we had an airline. More than three decades after Yuri Gagarin's flight, we still have no spacelines. Why?"

Player points out that Congress in the 1920s recognized the value of aviation for commercial and military uses. Support for aviation was readily undertaken by government through the years. Funds were provided for airports and navigation, and for research. The government support bolstered the fledgling aviation industry, which attracted private investment. The space story is one of contrasts. Congress showed little foresight, deciding that the civil space-transport system should be the exclusive domain of the government. Private enterprise has played second fiddle. No program exists that is in any way comparable to the research support received by civil aviation in its early years.

As usual, technology is ahead of politics and economics. Some of the visions, movie or real, will not become realities unless they are supported by the appropriate institutions. An SST or a superjumbo is very possible in 15 to 20 years. The real question is, how will a financially strapped industry buy a fleet of those aircraft of tomorrow.

## FINANCING THE BIG BIRDS
*Long Beach, California:* **January 1993**

Traditionally, investors have not made money buying airlines [stock]. They have made money investing in aircraft [Equipment Trust Certificates].

—ROBERT L. CRANDALL,
   chairman, president, and chief executive officer, American
   Airlines, in an offhand comment made at the Wings Club;
   December 15, 1993, New York City

Southern California is getting soaked by rare heavy rains as 1993 gets under way. The downpour puts a social damper on the high-level annual gathering of airline analysts and consultants sponsored by McDonnell Douglas Corporation. The four analysts who follow airline stocks, called *equity analysts,* are joined for the first time by a debt analyst who trades in bonds. There is a naked, down-and-dirty rawness to these meetings. The Wall Streeters voice their opinions on the state of the airline industry and its direction, and they provide candid assessments of winners and losers. Disagreements are routine. After three years of industry losses in a sluggish, strange economy, reading its future has become harder than ever.

As the discussions proceed, one of the equity analysts lambasts the credit-rating agencies for becoming pessimistic about the airlines. He has a good point. The Big Three carriers—American, Delta, and United—own dominant market positions, but they certainly aren't impregnable. In fact, they are more vulnerable than they have been in several years. The short-term futures of these big operators isn't in serious doubt, however; a strong point bolstering his position. Consequently, each of the Big Three has investment-grade credit ratings. The analyst expresses concerns that the agencies will reduce the ratings to noninvestment grade, causing debt markets to punish the big-borrowing majors with higher costs of capital.

It is clear from the tone of the comments that the sustained length of the industry debacle has damaged the confidence of all. Losses are closing in on $10 billion. The Value Pricing bloodbath of 1992 has deepened the losses and raised the spectre of airlines as financial kamikazes. Another factor the rating agencies have ignored is the return from near-death of bankrupt second-tier carriers, and the growth in the marketplace of the low-cost, low-fare airlines. Their presence is restraining the Big Three from forming the oligopoly many had predicted and some had feared. The analysts know that investors are growing concerned over how the rating houses will read the tea leaves after the recent spate of airline losses.

The debt analyst present at the meeting offers the contrary opinion, that credit agencies have been too lenient and slow in their assessment. The huge airline losses beg for changes, he says, to accurately reflect that arid earnings landscape and the harsh impact of increased competition. He admittedly plays the "smartass" by comparing the soft ratings for airlines with those of companies such as Caesar's World, part of the casino industry. Major airlines operate on high cashflows, but even so, the airlines can cover only one to one-and-a-half times their interest expenses. Yet the Big Three airlines are rated in the positive triple B category. By contrast, the casino possesses a cashflow to cover its interest expenses five times over. It has a lesser rating, BB+. The debt analyst is playing devil's advocate.

That very night, Standard & Poor's, places the Big Three airlines on a credit watch, for possible downgrading to non-investment junk-bond levels, a move which jolts the upper echelon of the airline industry. The ratings for the major airlines later are reduced, but, appropriately, not to as low as single B. The new ratings reflect the changed marketplace and the clouded future of the airlines, but they don't fully reflect the three-year drought in earnings.

This kind of dynamic is constant on the debt side of the world of airline finance. Credit ratings are crucially important for the carriers. Ratings should reflect realistic views of the future of individual airlines, because they will relate directly to the cost of borrowing in public markets for future projects.

## The Search for Capital: Where to Go

The airlines, consistently low earners and highly capital-intensive, are always on the lookout for financing. Aircraft-fleet needs keep chief financial officers on the move, looking for capital and creative ways to finance expensive projects, from aircraft to airport facilities. World capital for purchase of new aircraft amounts to about $30 billion a year in what *The Economist* calls a good year.

The days of easy financing for all airlines in the United States are long gone. When the airlines were regulated by the government, prior to 1978, raising capital was comparatively simple. Airlines could borrow from lenders who felt secure about their investments. The investors had a credible faith that the overseeing federal government would bail out a failing carrier, and that their investment would be protected. In those days, lender confidence was bolstered by a second belief: that route franchises had value in and of themselves. The insurance companies were first at the airlines' door in those days, and financing was largely through private placement-secured deals. Today, the process of financing is much more complex. Some of the important methods are presented in Appendix B.

## THE FINANCIAL CRAZE OF THE 1980s
### *New York City:* Late Summer, 1989

The prediction that United Airlines' stock would increase to more than $300 a share, more than double its value that summer of 1989, had divided the investment community. Most thought the prediction outlandish and without foundation. The prediction, by the investment bank of Dillon Reed, New York City, seemed bold, but it was rooted securely in the experience of the then-recent Northwest leveraged buyout. Northwest had been sold to Wings Holdings for about a six-times multiple of its projected annual cashflow. The prediction for the United share value was based on the Northwest buy-out formula, on the theory that the market would react similarly to the United buyout. The multiple in United's case was seven times the cashflow, in deference to United's better-known name, its strong route structure, and its market reach, and because of the increasing feeding frenzy in the market.

In the debt, however, there was a rub. To finance the $6.75 billion purchase, United's debt would have been increased by $4.85 billion to $6.65 billion of total debt. Several months later a cashflow analysis, to preview the probability of United servicing the $6.65 billion debt in a normal economic downturn, indicated that catastrophe was awaiting the carrier. Even in the mildest downturn, not the three-year slump actually experienced, United would have defaulted on servicing its debt had the deal been completed as proposed. Shortly thereafter the junk-bond market crashed and prevented the deal from concluding, thereby saving UAL Inc. from a sure trip to the bankruptcy court.

## The Inside View of LBOs

Leveraged buyouts (LBOs) are returning to a limited degree at other industries but they probably are not suitable for the airline industry, and are not expected to return any time soon. In the LBO craze of the 1980s, the airlines acquired under leveraged buyouts were badly damaged by the economic downturn of the early 1990s. Therefore, it is not expected that airlines will be likely future targets, at least in the foreseeable future under their current capital structures.

Two airlines were acquired by leveraged buyouts, Trans World Airlines in 1987 by the corporate raider Carl Icahn, and Northwest Airlines in 1989 by the Wings Holding Group headed by former hotelmen Alfred A. Checchi and Gary L. Wilson. Trans World resorted to bankruptcy on January 31, 1992, and Northwest escaped it only by gaining large-scale concessions from their unions.

What happened to these airlines? First, a leveraged buyout is defined as a takeover of a company using borrowed funds. More often than not, the assets of the targeted company serve as security for loans taken out by the acquiring firm. A group of investors also may borrow from banks first, offering their own assets as collateral, in order to acquire another firm.

Either way, debt for the acquired company increases significantly. To induce the completion of the deal, the public shareholders receive a premium payment over the current market value of their shares, making the deal advantageous enough to entice them to sell. The new owners direct the cash flow of the acquired company to service debt. In many instances, the new owners convert the acquired company from a public entity to a private one, and derive tax benefits by being able to deduct interest expenses on debt.

The real danger for an LBO'd company lies in the weakened balance sheet and the huge financial obligation taken on to meet debt service requirements. The company loses financial flexibility as a result. It is akin to the same type of drag on spending that the U.S. national deficit creates on the federal government. However, management of an LBOed company may gain some flexibility if the company shifts from public to private. The company's earnings reporting obligations are relaxed to an annual basis in many cases, and there may be less concern for making quarterly gains to satisfy the closely monitoring public stockholder. Both TWA and Northwest turned private for a time.

Increasing a company's debt load isn't all bad, however. It can change the work attitude of its executives, forcing them to cut excess fat in operations. Because of the debt, they will be focused on timely decisions and efficient operations. The pitfalls of an LBO can be as numerous as the advantages, however—perhaps deadly. The new owners may be locked out from access to public markets, limiting financial flexibility and withholding access from the company to new capital.

Many analysts warned that a day of reckoning would come for leveraged buyout companies. The LBO craze spread from one industry to another, and reached the airlines in the late 1980s. Airlines were perceived to be rich in assets. They owned aircraft as well as numerous facilities, real estate, and other assets such as landing slots at the high-density, restricted airports and overseas routes that came about through government designation.

The financiers who structured LBOs believed that many airline assets were hidden from the balance sheet but were valuable as a means to support additional debt. To their way of thinking, if the debt burden became too great, the assets could be sold even in a down market as a last resort. Further, some investors in this period believed that the stock market was giving short shrift to full valuations of airline shares, particularly to the rich cashflows these carriers generated, even as cashflow was thin and inconsistent.

The LBO trend in the United States was quickly terminated by a series of international crises. Passenger traffic fell, under the rising threat of terrorism, while a long economic downturn gripped the country. Coming out of the prosperous period of the 1980s, even the financially sturdy U.S. carriers became over-leveraged as they ordered aircraft in unprecedented numbers and aggressively expanded. In the same period, starting in late 1989, weak airlines grew weaker, watching with dismay as steady losses eviscerated their equity positions. As the economy lagged, even the stronger carriers felt the equity pinch, and losses mounted.

LBO investors miscalculated. They properly perceived the airlines as owning undervalued hidden assets. The problem was that many were illiquid. Their values fell sharply in the economic downturn, which is inevitable in the cyclical airline industry. For example, the value of Northwest's real estate, aircraft, and route system fell drastically in the downturn.

The worst that could have happened did happen. The two major airline LBOs, at TWA and NWA, occurred on the eve of the longest downturn in commercial aviation history and the worst losses in history. Airlines and LBOs did not mix well. The experiences of Trans World and Northwest taught the investment community and capital markets a lesson about the unchanging nature of the cyclicity of the airline business.

As airlines enter the mid-1990s, they are strengthening their balance sheets. The LBO threat is gone. Gradually, they are improving their position to finance new aircraft either through purchases or leases, assuming that a reasonable record of earnings can be established.

# TEN

# Future Trends for the Industry

My crystal ball projects a half-dozen or so large carriers, comple-
mented by another 20 to 30 smaller carriers who either provide a
specialized service to a discrete market or who dominate a small geographical area by feeding to one or more of the major airlines.

—JOSEPH F. SUTTER,
   Executive Vice President (retired), Boeing Commercial
   Airplanes; twenty-third Wings Club General Harris "Sight"
   Lecture; May 21, 1986, New York City

## A DIALOGUE ON THE FUTURE
## OF THE U.S. AIRLINE INDUSTRY

JOURNALISTS ARE ALWAYS on the lookout for a telling comment on developments in the aviation/aerospace field. Wall Street
analysts are among the primary sources of information and opinion.
Airline analysts are specialists who delve deeply into the workings of
carriers, and frequently they can aid the journalist in finding the real
story that may exist behind the official story as released by an airline.
Their comments usually are quotable, and their opinions often reflect
contrary judgments, which offer readers balance and perspective.

   In the following dialogue, aviation writer James Ott queries his
coauthor, analyst Raymond E. Neidl, on the future of the U.S. airline
industry.

People are asking what's wrong with the airline industry. The concerns seem to be as great as at any time since the 1978 deregulation. The airline business is, as former United president Jack Pope said, capital-intensive and costly. Further, the airline business is cyclical, and driven by the state of the economy. How can such an industry survive, much less prosper, without heavy government regulation, or some kind of government support or control?

People asked the same kinds of questions about the railroads before the passage of the Staggers Act that deregulated the rail industry. Today, freight rail is prospering, and easily attracts investment capital to meet its maintenance and growth needs. Under rail deregulation, the industry was liberated. Management was forced to make bold decisions and take actions that never were allowed to it under tight government regulation. The managers have spun off to low-cost, short-line railroads many of the peripheral rail lines that the big railroads couldn't economically operate. They also tackled employee featherbedding work rules that dated back to the turn of the century.

Does this sound familiar? Can the same thing happen to airlines with the right type of management? With deregulation, a fundamental restructuring of the airline industry was begun, and currently we are witnessing even more changes. The questions are these: What form will the industry ultimately take? What is the timing of developments? Are current managements capable of implementing changes?

Railroads had the basic problem of having too many employees, servicing a system that was too large. They solved this problem by getting the work rules changed, which permitted a reduction in the work force, and by either abandoning or spinning off to short-line railroads surplus assets and employees. Airlines, on the other hand, don't suffer so much from surplus employees, though some of that exists, but far more from not getting enough productivity out of existing employees, who generally receive very high salaries.

## Why are credit-rating agency ratings important for airlines?

Credit ratings tend to give an indication to the bond markets of what the cost of money should be for the rated company. In my opinion, a credit-rating opinion is more useful for investment-grade companies (Baa3/BBB+ or above, by Moody's/Standard & Poor's) than for non-investment-grade rated companies. For companies rated in the later category, specific credit analysis is usually much more intense by individual investors, and developments sometimes cause credit ratings to become obsolete fairly rapidly.

Nevertheless, credit ratings are important. When I first came to Wall Street in 1984, I was a rating analyst at Standard & Poor's. AMR was due for a credit review, and with the progress they had been making in returning to profitability at the time, the company believed that their senior unsecured debt should cross that magic barrier and be upgraded from BB+ to investment grade. This was an important event for the company, which sent their full team of high-level management at the time—chairman (Albert Casey), president (Robert Crandall) and CFO (Jack Pope)—to plead their case. We agreed with their argument and raised their ratings, which in turn would lower the cost of borrowing money for American in the public bond markets.

Though companies can borrow when they are non-investment-grade rated, costs tend to be higher. Before the development of the so called "junk-bond market" in the early 1980's, companies that couldn't achieve investment-grade rating didn't even bother to seek a rating on their debt, since the public markets wouldn't accept the company coming to the public market anyway. Most of the non-investment-grade ratings were held by so called "fallen angels," companies that had had investment grade ratings but due to deteriorating business developments had been downgraded. With the development of the junk-bond market, companies that previously had been excluded now had access to this new source of capital, giving them greater financial flexibility, though at a cost.

**If the industry restructuring fails for any reason—whether management incompetence or labor recalcitrance—what's in store for the U.S. airlines?**

If problems can't be solved, then the old must die to make way for the new. It's adapt or perish, in this environment.

The airlines would be in danger of dying a slow and agonizing death. The loss of one of The Big Three airlines would damage the industry, but not cripple it permanently. In that eventuality, a second-tier carrier would grow to take its place. But from a cost viewpoint, an industry comprising unrestructured airlines would be operating on borrowed time.

Some danger signs to watch for, in that case, are a deteriorating level of flight service, highly overpriced fares, continuing labor strife, and an inability of airlines to raise capital. The airlines have a mission: to serve as a vital transportation link in the nation's economy. A troubled airline industry, threatened with collapse, would invite a political solution, and few in America would find the solution desirable.

A successful restructuring could usher the airlines into a new era in which they would earn an adequate rate of return and continue to attract investment. Private investment provides financial flexibility, and a shortage of it would hurt the airline business, possibly forcing the carriers to seek from the government a form of government loan guarantees to meet capital needs. In that event, decisions made on political grounds will begin to replace economic decisions. Reregulation and price controls won't be far behind.

**There is constant talk about the power of The Big Three in the United States: American, Delta, and United airlines. What has been their impact on the industry, and do you see them as still being the dominant players in the future?**

Well, Harding Lawrence, the chairman of Braniff International, saw it that way, when he testified before Congress in 1977. United was to become the General Motors of the industry, American the Ford Motor Co., and Delta the equivalent of Chrysler. Many analysts bought this theory. The Bush Administration appeared to accept the notion that The Big Three carriers would assume a dominant role. The Department of Transportation under President Bush awarded new international routes to The Big Three, who were perceived as being sure survivors. They also were seen as the strongest competitors the United States could muster for international markets.

But to my mind, The Big Three have believed their own press clippings. They went on a buying binge, putting in orders for many new aircraft and flooding the market with capacity. Big Three managers felt they needed to dominate every market, or at least have a strong presence, which was a mistake. The industry suffered for this mistake, but The Big Three are now making adjustments. Each is now on a comeback trail, but each still has a long way to go. My guess is that they are the top candidates for survival—their basic route systems are very strong—but only if they can make the necessary adjustments and reduce costs.

**Airline executives believed in developing critical mass, having that strong presence in many markets. But what's so wrong about having three large carriers dominate the U.S. market?**

Consolidating the industry to only three large carriers would lead to domination by those few and a lack of competition. Prices would rise to meet each of the company's high costs. If this situation did develop, it would destroy the viability of the industry as an unregulated business. The passenger transportation system would shift into the hands of a few management teams, who would exercise all control over pricing and services.

Another downside would be a sharp increase in the power of the airline labor unions, possibly to an unacceptable level. A strike at one carrier could severely cripple the whole transportation system. Unlike the steel or the automobile industries, airlines can't stockpile inventory for a strike. Seats on an airline flight are perishable commodities that spoil if they are unfilled when the airplane takes off. My guess is that an industry consolidated to three big operators would bring on increasing pressure for government intervention, increased price and labor regulations, and possibly even reregulation of the industry.

I have felt all along that the U.S. industry would best be served by a solid, second-tier level of carriers whose financial positions would be strengthened by restructuring their finances and reducing their costs—either through bankruptcy or the threat of it. In this way, the second-tier carriers would become effective competitors of The Big Three, and their lack of size would be made up for through code sharing and marketing agreements with foreign carriers. That is precisely what has happened with Continental and Northwest. I have maintained that five or six full-service airlines could exist in the

United States and provide a competitive system with the airlines serving most sections of the country through a dispersed hub-and-spoke network. Some of these networks, such as United's, will be worldwide. Other airlines will be part of the trend toward globalization through partnerships with other carriers, like that between Northwest and KLM Royal Dutch Airlines.

In the late 1980s, Bob Crandall of American Airlines predicted that an investment banker would invent the equivalent of the junk bond of the 1990s, in other words, a brand-new product to take to the financial markets to enable financing to be done by companies that otherwise would not have been able to raise capital. As a result, there would be many start-up carriers coming into the market. He was a prophet with that very accurate prediction.

### What are the circumstances that led up to start-up airlines and low-cost carriers?

When the hub-and-spoke system evolved, consumers began to complain about the need to change planes at hub airports. To passengers, the transfer at a hub is an extra stop on the way between points A and B. Consumers who reside in the hub cities have the advantage of frequent flights and many destinations, but they complain about one-airline domination, less competition, and higher fares. Clearly, the airlines have over-hubbed their networks.

This sense of dissatisfaction with changing planes has led to the start-up of short-haul niche carriers. Investors have been cautious, since some were burned in the first growth-spurt of start-ups in the eighties. They have to be convinced that new and risky ventures were worth investing in. The consumer demand for the product is clear, and with the free entry of new carriers under deregulation, the market has begun to respond. The new airlines have the advantage of a surplus of good used aircraft, trained crews dislocated from failed airlines, and some favorable lease rates. They fly direct, from point to point, and can charge low fares because of their low-cost structures. It's a hard combination to beat, particularly when the work forces are highly motivated and there is no adversarial relationship between unions and management. Many airline managers estimate that there is a natural market for point-to-point flying of as much as 25 to 30 percent of all domestic RPMs.

Southwest Airlines has been an outstanding success as a low-cost carrier. Why did Southwest move into the East Coast market, which it had studiously avoided in the past? What role do you see the start-ups playing?

Many of the start-up carriers are trying to imitate Southwest by keeping the operation simple and offering low-cost, direct air service. Southwest has demonstrated that an airline can make a profit even in an economic downturn. They offer low prices and, in many cases, high-frequency service in dense markets. This combination is competitive against the full-service carriers, which are hamstrung by complicated fare structures.

Southwest made its move to the East Coast when many of the new carriers showed interest in the markets there. Previously, the region had been avoided. Bad weather conditions and congested airports could play havoc with a flight schedule and ruin the 20-minute turnaround of an airplane that is a central feature of the Southwest operation. Landing fees are higher on the East Coast, work forces tend to be unionized, and the airways are crowded. But the region offers potential to any airline because of the high average income levels, the big population base, and the ability to attract travelers away from ground transportation.

The new carriers aren't an immediate threat to the full-service carriers. They have less than 2 percent of the total seating capacity in the U.S. fleet. Eventually, the survivors among them will prosper and will carry some weight. At the very least, niche carriers may drive major airlines out of short-haul markets, possibly out of some of their smaller hubs. American Airlines, for example, was pushed out of San José by Southwest. Still, few of the newcomers want to take on the big airlines directly. Those that survive will remain niche carriers, stepping in where opportunities or vacuums emerge. In time, the larger airlines may decide that they would rather work with these new carriers than fight them. That's where I see an expansion of inter-airline agreements, or even the turning over of hubs to up-and-coming niche operators.

I expect that the airline business will develop into a multitier system. The majors will serve the international markets and the heavily traveled domestic arteries, using their hubs to transfer passengers. Smaller carriers will develop and have regional niches and provide feed for the broader systems, and there will be carriers serving point-to-point markets.

**Let's talk about the current marketplace. What is behind the drive at every airline to bring down costs?**

Success will be determined by three criteria: low costs, high yields, and high load factors. An airline ticket is a commodity, and though people may complain that airline service isn't what it used to be, most consumers still shop for price and flight convenience. The marketplace has dictated that prices will be lowered; therefore, cost structures have to come in line with the new market realities. Many old line names have disappeared—Pan American, Eastern, and Braniff—and the chief reasons are that the managements couldn't lower their cost structures to meet market demands. If management and labor can't work together to find solutions to their problems, and together sharply lower costs, many more familiar names will disappear from the airline register.

If the industry consolidates again—and it could—I expect that new airlines will spring up to take up the slack. In 1994, airline managements began to take hard looks at their systems, in the context of their particular strengths. Northwest Airlines and America West were among the first to seriously rationalize their systems and restructure them to their strengths. Delta has had an advantage in its quest for a huge cutback of its system and personnel. Since it is largely nonunion, Delta is doing what it has to do and worrying about employee reaction later. The downside to layoffs is the bad effect on morale and possible unionization.

Bankruptcy, the route taken by some airlines, is a very dangerous way to reduce costs. It creates antagonisms with company employees, investors, and creditors. Further, cutting costs unilaterally by management is difficult in a highly unionized industry, even in the bankruptcy process. Lastly, just the term *bankruptcy* tends to scare away customers and the important travel agents, costing the carrier revenues right at the time they can least be afforded.

**What is your long-term projection for an industry trying to cut costs? How are the airlines to maintain good labor rela-**

tionships, if their whole corporate lives are dedicated to cutting costs?

Ultimately, airlines may divest themselves of many high-cost functions and rely on outside contractors for much of the work. Many of the start-up carriers do business that way, and several majors are trying to outsource in a limited way. I see this happening as airlines seriously look at spinning off operations that have no direct customer contact, such as maintenance, food service, and computer operations. If airline executives become convinced that third parties can perform functions as reliably as, and more cheaply than, the airlines can, you will see this trend accelerate.

The economic appeal of contracting out has to do with the removal of huge capital burdens. The biggest of these is aircraft ownership. For years, airlines have been evolving more toward leasing than owning their aircraft. I see that trend continuing. Someday we may see "asset-less" airlines operating in the systems.

Airline executives will want to maintain controls on the functions and services provided by employees who are in contact with customers. These would include their agents for reservations and ticketing; personnel at airline gates; the pilots; and flight attendants. I don't expect any major change in airline policies toward these kinds of employees, at least not in the immediate future. American Airlines is experimenting, however, with a program to contract for personnel services at small airline stations. Two companies bidding for the business are American Airlines affiliates. If contracting-out proves successful, you can depend on it that the idea will spread. Some airlines are using outside contractors to handle the overflow of calls for reservations.

Old-line management may be opposed to contracting out for services, but new managers may be more receptive to the trend, particularly as new blood comes into the industry.

**If airlines were to spin off assets and peripheral services, what effect would this have on how capital markets look at the industry as a vehicle for investment?**

The airline business always will be cyclical. This is a risk for any investor, but especially so for equity (stock) investors. However, capital markets rate the industry as risky for other reasons as well. Let's look at this in terms of an assetless airline.

Airlines are labor- and capital-intensive and most are highly unionized, which restricts management flexibility. A large portion of the operating expenses are dependent on the price of fuel, which can be volatile. Airline managers have tended to come from within the industry, due to the high degree of technical knowledge that is required. Because of this, a certain insularity has set in, which prevents new ideas from being tested and implemented.

If airlines begin to spin off peripheral functions, investors will face less risk. The heavy capital burden will be eliminated for the airline, improving its credit rating and probably its return on capital. Union restrictions will be curtailed, since contract employees will realize that production is needed. The companies doing the contract work will be specialists that can perform the work with economies of scale on their side. New managers from outside the traditional airline sector are likely to be attracted to the contracting sector, or even to running the core airline that remains, thus bringing in fresh ideas.

Under this scenario, the core airline could be devoted to its primary function of transporting people and goods in the most efficient manner. The airlines would have less need for capital, a condition that would enhance their position to attract capital. As the old saying goes, "Bankers always want to lend you money when you don't need it."

In summary, if airlines became less capital-intensive, I see a possibility of new management and fresh ideas entering the field. With a reduced need for large borrowings, airline credit ratings would likely improve, and the potential for improved return on equity (ROE) would increase, generally driving up stock prices and opening the equity markets to a greater degree for the airlines. Incidentally, it might also revitalize a certain sector of Wall Street, analysts who follow this industry, in that it would finally give them something to recommend.

**With the sorry record of airline earnings, how can you as an analyst recommend that professional money managers or the investing public put their money into airline securities?**

There are different instruments worthy of an investment, with various levels of risk and potential return. Some investments have produced very good, others not so good, returns. Investors usually think in terms of stocks, or equity for ownership in a company. With a certain few exceptions, such as a growth company like Southwest Airlines (at least until mid-1994), investing in airline stocks has not provided a good return, unless you traded frequently on temporary strengthening or rumors. Since few dividends are paid and the appreciation of stock price has been minimal, airline stocks probably aren't a good investment for the average investor.

Publicly traded debt, on the other hand, offers the investor more security. In almost all cases there is current income from interest payments, and a fixed time limit on the security. If interest or principal payments aren't met the company will be forced into bankruptcy, which is a good incentive for the company to pay its bills. There are times when companies don't have the cash to meet these obligations, in which case the bond-holder has a higher claim than equity-holders in bankruptcy court, which adds to the values of these debt securities. Industry debt is generally rated in the non-investment-grade sector, sometimes known as "junk," but historically returns have been more than sufficient to cover the risk. In some cases, smart investors have done very well with airline junk bonds. Let me give you an example.

In the winter of 1992, industry analysts expected a recovery in airline profitability after two years of losses. It was a presidential election year, and it was logical to assume several developments: The economy was expected to perk up and consumer confidence was expected to rise, inspiring more travel and returning the airlines to profitability.

I discussed this possibility with an astute Boston-based money manager, Arthur Calavritinos of John Hancock Advisors, who was looking for undervalued situations. Northwest Airlines had completed its leveraged buyout in mid-1989, leaving no public stock available for the investor. However, Northwest had about $200 million of public debentures (nonsecured bonds) trading. Due to the spiral of losses and the uncertainty, the 8⅝ percent bonds were trading in the low eighties ($800 for $1000 face amount), with a relatively short maturity date of August 1, 1996. This would allow the investor a total return, yield to maturity, of about 14.5 percent. Not only would the investor gain a general current return of over 10 percent, there would be capital appreciation as well when the bonds matured in four-and-a-half years. The Boston money manager decided that the Northwest buy was a real investment opportunity, and took an aggressive position.

Unfortunately for that investor, and for President Bush, the economy didn't recover as quickly as had been hoped. More seriously, the infamous Value Pricing fare wars started shortly thereafter. As a result, prices on the bonds began to drop sharply and continued a downward spiral until they bottomed out in the mid-teens (15 cents on the dollar face amount) and then stabilitized in the mid-twenties. The money manager did his homework, and he still believed that Northwest was a good investment. He liked the new management and policy changes, and he saw a hope that management and unions at Northwest would reach an agreement on cutting costs and that the banks would defer debt payments. He felt secure that his investment had additional protection, since his evaluation showed that there would be ample value for investors if Northwest couldn't recover opeationally. There appeared to be ample asset value in overseas route authority and real estate, and in aircraft ownership. He kept buying the securities, and the prices rose into the thirties on speculation of union agreements. He continued to buy as prices rose into the forties and higher.

The money manager's confidence in Northwest was justified. The union and bank agreements were completed in the middle of August 1993. From that time on, Northwest has achieved near-record profitability. The money manager was amply rewarded for his research and patience with over-size profits, as bond prices skyrocketed to near par value.

**That course of action may be fine for risk takers, but is there any other way a more cautious investor can invest in airlines?**

Transportation companies are unique, in that they can offer secured debt backed by equipment, which are known as Equipment Trust

Certificates (ETCs). They also are unique in that they offer extra protection, even beyond having a claim against a hard asset as one would have in a mortgage loan. In many cases, the bond-holders are allowed to repossess the aircraft if there is a default. The investor bears the risk of having to remarket the asset once repossessed, however, and aircraft prices can vary with market demand. Though it may be more difficult to remarket aircraft in a down period, nevertheless having a hard asset limits the downside potential of the prices of the bonds, and of losses for those investing in this type of instrument. It also gives the investor greater leverage in negotiating with the company in case of a default. There tends to be less liquidity in this type of paper, but yields at times in the double digits make this a good instrument for the more conservative, non-trading-oriented investor.

## Are ESOPS a good, long-term answer to the airlines' difficulties? What are the problems associated with them?

The number of companies in which workers own a stake in the company has dramatically risen since the 1970s, to about 10,000 today, with roughly 11 million employees at companies of all sizes taking part in stock ownership plans. In only about a quarter of these, however, do the workers own a majority of the stock.

Employee Stock Ownership Plans (ESOPs) are programs that encourage employees to purchase the stock of their companies. Employees may participate in the management of the company and even take control of the company. This is done in many cases to save a company that might otherwise go out of business, go into reorganization, or just need some cost relief to remain competitive. In return for ownership, employees may offer wage and work-rule concessions.

There are both potential advantages and risks involved in Employee Stock Ownership Programs (ESOPs). They have been used in other industries, particularly in declining businesses in declining industries where a sharp lowering of costs was necessary if the company was expected to survive, much less prosper. In many cases, they occurred in industries that were becoming just technologically obsolete. Though the airline industry isn't declining or technologically obsolete, it was a prime candidate for ESOPs since the structure and composition of the industry was rapidly changing. Robert Reich, former Harvard professor and current Secretary of Labor, has persuaded the Clinton Administration to encourage employee ownership in industries that are undergoing major changes and have to rapidly reduce costs and restructure the way they do business. He feels that productivity will improve with employee ownership and greater participation in the decision-making process. The alternative would be employee discord and the possible demise of both the employee and the company, as has happened in the case of Eastern Air Lines. Though the idea has merit, it nevertheless is largely untested on a wide-scale basis or in the airline business.

The question is whether employees and their union representatives will begin to act more as owners, wanting to put more resources back into the company, or as traditional employees, wanting more compensation now and fighting unpleasant changes that would make the company more productive. Employees tend to think more in the short term, regarding compensation and up-or-down answers to their job problems, whereas ownership entails more strategic long-term thinking and more gray areas that require more than a yes or no. It's hard for employees to adopt to thinking in those terms and does raise an internal conflict as to which way to go, what is best for the employee short-term, or what is best for his/her investment in the company long term. Union negotiators now have to sit down and try to figure out how to guarantee the long-term success of the company and how they can share in its profits. There has to be more "us," less "us versus them."

Long-term, ESOPs probably won't be the ultimate solution to either operational or cost problems. Though they will save airlines in many cases, or enable them to become more competitive over the short to intermediate term, they probably don't represent a long-term solution. Employees may try to interfere in vital management decisions if employee groups feel, that a certain action deemed necessary by management is not in a particular employee group's interest. The key would be to weld employee group interests into company interests, as possible. Over time, and once a temporary danger has passed, employees become disillusioned with it, creating morale problems which could affect service or slow down the management decision-making process. In addition, over a period of time, the ESOP may begin to liquidate, since employees and not employee groups have ownership. As employees retire or leave for other reasons, they take their interest share with them and at some future date will be allowed to sell this interest.

As far as analyzing the company from an investment point of view, ESOPs add to an already difficult job in forecasting earnings and cashflow, and the general feasibility of investing in or loaning money to the company. Simply trying to determine what the earnings will be, or the projected earnings per share, becomes more complicated. Besides all the usual variables that the investor must look at in trying to forecast what the airline will earn and the merit of making an investment in it based on this analysis and forecast, the money manager must now take certain extraordinary things into account, especially the employee ownership percentage, additional stock that will be issued to the employees as part of the ESOP deal, and how new share issuance to employees will affect operating earnings. If shares are issued, this cost must be expensed, and the ironic thing is that the better the stock performs in anticipation of increased operating earnings, the larger hit the company will take on operating earnings due to the fact that the stock being issued to the employees will be that much more expensive. A further complication is that in many cases this figure may have to be adjusted for back quarters, to bring it into balance for fiscal year-end.

Early indications are that modifications are being made in the way a large part of the work force thinks, but the real test will come if the individual company deteriorates, knocking down the value of the employee investment (through lost wages and changes in work rules) in the company. We are only in the early stages of this test. However, one thing has been accomplished. In certain cases, costs have been sharply reduced, giving some individual air carriers a good shot at reversing their deteriorating financial or operational situations. On a net basis, ESOPs are still worthwhile in today's environment, where costs must be lowered. ESOPs do this while maintaining labor peace, and the current Administration seems to be giving great support to this experiment.

You speak of the need for new ideas and new management in the airline business. What can they do that current managers cannot?

Airlines are businesses that must operate in a real economic environment if they are to attract future capital and properly serve the consumer. The major airlines must adapt to the new competitive environment or perish.

Airline competition is growing in a way that the big airlines haven't been able to counter effectively. That is, the pricing level for an airline ticket is based on low costs. Even with all their networks, computer systems, and frequent-flier programs, the big carriers are at a disadvantage against the low-cost operators in the late-twentieth-century marketplace. So we have a labor-intensive industry with high fixed costs and enormous capital needs. Labor costs are the first candidate for reduction.

Further, management has come to the conclusion that airline problems are due to the structure of basic business and represent more than a cyclical downturn. If major restructurings aren't successful, we can expect quick exits from executive suites. New management, from outside the industry, will bring in some fresh ideas and new approaches to old problems.

Some have said that outsiders can't adapt to this industry, but there have been notable examples of turnarounds. Gerald Grinstein, currently the chairman and chief executive officer of Burlington Northern Incorporated, was the chief reason that Western Airlines pulled out of its tailspin in the mid-1980s. Prior to joining Western in 1983 as chairman of the board, he had had no direct airline-management experience. He was successful in bringing about lower costs and in persuading union employees to become more productive. Northwest and America West are examples of carriers managed by executives from outside the industry who have successfully brought business sense to their carriers.

One airline executive told me, "It's hard to shrink yourself to profitability." And this is definitely true when an airline fails to address its key problem of high costs. The rail industry was able to implement major changes vis-à-vis "featherbedding" work rules, and thereby sharply lower costs. The problem in rail was over-manning. The problem with the airlines is more complex. Featherbedding is less of an issue. Salary levels of airline employees are high by comparison with those in other industries, resulting in high costs and low productivity.

**What will the U.S. industry of tomorrow look like? Will it resemble the structure we have today, will it revert to pre-deregulation standards, or will it become something entirely new?**

Based on observations and trends that can be currently detected, something entirely new is evolving in the United States. We are heading for an industry that is segmenting into three or four tiers. There may be some overlap from one tier to another, as some airlines try to fit into more than one market niche.

We have talked about the first two tiers: the large, full-service carriers in the first tier, comprising American, Delta, and United. In the second tier we have the reconstituted carriers, Continental, Northwest, and USAir, each with connections with overseas airlines. A third tier is made up of some regional airlines that have expanded. These would include Southwest Airlines and America West. Finally there will be the niche Southwest clones that have found a place in the short-haul market. Some of the regional/commuter carriers fit into this category as well, such as Comair, based in Cincinnati, and Atlantic Southeast of Atlanta.

**What about the globalization trend? The U.S. airlines have always been a big factor in the international market. How will they perform in the future, and with what impact?**

U.S. airlines will need to be bigger and stronger to compete on a global basis, as foreign carriers begin to emerge from government protection. However, the foreign airlines may still have some form of government backing, either overtly through some kind of ownership or covertly through favoritism.

I expect that there will be fewer, better-financed airlines or part-nering airlines that will meet consumers' needs. I don't believe that cabotage—foreign airlines competing in the U.S. domestic mar-ket—will occur at any time soon. Labor unions would resist cabo-tage because of its effect on local jobs, and they would have the backing of politicians. Further, airlines can share their computer reservations systems (CRS) codes and obtain practically the same result through an inter-airline partnership. Finally, I don't believe foreign carriers will bother with the high capital investment that would be required to begin flying in the U.S. domestic market, even if they had the right to it.

Most foreign airlines are still predominately government-owned, and many are subsidized. This is changing, but these airlines still lack the culture to operate in a disciplined, competitive free market. Most international fares are set by traffic conferences of the International Air Transport Association (IATA) rather than by mar-ket conditions. This may change as deregulation sweeps the rest of the world, although the process has been slow.

### What is your general outlook for international services from the United States?

America is becoming a mature market. There is still growth in the domestic side, but it has been slowing on an annual basis. The inter-national sector holds more promise. Airlines will be forming global systems, and deregulation or liberalization is gaining a foothold in many countries. Much more price competition can be expected when this occurs.

Pan American and Trans World lost their franchises in the 1980s. Foreign carriers began to compete more earnestly with the two U.S. flag carriers at New York's John F. Kennedy International Airport. Other U.S. airlines became tough competitors, offering nonstop flights from heartland hub cities to important European and Asian destinations. Eventually Pan Am and Trans World were superseded by other U.S. carriers in the international market, in part due to sales of route rights.

U.S. majors will be under an obligation to continue to grow internationally. Otherwise they will not be using their hub facilities to full potential. Competition on an international scale will require them to control passenger traffic over a wide area, and have the right mix of aircraft equipment for their route structure. Globalization may be advanced even further when the second-generation supersonic transport (SST) arrives. SST airline partners could join in financing the expensive aircraft, and improve the utilization rates by flying from one end of the globe to the other.

### Can you describe a model future airline?

The assetless airline may be the long-term product of deregulation. Companies are contracting out more and more functions, so airlines should be no exception in this trend.

The contracting of work outside of the airline has been growing quietly and slowly at the U.S. carriers. Executives used to argue that control over certain vital airline functions, such as aircraft maintenance, was necessary, to ensure, for example, the disposition of the fleet. The latest trend in U.S. companies is toward outsourcing work to independent companies, which can perform the work economically and efficiently. At the same time there is a trend toward sharply cutting back on fixed overhead and capital needs. If that trend takes hold at U.S. airlines, as I think it will, the carriers will become more flexible and efficient by concentrating on their primary business, which is moving people.

Control of all the phases of an airline's operations harks back to the period of total regulation of the industry. Bringing all functions in-house was thought to be more efficient and more prudent, and the high costs were passed on to the passenger through fare increases approved by the government. The large carriers control operations ranging from maintenance of owned aircraft to customer sales, reservations, ticketing, in-flight service, pilot training, ground handling, security, and food service. Airlines have even entered related fields such as hotels and car-rental agencies. But ever since Richard Ferris, the former chairman of UAL Inc., then known as Allegis, lost his job trying to integrate these diverse operations, virtually all airlines have scaled back to their basic business. Given the pressure for economical operation, I expect that the emotional commitments to the past will be put aside, and that more outsourcing is to be expected.

**What additional functions can be spun off while still allowing an airline to maintain its marketing identity? And can this be done with labor peace?**

It's highly possible that airlines will evolve into very different types of organizations than the capital-intensive behemoths they are today. But this transformation won't happen overnight. Changes in the industry will occur over this decade, and dramatically impact the industry as much as, if not more than, deregulation did. I expect that the airlines ultimately may divest themselves of maintenance bases, reservations systems, and aircraft ownership. A similar evolution is happening in the hotel industry, where old-line hospitality companies are opting to manage rather than own assets. Under such a scenario, airlines could become assetless entities, contracting out most functions and operating only as service companies that bring a customer into contact with an airline seat. Functions that require direct contact with the customer—passenger-handling at ticket counters, for example—may be more difficult for airlines to divest, since it is through these functions that an airline can differentiate itself from its competitors.

American Airlines broke new ground by hiring contract-ticket and gate agents, not American employees, at small airports. I see this as the beginning of a trend. United Airlines was heading in the direction of becoming an assetless airline before the employee ESOP proposal was accepted. Cost reductions by other means may temporarily shelve the trend to assetless carriers. But internal cost pressures will continue, and hold out the possibility of outsourcing in the future. This kind of future airline would need far fewer employees than it has today, which would give management much greater flexibility in controlling costs.

As for labor peace, the restructuring of the industry is almost bound to bring some additional upheaval. Some employee groups will fight it tooth-and-nail. The railroads used employee buyouts, early retirements, and the like, to attack the featherbedding in that industry.

Airline executives will be walking a tightrope as they try to downsize and work with the unions at the same time, but it can be done.

**The benefits of the airlines' frequent-flier programs were reduced in 1994. What is the long-term prospect for these programs?**

Frequent-flier programs are like the Green Stamps craze of several decades ago. Consumers used to get Green Stamps for purchases. These had to be pasted into booklets, which were redeemable for appliances and other items. Airlines claim that the frequent-flier programs are popular, and one of the more successful of their marketing programs. They have developed frequent-flier programs as a way of building customer loyalty even when service levels are similar.

There is little evidence that these programs have stimulated travel, but there is evidence that fliers may more carefully choose the airline they fly. Now that all the major carriers have competing programs, they tend to cancel one another out, but also act as a weapon against smaller and weaker carriers. This advantage may be beginning to disappear, as the leisure traveler becomes a greater factor and as price becomes a more defining factor.

The ways to earn and redeem miles are growing rapidly, causing airlines to restrict seats and timing of usage and to raise the number of miles needed for free seats, upsetting customers in the process. Mileage benefits can now be earned for automobile rentals, hotel stays, and restaurant visits—even credit-card charges. In some ways, frequent-flier miles are becoming an alternate currency. Airlines try to restrict the sale of miles, but the restriction hasn't been widely enforced, and there are no restrictions on giving them as gifts. Working frequent-flier programs with non-airline companies, as incentives to buy products, is becoming a large source of revenue for the airlines, but it is ballooning the amount of miles that have to be serviced by the carriers.

Frequent-flier programs are popular with the individual who flies and gains the mileage benefits. The question has to be asked, however, "Would this individual have taken the trip if the travel reward wasn't a factor?" And more and more employers are asking the question, "Are the mileage benefits built into the cost of the ticket?"

Companies that pay for the tickets are growing more interested in controlling frequent-flier miles, using them on future business trips, or forsaking the programs altogether in exchange for cheaper fares.

### What will trigger the airlines to abandon so popular a program as frequent-flier miles?

The Green Stamps fad was popular, and it faded away. In the case of frequent-flier programs, the airlines will drop them when the programs grow so massive that the airlines begin to lose control of the product. The programs will come under greater pressure when leisure travel grows as a percentage of travel. Airline officials say that customers who redeem frequent-flier miles don't take seats that otherwise would have been sold. But as consumers have the opportunity to earn miles through non-airline-related purchases, paying customers are bound to be squeezed out. It is these types of pressure that eventually will force the airlines to take a good hard look at doing away with their frequent-flier programs.

### Travel agents sell most of the airline tickets, and the commissions they receive have grown to more than 10 percent of an airline's operating costs. Airlines are anxious to reduce those commission costs, but don't want to antagonize the travel agents. What are the trends here?

Travel agents have become the big sellers of airline tickets, but at a cost. Travel agents earn commissions on each ticket sold that have varied from 8 to 10 percent to as high as 30 percent of the value of the ticket. This stream of income has come under pressure as the discount airlines have gained a larger share of the market.

Automated ticketing machines have been waiting in the wings for several years. Delta has abandoned commission rates and turned to a fee-based system to reward travel agents. I expect this trend to continue.

New ideas spring up from new airlines and new management. ValuJet has been successful with its ticketless travel, and I can't believe that the airlines haven't tried to eliminate all of the paperwork associated with ticketing long ago. After all, airlines were among the first businesses to use computer technology, which was supposed to cut back on paper transactions. The cost of producing tickets and processing them can range between $25 and $30 per ticket. Ticketless operations may pose problems for a full-service airline that permits interlining with other carriers. But I expect those problems to be overcome, and I believe that the airlines could save up to $1 billion a year through ticketless operations.

### What are some of the effects of cost-cutting at the airlines?

As the airlines reduce service in certain parts of the nation, national advertising and promotions will be curtailed. I expect that there will be more concentration on regional and local advertising in those areas where an airline is strongest.

The industry will continue to go through fundamental changes. In the short term, the major carriers will continue to adjust their route structures, reduce unit costs, work to reach agreements with unions on productivity improvements, and search for partnerships—with niche carriers on short-haul routes and with international carriers on connecting traffic overseas. They also will try to better control pricing.

I foresee, over the long term, some major restructurings among the major carriers. The number of hubs will be reduced, some hubs will be downsized, fleets will be reduced, and I expect greater commonality of aircraft as other ways to keep costs down. Airlines will continue to sell assets and outsource for work, to achieve sharp reductions in unit costs. Right-sizing each airline, though painful to management egos, will be necessary. No single carrier will be able to be all things to all consumers in the segmented future marketplace of this industry. The majors are likely to look very different a decade from now.

Cost-cutting may mean the end of in-flight food services on flights of under 500 miles, which means the bulk of the domestic system. The focus for now is on safe, efficient, and low-priced transportation, at least for the short hauls.

### Airlines have gone on cost-cutting binges before. Why will future ones be any different from the others?

Ever since airline deregulation, airline executives have paid lip service to their mission of setting up route networks that make profits. Success in the business has more and more become equated with size and destinations flown to. That picture is changing. Airlines are looking to their own strengths and weaknesses, and abandoning whole areas if they don't fit into their strategic system. The danger here is that as operating costs are reduced, some airlines may be tempted to aggressively grow and rejoin the rush for market share. If that were to happen, the negative cycle would return.

### What will happen to the hub-and-spoke networks that so many people love to hate?

The major airlines have reduced operations at secondary hubs and are strengthening their main hubs. When the majors operated more than 30 around the country, the United States became over-hubbed. Some mini-hubs were too small to ever be economical. Some hubs were too close to one another and didn't work out well. In some cases, hubs were situated in areas that could be served better by point-to-point service. It was more economical for start-ups to over-fly hubs, and therefore hub strength was diluted. The large hubs will remain, but the airlines must bring down the costs related to their operation if they are to be successful.

You may have heard the criticism that the traditional air carriers have a high cost structure because of their hub-and-spoke systems. It's true that hubs build in some inefficiencies. Many aircraft are trying to use the same facilities, the air space, the runways and taxi areas, and the assets of the airline—the personnel and gate facilities—at the same time. This leads to an inefficient use of aircraft as they wait on the ground for connections. Airline officials maintain that hubs generate additional revenues through cross-feeding, and that this more than makes up for marginal increases in costs. There are many mid-sized markets that cannot support frequent nonstop service, which makes hub-connecting service necessary. In my mind, there is sufficient proof that hubs are economical, if they are run properly and at the right size.

The globalization trend has been with us for more than a decade. How do you expect it to pan out over the long term?

There are some who disagree, but I think the trend will accelerate. Airlines from different countries will coordinate their marketing, and make financial investments in each other. The best-case scenario would be the elimination of all barriers that hamper capital flows and route entry, but I don't expect that to happen easily or any time soon. In time, rules on investments will be liberalized. Second-tier airlines in the United States will depend on foreign investment to survive, and I expect that the U.S. government will recognize this. Perhaps even The Big Three will require foreign investment.

The airline alliances will grow, and may include merged identities. If U.S. law is liberalized, some form of control by the investing carrier could emerge. Most likely, investment will not be only one way. The Big Three may be forced to form partnerships of their own to combat this encroachment on their territory. Much depends on how fast and how far foreign governments open their domestic industries to investment, and the pace and breadth of the deregulation and divestiture of their carriers. I also believe that major questions would be raised about a government-owned airline—a subsidized carrier—taking a major position in a U.S. airline.

Second-tier U.S. carriers will rely on foreign investment and alliances with big foreign partners. They will need these connections to compete with The Big Three, and also due to the high cost of capital. Top-tier U.S. airlines will do some international investment to strengthen their own positions.

Where will the upheaval in the industry lead it, and do you have any reservations about it?

The airline industry in the United States is boiling down to a half-dozen full service network carriers. With the survival of the second-tier carriers, along with the rebirth of start-up, low-cost airlines, consumers have been assured that there will be service by a host of airlines meeting their demand for safe, efficient service at relatively low prices. The restructuring is not yet complete, but its form can be discerned. The survivors among the top six will operate both domestic and international systems and major hubs.

Leisure travelers will become more numerous, which will require mass and price-sensitive marketing by the airlines. Business travel will decline as a percentage of total travel, due to the rise of videoconferencing, the layoff of middle managers, and new attitudes toward business travel. Airline travel will become more of a commodity business, in which the high-cost producer will suffer the most.

Some people over the years have called for reregulation of the industry, because of the recent years of turbulence and heavy losses. Reregulation would bring stability to our business, but at a high cost, and I think it would be a mistake. The industry is undergoing structural changes that are challenging management as never before. The industry needs flexibility and innovative thinking, and some of this could come from new approaches by managers who have come from outside the industry. Reregulation would prevent this.

Politicians will want to avoid reregulation. The new Republican congressional majority is more inclined to privatization than to a return to regulation. They don't want another Amtrak on their hands. I expect that other means will be found, such as privatization, or a change in laws governing foreign investment, or investment tax credits. For now, cost-cutting is the answer for the airlines.

## What's happening with European Airline Developments?

There is currently an upheaval going on in Europe, where the industry is being deregulated similar to what happened in the United States in the late 1970s and early 1980s. However, it's being done more caustiously than it was on this side of the Atlantic. What's developing in Europe is an evolution that will steadily lift barriers until January 1, 1997, which is the target date for fully open skies in European markets. Airlines from the 11 European Union countries are now moving into each others markets, that previously were off-limits.

Northern-tier carriers generally continue to make progress in privatization. Most recently, Lufthansa (51 percent state-owned) has taken another major step towards its goal of privatization through a restructuring of the company. Lufthansa is about to join KLM, Swissair, as well as British Air in being less than 50 percent government-owned through a new rights offering. British Air, totally privately owned, has established subsidiaries in France and Germany, and shortly will be flying directly between Rome and Paris. Swissair is outside the European Union, but is entirely privately owned and as a result could be at a disadvantage against other European-based carriers.

Southern-tier European carriers generally continue to produce large losses, resulting in the need for continuing large government subsidies, to the distress of the countires that are privataizing their air carriers. Included in the later category are TAP–Air Portgual, Olympic Air of Greece, Aer Lingus, Air France, Alitalia, and Iberia. These inefficiently-run, government-controlled carriers not only face additional competition along with the European Union from the more efficient foreign carriers, but even within their own borders they are beginning to face the start-up of new private carriers that want to enter their most lucrative routes.

The less-efficient carriers, in particular, have been effective in lobbying the European Union to retain extra barriers against outsiders. There are questions, also, regarding just how serious the European Union is in wanting to foster open competition, even among airlines of the member countries. The bottom line question is, will national governments allow national carriers to scale back to meet economic needs, or even to fold if they can't adapt to competitive pressures?

Airline subsidies worsen airline fortunes in several ways. Subsidies perpetuate overcapacity. In a free market—one without subsidies—the least-efficient carriers would be forced to cut capacity or go out of business. With subsidies, excess capacity remains, precipitating fare wars that make it difficult if not impossible for anyone to make money. Generally, U.S. based carriers, which have made great productivity gains in recent years due to deregulation, are operating much more efficiently than their foreign counterparts, but aren't receiving the appropriate traffic share or achieving profitability on international routes, due to the effects of subsidies on much of their competition in this arena.

## Could a Southwest-type of airline make it in Europe?

As a newly graduated college student, I decided to spend a summer touring Europe by rail before embarking on my work career. I bought a EuroRail Pass and set off to see the old world. I was thrilled at being able to travel the breadth of the Continent by rail, since I come from a longtime rail family. As a child, my father would take me to Albany's Union Station to see the many great trains of the New York Central System stop off after their late-afternoon or early-evening journey up the Hudson River from New York City to begin their overnight sprint to the many giant cities of the Midwest, the great interior of the American continent, which as a young boy seemed to be such distant places.

By 1971, intercity passenger rail service had almost become nonexistent in the United States, with freight railroads having all but given up on it and with a government-supported corporation about to try to salvage the skeletal remains of a once-great system of transporting people. I couldn't believe that it would be any different in Europe.

Upon arrival in Amsterdam's main station, I was amazed at the activity going on, on the dozen or more platforms that warm summer evening. Not only were the great train stations of Europe still in place, but they also were beehives of activity as an incoming train would immediately replace a recently departed one. Every track was constantly full, every platform crowded. This was still the "golden age" of rail transportation. This same situation still exists today in most of Europe.

Passenger trains in Europe, as in this country, lose large amounts of money, made up through government subsidies. The government contributes to capital as well as operating deficiencies in revenues, enabling train fares to remain relatively low. The big difference is that the trains in Europe are still thought of as being the main form of transportation between cities. The system is convenient, efficient, and heavily used. European city centers still remain the hub of all activities: business, shopping, tourism, and general commerce. European cities also tend to be closer together than American cities (outside of the high-population-density Northeast region), which tends to make ground transportation more efficient when compared to air travel. This, along with airport and air-traffic constraints, ultimately will cap any local European air-traffic growth.

**What can the passenger expect to see in the way of changes in airplanes? How will new aircraft affect the economies of air carriers? How will they be paid for?**

In the near term, I expect aircraft developments to be more evolutionary rather than revolutionary, with most developments being unseen by the consumer except for the fact that there may be more long-distance, nonstop flights for the international traveler. Many new aircraft types are more derivatives of current aircraft rather than totally new designs. New aircraft coming out now incorporate new technology for cost savings and greater efficiency, but may not be noticed much by the traveling public. There will probably be new gimmicks for the customer, such as computer games, but these can be put on older aircraft as well as being built into new aircraft types. Because of current financial conditions, airlines are buying these aircraft very cautiously, and must be convinced that the large capital expenditure required does really produce a more economical product that can better help the particular carrier to serve targeted markets.

Early in the next century, financing and economics permitted, we may see the dawn of some truly new aircraft types. The first would be the very large transport, possibly seating up to a 1000 people on multiple decks. There still are many questions to be answered, the main ones being, will there be a real demand for this type of product, and can it be economically developed without bankrupting its developer?

From the passengers' viewpoint, the question has to be asked; Having up to a 1000 people confined in one cabin for a length of time, what problems would be created? There would be noise problems with so many bodies crammed into a given space, and boarding and deplaning such a large aircraft would require more time. And what would be the potential human and political loss if one of these aircraft had a fatal accident? Evacuation of such a giant aircraft could present problems. Such large aircraft would present many potential ground and gate problems as well. Though such a plane would provide for substantially lower unit operating costs, there are only a limited number of routes worldwide where the high load factor needed to make the plane economical could be achieved.

**Finally, how will new technology in communications affect traffic on air carriers and any potential growth? After all, if a businessperson can avoid the stress of fighting airport traffic through teleconferencing, how can there be any competition in what the choice would be?**

I expect the growth areas in air travel to be leisure and international, where advanced telecommunications will have limited or no effect. Until technology is developed such as was available in the movie *Total Recall,* where customers can go to a travel agent and mentally travel to their desired locations, people are going to need airplanes to get to exotic vacation destinations. Additionally, as business contacts become more global, some personal visits will be needed to cement personal relationships and overcome cultural differences that cannot be accomplished by teleconferencing. Finally, there are many business transactions that will always require personal contact.

As William H. Whyte, the author of *The Organization Man,* has penned, "Increased communications and travel have not obviated face-to-face interchange; they have stimulated it." I believe that the more interchangeable the business world becomes, the more there will be a desire for personal contact. In fact, cheap airfares may stimulate business travel in many instances where there may only be a marginal benefit of face-to-face contact, since a trip could be almost as economical as a call.

# ELEVEN

# Summary and Post-Analysis of the Industry Worldwide

It's not the earth the meek inherit, it's the dirt.

—A line by Mordred from the Broadway musical *Camelot*

## THE U.S. INDUSTRY

AS WE HAVE POINTED OUT in this book, the U.S. commercial aviation industry was stood on its head in 1978, and it will never be the same again. There are perceived losers such as airline unions, complacent management, and bureaucrats, but there is at least one winner as well: the customer who puts down hard-earned earnings in return for safe, efficient, and economical travel. After all, isn't the reason for running a business to provide the consumer with a cost efficient product? Despite bankruptcies, loss of jobs at particular carriers, and management changes, it's hard to dispute the fact that more people are traveling at more economical rates than were available in the regulatory period. This trend is now catching on around the world, and should bring the ability to travel at affordable prices to new masses of consumers. The airlines must be bold in making the necessary changes that will enable them to achieve profitability over the economic cycle. The airlines that can produce a good product in a cost-efficient manner will inherit the earth; those that don't will eventually be buried in the dirt.

## TRENDS RESHAPING THE REST OF THE WORLD

The upheaval taking place in world air transport can be traced to the deregulation of the U.S. airline industry. Deregulation is the United States' modern-day version of "the shot heard 'round the world." The transition from a government-regulated industry to one in which the airlines were free to choose their own routes and set their own prices represented a triumph for many economists and consumer interests. And now, slowly, deregulation is becoming acceptable around the globe. This trend will continue for as long as the world economy is viable.

As of this writing (March 1995), the airline business in Europe is undergoing changes similar to those that occurred in this country 15 years ago. The process of European change is evolutionary, as governments have moved in stages to remove barriers to free competition. The final barrier will be lifted on January 1, 1997, the target date for fully Open Skies in the European Union, meaning that the air carriers of any European Union nation will be permitted to operate in any country of the Union.

The sections that follow offer some specific observations about Europe and other regions.

### Europe's Liberalization: One Step at a Time

Europe's liberalization is going slowly for several reasons. Access to European airports by airlines is a far more crucial issue in Europe now than it was in the United States in 1978. Most of Europe's major airports already are congested. Furthermore, the air-traffic-control system is a patchwork of national systems and represents a hard constraint on the growth of flights.

The structure of the European air-transport system, which traditionally has relied on charter operations from large cities to leisure destinations, will tend to slow the entry of new start-up carriers in comparison to the U.S. experience. The European system of railways connecting major centers represents another constraint on airline development. Major European centers are close to each other, and easily accessible by train.

The deregulation genie is, however, out of the bottle. In time, new technologies will ease constraints on airports. Aircraft noise and pollution problems will be minimized, under new regulations scheduled for implementation under the standards promulgated by the International Civil Aviation Organization (ICAO). As competition increases in Europe, the trend toward the consolidation of Europe's flag carriers and privatization can be expected to accelerate. Airlines in the union will seek further partnerships with airlines from around the globe.

## Airlines in North Europe Are Leading the Way

The northern-tier nations of Europe are leading the way toward the privatization of flag carriers. Airlines of the southern tier, where losses have been heaviest, have been slow to adopt privatization. Pressures are increasing from the privatized carriers for the European Union to require an abandonment of government subsidies to failing carriers, a crucial issue of governance for the EU. Subsidies disturb the marketplace in several ways. They contribute to excess capacity of aircraft—a major cause of crippling fare wars—and perpetuate the least efficient operators. In a free market the inefficient would be required to cut capacity, change, or leave the market.

Airlines in former Communist countries are likely candidates to serve as feeder carriers to the surviving larger European airlines. A few of the Eastern Bloc airlines will survive on key routes carrying ethnic traffic.

## Airlines of the Former Soviet Union
## Will Develop in Time

A successor to Aeroflot is operating internationally, and the one-time monopoly has fragmented into regional operations. If the old republics of the former Soviet Union continue on the road toward democratic capitalism, the airline industry will develop along the same lines as it did in the United States. The C.I.S. constitutes a vast country in which there is a strong demand for travel. Once these new nations are well situated economically, growth in the airline sector will follow. The mass privatization of Russia and its former allied republics began to attract foreign capital late in 1994. In 1995, Russian companies will begin to active seek capital in world markets. For foreign airline interests the only question is, "When will it be economical to start service to the C.I.S.?"

## China's Strides Toward Democracy Are Boosting Its Airlines

China is moving in the right direction. Its limited experiment in airline competition has been successful. Though the nation still lies under the heavy hand of bureaucracy, China is making strides toward democratic capitalism and the airline industry is following the same trend. Chinese airlines are closer to accessing western capital markets than their Russian counterparts, though Russia has made advances lately. The vast land-mass of China, its huge population, and natural wealth offer great potential for economic growth. Hong Kong, which will transfer authority from the British to the People's Republic in 1997, may serve as the trump card for China's future.

## The Pacific Would Benefit If Japan's Lock Was Opened

Asia is growing rapidly, but greater progress in trans-Pacific commerce would be possible if only Japan's lock on access could be opened. To be successful, a Pacific air carrier must obtain access to Japan, the economic powerhouse of the Pacific. The rights to fly from Japan to other Asian nations are an important asset. The opening of the new Kansai International Airport on Osaka Bay is a welcome development. Aircraft coming into use by trans-Pacific carriers have the range capability to overfly Japan. However, Japan remains the key to Pacific profits for airlines, and it will remain that for some time to come. The unlocking of Japan is likely to be a long and difficult process.

## The Case Against Frequent-Flier Programs

Along with tax cuts, leveraged buyouts, and Yuppies, frequent-flier programs may eventually become relics from the 1980s. The programs are growing out of the airlines' control, as the number of ways to earn benefit mileage points continues to increase. Airlines in the United States have modified the programs several times, in the process usually upsetting frequent flyers, the very customers that the programs are trying to please. In steps taken in 1994, the carriers have raised the requirements for redemption of mileage points and some customers have threatened to sue. Mileage benefits are becoming expendable and time-limited. Moreover, the top officials of some companies that have employees who travel frequently are becoming skeptical about the programs and their costs. In the drive common to all businesses to drive down costs, one can expect them to confiscate earned mileage benefits for other business trips or to negotiate for lower fares.

## Globalization Will Move Along with New Impetus

The globalization trend will accelerate, as airlines increase the number of alliances and partnerships with other airlines. Even certain big-name U.S. airlines could become feeder carriers to partners. The use of CRS code-sharing, already important, will become even more so. This will occur in the short term, as airlines retrench to their basic geographical areas of strength and still attempt to attract traffic into world markets.

## Closing Thoughts

We close with a few conclusions about this world industry.

1. *The industry's problems are attributable to a few general causes.* Airline managers must take the responsibility for failing to prepare airlines for the competitive environment. Too often, union labor has ignored the realities of the changed environment and laid down roadblocks in the path of management. Finally, governments have been slow to respond to needed infrastructure improvements.

National policies have been ineffectual or overdone, as in the cases of airline subsidies. These forces will have to learn to work together more closely.

2. *The consumer pressure for low fares will continue, requiring airlines to become cost-effective.* The low-fare trend will continue because of excess capacity in aircraft. This surplus is the primary reason for low fares and the frequent, damaging fare wars. Aircraft manufacturers are pressing sales of new aircraft in order to keep their production lines moving, and the airlines, at least in the past, have been willing buyers.

3. *Continued worldwide privatization will help the industry out of its doldrums.* The airline industry will be better off if airlines privatize and governments are removed from the airport and airway systems. An injection of fresh, new leadership could bring new business approaches to an industry that has grown stale and even insular.

4. *The advance of technology has outpaced political progress by a wide margin.* A good example of outpacing technology is the constellation of satellites spinning above the Earth. The satellite system is available for commercial use, but slow-moving governments, global politics, and shortages of funds have prevented its implementation. Airport expansion is another need that has been stymied for the same reasons.

5. *Expect continued shocks.* The new economics of the industry favors consolidation, which means that old names will disappear. The truly global airlines of the future will be few in number. Most airlines will depend on alliances to fill gaps in their global route networks. Smaller carriers will operate in exclusive niches, and some may provide traffic feed to the larger airlines.

The only thing that is certain is that the industry will continue to change and evolve. The only question is, will government regulations, airline management, and unionized workers be flexible and quick enough to adapt, or, as in the case of the dinosaurs, will others inherit the earth? In mid-March 1995, we look out upon the future and wonder.

# Notes and Sources

## CHAPTER 1: FLYING IN THE FUTURE

12 *Airline Deregulation Act of 1978:* Under deregulation, competition has been more keen than ever. Prior to 1978, few routes had more than two competitors, and many were monopoly routes. A 1976 study of the top 50 city pair markets showed 7 monopoly city pairs, 33 city pairs with two competitors, 22 city pairs with three competitors, 8 with four competitors, and 5 with five. Under deregulation, competition has increased on a point-to-point basis but also through the hub networks of the major airlines, which provide ample choices of airlines and flights. Source: *Airline Deregulation:* The Early Experience, Meyer, Oster, Morgan, Berman, Strassmann, Auburn House Publishing Company, Boston, 1981.

14 *". . . an international consortium":* International Aero Engines is a joint venture of companies in five nations: Fiat Avio S.p.A., of Italy; Japanese Aero Engines Corp.; MTU Motoren- and Turbinen-Union München GmbH, of Germany; Rolls-Royce plc, of Britain, and United Technologies Corp., of the United States.

## CHAPTER 2: THE BIG THREE FACE THE CRISIS

21 *"A problem for employees":* Wolf's 1992 salary was $625,000, and he received performance-based stock options in 1990 and in 1991 amounting to 200,000 shares. As of March 1, 1993, Wolf

beneficially owned 182,584 United shares. These shares include 87,500 shares for which he has the right to acquire within 60 days and 20,000 shares he had bought for $3 million on the open market in February 1992. Wolf commented that his and other executives' salaries were low compared to those of their peers in the industry, and that "the upside" came with the stock options.

21 *"compensation for directors":* Directors who are not corporation officers are paid a $20,000 annual retainer and qualify for 100 shares of common stock each year. They receive $1000 for each meeting attended. Certain committee chairpersons receive an additional annual retainer of $3000.

34 *"industry through the decade":* Between June 1984 and January 1989, American Airlines interviewed 22,287 pilot job applicants in its growth plan. Some 4426 were hired and on-duty in December 1989. Source: Flying Through Time, a FAPA Publication, Atlanta, Ga., Copyright © 1993.

35 *"enough to become profitable":* American management rejected the findings of a study, funded by the Allied Pilots Association (APA), the company union, which concluded that American should restructure its short-haul flights into a more efficient, high-productivity operation and compete directly with rival Southwest in the short-haul market. While the APA attacked the network for high costs, American's executives took aim at the labor costs and the work rules, basically the regulations covering pilots' duties and trips—the "rigs," as they are called, that guarantee pilots a certain level of pay no matter what their level of actual flying.

Small hubs tend to be less efficient than bigger ones, because of their irregular and limited use of facilities and personnel during the workday. More active hubs, in which there are as many as 10 rushes of flights arriving and departing per day, are efficient. Airline managers contend that added revenues from the cross-feeding of passengers at hubs is more than sufficient to counter the marginal increases in costs resulting from downtime of aircraft and personnel.

## CHAPTER 3: INDUSTRY HOT SPOTS: THE MIDDLE THREE AIRLINES

PAGE

43 *"revenue passenger miles"*: A revenue passenger mile (RPM), a standard measurement of airline finance officers, represents one paying passenger flown one mile. Thus, it is the passengers in a period of time multiplied by the miles flown. Northwest ranked fourth in RPMs in 1993, behind United at 101 billion RPMs, American at 97 billion, and Delta at 83 billion. British Airways ranked fifth, at 49 billion RPMs.

47 *"after World War II"*: Exercising what are known as "fifth freedom rights" (see the Glossary for the definition of other freedoms of the air), Northwest flies from the United States to Japan. The fifth freedom is the right to carry passengers from Japan to other Asian destinations. These passengers would include those who boarded in the United States and those boarding in Japan.

50 *"3100 seats per week"*: The service began in a KLM Boeing 747 combination passenger-cargo aircraft, known as a Combi, which seats 300 people. The aircraft flew three times a week in April 1992, totaling 900 seats in the market. A year later, the thrice-weekly 747 was replaced by daily service in a McDonnell Douglas DC-10, increasing the weekly seating to 2100. The following April of 1994, the aircraft was changed again to a 400-seat Boeing 747-400, bringing the seats-per-week in the market to 2800. In the summer of 1994, the joint venture added an eighth weekly frequency in a DC-10, bringing the seat total to 3100. The aircraft have been 80 percent full, and in summers the load factor reaches 90 percent.

51 *"Northwest flight to Cincinnati"*: The U.S. Transportation Department has authorized KLM to code-share with Northwest to 108 points beyond its U.S. gateways, and in 1994 the Dutch carrier was adding four new code-sharing stops per month.

60 *"Continental Life has suffered"*: It was restored from a low, undetermined level to 98 percent in the spring of 1994, after a difficult winter.

## CHAPTER 4: THE POPULIST OF THE PLANES
PAGE

76 *"Judiciary Committee Hearings in June":* For an academic justification of airline deregulation, see *Regulation and Its Reform,* Stephen G. Breyer, Harvard University Press, Cambridge, Mass., 1982. Mr. Breyer served as counsel to Senator Kennedy's Judiciary Committee during the airline deregulation hearings. He was nominated as a Supreme Court justice by President Clinton in May 1994.

77 *"Muse took the operational reigns":* Muse served as president until his resignation in 1978. He founded Muse Air, later known as TranStar Airlines, after Southwest acquired the carrier, in 1985, for $409.5 million in cash and $20 million in stock.

87 *". . . the Mueller family":* Comair was started on an intuition of a young pilot, David R. Mueller, who was flying in the mid-1970s for a corporation at Cincinnati's Lunken Field, an old municipal airport, situated on bottomland near the Ohio river, known to regional aviators as Sunken Lunken. Mueller overheard the grumblings of local businessmen about the lack of air service to large midwestern cities. He discussed the idea of a short-haul commuterline with friends. The project won the backing of David's father, Cincinnati businessman Raymond A. Mueller, who ignored a host of doomsayers and doubters in their rumblings about the hazards of investing in aviation.

Within several years, the Muellers had become the principal owners of Comair, and the investment has paid off handsomely. The young pilot is now the chairman and chief executive officer of Comair. He turned 40 years old in 1992, when the airline celebrated its fifteenth year. Like many successful Kentuckians, David is developing a horse farm in the rolling countryside less than a half-hour's drive from the airport.

87 *". . . in a Midwest aviation renaissance":* For 80 percent of those who live east of the Rocky Mountains, the Cincinnati/ Northern Kentucky International Airport is centered geographically. It is one of the few surviving hubs among the dozen established in the 1980s rush. In 1994, Delta Air Lines

opened a $375-million flight center, increasing its number of gates to 52. With Comair's new facility, the Comair–Delta combination offers 105 gates at the airport.

## CHAPTER 5: LOW FARES FOREVER
PAGE

97 *". . . anticompetitive behavior in the industry":* The investigation of price-fixing allegations didn't deter American from innovation. In 1985, the carrier introduced a new version of the SuperSaver that carried the first-ever penalties if the discount ticket was not used as prescribed. In time the airlines put further controls on the process, with the creation of the nonrefundable ticket.

Nonrefundables are plentiful today, but a full-scale passenger revolt in 1990–1991 caused the airlines to be more flexible in their use. In a mid-1991 analysis by her office, USAir's consumer affairs director, Deborah Thompson, noted a doubling of complaints regarding nonrefundable fares. She brought the fact to the attention of USAir executives and worked with them to relax the strict rules regarding nonrefundables. In most cases now, a passenger may revise his or her itinerary after purchase of a nonrefundable ticket and lose only the cost of an administrative fee.

## CHAPTER 6: THE ODD COUPLE:
## GOVERNMENT AND THE AIRLINES
PAGE

109 *". . . paid off for both sides":* See unpublished paper, "Congress and the Founding and Success of Our Airlines," by Willis Player, a former aide to the pioneer aviator C. R. Smith at American Airlines and a former vice president of Pan American World Airways.

109 *". . . made faster aircraft possible":* See Laurence K. Loftin, Jr., *Quest for Performance, the Evolution of Modern Aircraft,* National Aeronautics and Space Administration, Washington, 1985.

110 *". . . federal funding of locally operated airports"*: See *The Federal Aviation Administration* by Robert Burkhardt, Frederick A. Praeger, Publishers, New York, 1967

110 *"In a recent fiscal year"*: Between October 1, 1993, and June 30, 1994, the Airport and Airway Trust Fund grew by $3,760,253,700.00. Of that figure, $3.26 billion came from ticket taxes. Net receipts, including $615.3 million in accrued-interest income, totaled $4,351,969,207.80.00. As of the June 30 date, the Department of Transportation had taken in a non-expenditure transfer $4,702,099,800.12, leaving a deficit of $350.1 million.

110 *". . . welcome every cent"*: Government budget officials have welcomed the slow pace of allocation, because the surplus in the fund serves to counterbalance the national debt.

116 *". . . the ASD system"*: The problem arose again when the FAA developed the Aviation Situation Display (ASD), which integrates radar target information from across the United States into a single screen. FAA Administrator James Buchanan Busey IV, a retired three-star Navy admiral, held up the distribution of ASD information to airlines until a means was found to deprive the airline screens of radar information on certain military and Central Intelligence Agency (CIA) aircraft.

## CHAPTER 7: LIBERALIZATION UNFOLDING
PAGE

125 *". . . globalization of the airline business"*: Loosely translated, the term *globalization* means the development of international airlines, largely through partnerships and alliances, in which the airlines serve most or all of the major regions of the world.

128 *Cabotage:* Originally meaning trade in coastal waters, it is prohibited by the Federal Aviation Act. In essence, airlines must be citizens of the nation in which they provide domestic service. The laws against cabotage are similar around the world, and they have been supported by labor unions as a form of local job protection.

129 *". . . failed to produce an agreement":* Bilateral negotiations between two nations may be likened to contract talks between labor and management. Each side will have overall objectives and a set of goals, which more often than not are contradictory. The motivation for negotiations usually is the desire of an airline in one country to gain additional rights from another. Talks will center around two elements, pricing and capacity. This means the fares, the frequency of flights, and the number of seats offered in a market. A problem for all negotiations is the inherent tendency of bilateralism to create restrictions to trade, with one side limiting the other. The success or failure of negotiations often hangs on many variables, including human reactions and cultural differences. Political repercussions can arise from a failed negotiation. Politics always play a role.

130 *". . . tap into domestic U.S. passenger traffic":* See *Aviation Week & Space Technology,* August 3, 1987, p. 44; May 11, 1987, p. 42.

131 *". . . passed through Amsterdam to come to the United States":* These passengers are referred to as *sixth-freedom traffic.* The passengers were carried by KLM to Amsterdam from other points, and transferred to other aircraft going to the United States. The United States contended that the Dutch were violating a provision in the bilateral agreement that specified that aircraft capacity should be adequate for the market. The market by U.S. definition was Amsterdam–New York. The dispute resulted in a case coming before the U.S. District Court for the Eastern District of New York. A decision in 1973 supported the United States. For two years, the United States held the Dutch at bay. An order was written to require a capacity reduction. Finally, after the Dutch supported the United States in a North Atlantic Treaty Organization (NATO) purchase of U.S. aircraft, the United States agreed to extend the order and never did enforce it.

133 *"investments of more than $400 million":* A prospectus issued in March 1994 listed the KLM common shares at 16,189,030 and preferred shares at 5793, with an assumed current value of $479,272,686.00.

137 *"amass passengers through their domestic networks":* (2.2.9. CAP 489 Consultation on Airline Competition Policy, An Interim Assessment, Civil Aviation Authority).

145 *"28,000 commercial flights a week":* According to a 1993 study conducted by the aviation consulting firm, Simat Helleisen & Eichner, New York.

146 *"Because of its size, the United States":* Other 1994 assessments were: Japan, $5.578 million; Germany, $3.379 million; the United Kingdom, $2.58 million; France, $2.519 million, and the Russian Federation, $2.48 million.

## CHAPTER 8: CHINA AND RUSSIA

PAGE

153 *"Russia's Aeroflot":* Aeroflot represented the totality of U.S.S.R. aviation, from airline operation to FAA-like certification of aircraft and airport operations. Aeroflot has been broken up into nearly 400 separate companies. There is only one company that still is legally named Aeroflot: Aeroflot Russian International Airlines, which does not fly domestically. Of the other hundreds of companies operating domestically in Russia, products of the Aeroflot breakup, some are absurdly small. Of the many carriers that emerged from the breakup, some planes have been repainted with airline names, but most regional companies still operate under the name Aeroflot and the planes still look identical.

153 *"China's CAAC":* The acronym stands for Civil Aviation Authority of China, which combined the operations of airline, aircraft certification administration, and airport operator.

153 *Commonwealth of Independent States (C.I.S):* The former Soviet Union may be referred to as the Newly Independent States (N.I.S.) if the formerly Soviet-controlled Baltic nations are included. In 1994, the Baltic nations were authorized as observers to the Interstate Aviation Commission (IAC), the Russian equivalent of our FAA.

## CHAPTER 9: BIRDS OF THE FUTURE

PAGE

171 *". . . anticipated the market":* Narrow-body, twin-jet transports grew in the world market from more than 2000 to 3800 aircraft in the first 10 years of U.S. deregulation, 1978–1988. Wide-body aircraft increased from 800 to more than 1800 in the same time frame. *(Source:* ICAO's *Review and Outlook, The Economic Situation of Air Transport.)*

   Average airplane size grew from 175 seats in 1980 to approximately 180 in 1985. The average dropped slightly in 1986 and flattened in 1987, before growing again in 1988. Boeing projects the average seating at 225 in 2010.

185 *"what* The Economist *calls a good year":* An estimate by *The Economist,* June 25, 1994, in an article, "Those foolhardy firms in their flying machines."

185 *Dillon Reed, New York City:* The prediction was the work of co-author Raymond A. Neidl, who was working at Dillon Reed at the time.

# Appendix A

The following is a list of FAA regulatory programs begun between 1989 and June 1993, showing their initial and recurring costs as compiled by the Air Transport Association:

| Regulatory Requirement | Initial Cost | Recurring Cost |
|---|---|---|
| *Equipment* | | |
| TCAS II collision avoidance systems | 660 | |
| Windshear detection | 254 | |
| Digital flight data recorder and cockpit voice recorder | 315 | |
| Protective breathing equipment | 8 | |
| Fire protection for cargo areas | 23 | |
| Type III overwing exit | 4 | |
| Safety seat standards | 33 | |
| Interior flammability retrofit | 525 | |
| | | |
| *Airworthiness Directives* | | |
| 1989 | 98 | |
| 1990 | 434 | |
| 1991 | 173 | |
| 1992 | 184 | |
| 1993 through May | 28 | |
| | | |
| *Drug Testing* | | |

| Regulatory Requirement | Initial Cost | Recurring Cost |
|---|---|---|
| *Air Carrier Access Act* | | |
| Aircraft accessibility | 382 | |
| Accessible lavatories | 171 | |
| Onboard wheelchair | 3 | |
| Training | 1 | |
| Exit row seating | 6 | |
| *Airport De-icing Facilities* | 100 | |
| Airline de-icing equipment and training | 10 | 1.4 |
| *Security* | | |
| Checked baggage screening | 28 | 42 |
| Airport access door requirements | 700 | |
| Level IV screening, Desert Storm | 200 | |
| **Totals** | **$4.317 (billion)** | **$58.4 (million)** |

# Appendix B

## ETCs, the Investor's Choice

THE AIRLINES AND RAILROADS—all transportation modes—
have similar capital needs. It was the rail industry that first developed the Equipment Trust Certificate (ETC) as a means to finance
railroad cars. Rolling stock serves as excellent collateral for an ETC,
since the cars are standardized and are easily transferrable to other
railroads. Because of the lack of standardization in avionics, power
plants, and other components, airplanes are harder to transfer from
one carrier to another. It can be done, but cost may be involved.

Legal protections extend to investors under the ETC. The legal
title for the equipment rests not with the airline or the investor but
with a third-party trustee. The trustee leases the equipment to the
airline and sells ETCs equal to the purchase price to investors. The
trustee collects lease rentals from the airlines, and uses the proceeds
to pay interest and principal on the certificates.

When the obligations have been paid off, the trustee sells the
equipment to the airline for a nominal price. During the lease
period, the airline doesn't own the equipment. If it defaults, the
investor/creditor may have to go through bankruptcy proceedings
before the equipment can be returned. Then it is the creditor's
responsibility to remarket the retrieved aircraft, which can be costly.
Creditors must be aware that claims by investors aren't all ranked the
same. The farther down the investor is ranked on the priority list, the
less his or her chance of recovering full value. This position should be
reflected in the yield of the security. The lower an investor's priority
ranking, the greater the importance of basic credit analysis and the
market value analysis of secured equipment becomes.

ETCs originally were conceived for long-term investors. The demands of deregulation on the airlines—basically, the need for flexibility in fleet and virtually all aspects of business—caused them to look for short-term leases. The aircraft-leasing companies obliged the airlines. In many cases, leasing is more economical for airlines than ownership. Airline profitability has been insufficient for some carriers to appreciate the tax benefits that airplane ownership can bring.

American Airlines took a leadership role in the 1980s. It worked out a financing arrangement for MD-80 aircraft with the manufacturer, McDonnell Douglas. Its finance expert, Jack Pope, later of United Airlines, toured the world to secure funding and tax-benefiting packages for overseas investors. When the insurance companies left the industry as negotiators for private funding, American led the way for the ETC to become a public instrument of finance, which is what it is today.

### Special Protection for Investors

Investors may enhance the value of an aircraft ETC with Section 1110 protection under the Federal Bankruptcy Code. The protection is available only when debt is used to finance aircraft that are new to an airline, or when the aircraft are on operating leases. The section provides automatic relief for qualified creditors. In the event of a borrower's bankruptcy, the debt-holders are assured of either received scheduled principal and interest payments even on the face of the suspension of other debt payments, or repossession of the collateral.

The best advice to an investor who is attempting to evaluate the collateral backing of an ETC is this: Review the equipment type and the specific features—engines in particular—and determine how widely the equipment is used, as well as the potential cost of refinancing in case of a bankruptcy. The value of the aircraft will be greater if its type is in common use. Newer-technology aircraft, which meet Stage 3 noise requirements and are labor-saving, tend to hold values and are easier to remarket.

As seen from one viewpoint, ETCs have played a critical role in modern finance, enabling the carriers to obtain large portions of their capital needs at manageable interest rates. From another viewpoint, ETCs have made it easy for the airlines to buy aircraft, resulting in overcapacity and leading to widespread discounting in order to fill surplus airplane seats.

## Junk Bonds

A history of low profit margins has hampered the airlines' funding efforts, yet extensive amounts of capital are required by airlines to support the infrastructure of airport terminals and ground equipment, and to acquire expensive aircraft. For many carriers in recent years, only junk bonds have been available to them.

The credit-rating agencies took due note of the airline debacle of the early 1990s. Airline debt ratings fell continuously until some carriers entered levels known in the trade as "junk." The junk bonds are high-yield and have become synonymous with airline financing.

"Junk" is an overstatement; it sounds terrible and wasteful. The technical definition of a junk bond is one carrying a credit rating in Standard & Poor's system of BB+ or lower. That rating is the equivalent of Bal under the Moody's system. Ratings at this level and below indicate the degree of speculation and level of risk.

These bonds are issued by companies that either have questionable credit or can boast no long track record of sales and earnings. Older and established companies that are facing difficulties and therefore deal in junk bonds are referred to in the trade as "fallen angels."

The volatility of junk bonds offers profit potential to investors, and the high yields attract specialist investors.

## Other Funding Sources

Airframe and engine manufacturers, boosted by their generally good credit ratings, at times have been reluctant sources of funding for new aircraft and engines. Government-financed packages have accounted for aircraft sales, through the Export-Import Bank of the United States and other facilities around the world. These funding sources will continue to be available.

Aircraft leases have helped airlines to meet their equipment needs. Higher-rated lessors (leasing companies) usually can obtain funding at low rates of interest, and can depend on a steady stream of profits on which taxes must be paid. With a middleman owning the aircraft, that aircraft can be acquired as part of a total package. When interest costs can be deducted from the profits, there is an additional inducement for third parties. Unfortunately, the airlines haven't been able to fully utilize the tax benefits of leasing because of their inconsistent and generally poor profit margins.

The growth of leasing has given a boost to the trend toward standardization of aircraft in cabin interiors and cockpit avionics. If this trend continues, greater standardization may prove beneficial in several ways. With greater standardization, unit costs of manufacturers may be reduced and aircraft transfers may be made more easily from one air carrier to another. Leasing will continue to grow as airlines trend toward a state that is less asset-, less capital-, and less people-intensive.

This developing trend is apparent in the larger amount of outsourcing of work related to airline operations, in particular specialized maintenance. Engine and component manufacturers are seeking to take over the maintenance of their own products, leaving airlines to the chore of flying the aircraft.

In the future, the cost of ownership will have to be reviewed by managers in the context of the overall cost structure of their airline. Leasing aircraft in lieu of owning them permits the airline to adapt more flexibly to fast-changing market needs. It reduces ownership risks, and lessens the need to raise capital for the acquisition of new aircraft.

# Glossary

**Available seat mile**   Known as ASM, and defined as one seat flown one mile. A transport configured with 100 seats flying 100 miles would have flown 10,000 available seat miles.

**Bilateral aviation agreement**   An agreement similar to a treaty between two nations concerning aviation rights.

**Cabotage**   Commonly used as part of the term *cabotage rights,* meaning the right of a company from one country to trade in another country. In aviation terms, the right to operate within the domestic borders of another country. Cabotage usually is not permitted.

**Code-sharing**   A growing practice in which airlines share the same two-letter designator code (NW for Northwest, for example) on certain flights, as they are presented in the computer reservations systems used by airlines and travel agents. Sharing of the codes permits a travel agent to sell a ticket that will include routings on both airlines.

**Computer reservations systems**   The electronic system that allows travel agents or airlines to reserve seats on commercial flights.

**Multilateral aviation agreement**   An agreement for air service among more than two nations.

**Revenue passenger mile**   Known as RPM, the principal measure of the airline passenger business. It represents one paying passenger flown one mile.

**Unit costs**   Costs obtained by counting total operating costs and dividing this number by ASMs. The result will be the unit costs in terms of cents per mile.

**Yield**   Basically, the price paid for transportation. It is a measure of airline revenue, and may be derived by dividing passenger revenue by passenger miles. It is expressed in cents per mile.

## Freedoms of the Air

These freedoms actually are norms of international commercial aviation, adopted at the Chicago Convention in 1944 that established the International Civil Aviation Organization (ICAO), the technical aviation arm of the United Nations. The rights, established and approved in aviation agreements, are as follows.

**First freedom**   The right of an aircraft from one country to overfly another country, provided the nation is notified and approval is granted.

**Second freedom**   The right of an aircraft from one country to land in a second country for technical reasons, such as for fueling and maintenance.

**Third freedom**   The right of an airline to carry traffic from the country of origin to another country.

**Fourth freedom**   The right of an airline to carry return traffic from the other country to its own country.

**Fifth freedom**   The right of an airline to carry traffic between two countries other than the country of origin. The flight must begin and end in the country of origin, however.

**Sixth freedom**   Not a right defined by the Chicago Convention, but referring to traffic originating in another country. An example of sixth-freedom traffic would be traffic originating in Mexico and flying to London via Miami.

# Bibliography

*Airline Deregulation, The Early Experience,* John R. Meyer and Clinton V. Oster, Jr. (eds.), Auburn House Publishing Company, Boston, 1981.

*The Airline Industry and the Impact of Deregulation,* George Williams, Ashgate, Aldershot, Hants, England, 1993.

*Annals of Air and Space Law,* McGill University, Montreal, Quebec, Canada, Vol. XIX–1994, Chicago Conference Anniversary 1944–1994, The Carswell Company Limited, Toronto.

*Change, Challenge and Competition,* The National Commission to Ensure a Strong Competitive Airline Industry, A Report to the President and Congress, August 1993.

*Deregulation and Airline Competition,* Organisation for Economic Co-Operation and Development, OECD, Paris, 1988.

*Diversification Strategies for Regulated and Deregulated Industries, Lessons from the Airlines,* Jonathan L.S. Byrnes, Lexington Books, Lexington, Mass., 1985.

*The Economic Effects of Airline Deregulation,* Steven Morrison and Clifford Winston, The Brookings Institution, Washington, D.C., 1986.

*The Effects of Deregulation on U.S. Air Networks,* Aisling J. Reynolds-Feighan, Springer-Verlag, Berlin, 1992.

"Flying Through Time, A Financial and Historical Overview of the Global and Major Airlines," David Jones, David Massey, and Andrew White writing in *Information Florida,* a FAPA Publication, Atlanta, Copyright © 1993.

*International Air Transport: The Challenges Ahead,* Organisation for Economic Co-Operation and Development (OECD), OECD Publications Service, Paris, 1993.

*Regulation and Its Reform,* Stephen G. Breyer, Harvard University, Press, Cambridge, Mass., 1982.

*The Sky Their Frontier: The Story of the World's Pioneer Airlines and Routes 1920–1940,* Robert Jackson, ARCO Publishing, Inc., New York, 1983.

*Strategic Plan,* Federal Aviation Administration, Office of Aviation Policy and Plans, December 1991.

*U.S. International Aviation Policy,* Nawal K. Taneja, Lexington Books, Lexington, Mass., 1980.

# Index

## ABOUT THE AUTHORS

JAMES OTT, a distinguished writer for *Aviation Week,* has covered the deregulation of the airline industry since 1978. He was the 1989 recipient of the Eugene Dubois award for international reporting, and has won several citations from the Aviation/Space Writers Association.

RAYMOND E. NEIDL is a managing director and research analyst with Furman Selz, Inc., an investment and brokerage house specializing in various industries, including airlines and transportation. His commentaries on airline developments can be seen frequently on network television, business news programs, and in trade publications.